Varieties of Alternative Economic Systems

Practical Utopias for an Age of Global Crisis and Austerity

Edited by Richard Westra, Robert Albritton and Seongjin Jeong

Routledge
Taylor & Francis Group

LONDON AND NEW YORK

First edition published 2017 by Routledge

2 Park Square, Milton Park, Abingdon, Oxfordshire OX14 4RN

52 Vanderbilt Avenue, New York, NY 10017

Routledge is an imprint of the Taylor & Francis Group, an informa business

First issued in paperback 2019

British Library Cataloguing-in-Publication Data
A catalogue record for this book is available from the British Library

Library of Congress Cataloging-in-Publication Data
Names: Westra, Richard, 1954- editor. | Albritton, Robert, 1941- editor. |
Jeong, Seongjin, editor.
Title: Varieties of alternative economic systems : practical utopias for an age of global crisis and austerity / edited by Richard Westra, Robert Albritton and Seongjin Jeong.
Description: Abingdon, Oxon ; New York, NY : Routledge, 2017. | Includes bibliographical references and index.
Identifiers: LCCN 2017000584| ISBN 9781138226579 (hardback) |
ISBN 9781315397344 (ebook)
Subjects: LCSH: Socialism. | Utopias. | Capitalism—Social aspects. |
Economics—Sociological aspects.
Classification: LCC HX73 .V3575 2017 | DDC 335—dc23
LC record available at https://lccn.loc.gov/2017000584

ISBN: 978-1-138-22657-9 (hbk)
ISBN: 978-0-367-25091-1 (pbk)

Typeset in TimesNewRomanMTStd
by diacriTech, Chennai

Varieties of Alternative Economic Systems

In this age of overlapping and mutually reinforcing deep global crises (financial convulsions, global warming, mass migrations, militarism, inequality, selfish nation-states, etc.), there needs to be more realistic dialogue about radical alternatives to the status quo. Most literature produced heretofore has focused on the surface causes of these crises without much attention given to the sorts of major societal changes needed in order to deal with the crises we face.

This book moves the debate beyond the critiques and the false or not fully realised alternatives, to focus on what can be termed "practical utopias". The contributors to this book outline a range of practical proposals for constructing pathways out of the global economic, ecological and social crisis. *Varieties of Alternative Economic Systems* eschews a single blueprint but insists on dealing directly with the deep structural problems and contradictions of contemporary global capitalism. It provides a diverse array of complementary proposals and perspectives that can inform both theoretical thinking and practical action.

This volume will be of interest to academics and students who study political science, ecological economics, international politics and socialism.

Richard Westra received his Ph.D. in Political Studies from Queen's University, Canada, in 2001. Currently he is Designated Professor in the Graduate School of Law, Nagoya University, Japan.

Robert Albritton is Professor Emeritus, Departments of Political Science and Social and Political Thought at York University, Canada. He is a prolific writer who has authored or edited 12 books and scores of articles in journals and book collections.

Seongjin Jeong is a leading Marxian economist in South Korea. He has written widely on Marxism, socialism and the Korean economy. He is currently a Professor of Economics at Gyeongsang National University and editor of *Marxism 21*.

Routledge Frontiers of Political Economy

Contents

Illustrations

Figures

Table

Contributors

Robert Albritton is Professor Emeritus, Department of Political Science and Social and Political Thought Program at York University, Canada. He is author or editor of 12 books, including *Let Them Eat Junk: How Capitalism Creates Hunger and Obesity* (2009); *Economics Transformed: Discovering the Brilliance of Marx* (2007); and "A Phase of Transition Away from Capitalism" in *The Future of Capitalism After the Financial Crisis: The Varieties of Capitalism Debate in the Age of Austerity*, eds. Richard Westra, Dennis Badeen and Robert Albritton (2015). He has also published scores of articles in book collections and journals.

Patrick Bond is Professor of Political Economy at the University of the Witwatersrand, South Africa. His books include *Elite Transition* (3rd ed., 2014); *Politics of Climate Justice* (2012); *Talk Left, Walk Right* (2006); *Against Global Apartheid* (2003) and *Uneven Development* (1998). His (1993) PhD at Johns Hopkins University was supervised by David Harvey, following which he worked as a policy drafter in the South African government, including the president's office. From 2004–16 he directed the Centre for Civil Society at the University of KwaZulu-Natal in Durban.

Al Campbell is a retired Emeritus Professor of Economics at the University of Utah, USA, and a long-time member of the Steering Committee of the Union for Radical Political Economy in the United States. His research interests are the nature of contemporary capitalism and its continuous evolution, and both theoretical and real-world more human-centered possible alternatives. His most recent book is the edited volume *Cuban Economists on the Cuban Economy* (2013).

Ann E. Davis is Associate Professor of Economics at Marist College in Poughkeepsie, New York, and chair of the Department of Economics, Accounting, and Finance. She earned her B.A. in American Studies at Barnard College in New York City, M.A. in Economics at Northeastern University in Boston, and Ph.D. in Economics at Boston College. She was the founding Director of the Marist College Bureau of Economics Research, 1990–2005, where she published quarterly reports of the Hudson Valley economy and economic impact studies. She has also published in a range of academic journals on economic history and methodology, such as the *Journal of Economic Issues*, *Science and Society*, and the *Review for Radical Political Economics*, as well as numerous book chapters. She has served three terms as an elected board member of the Eastern Economic Association, two terms as an elected member of the Steering Committee for the Union for Radical Political Economics, and is active in other professional associations as well. She served as Director of the National Endowment for Humanities Summer Institute "Meanings of Property," in June, 2014, with visiting leading scholars John Searle, Alan Ryan, and Mary Poovey. Among her most recent publications are "Bringing Politics Back In: Violence, Finance, and the State", *Journal of Economic Issues*, March, 2013, Vol. XLVII, No. 1, 1–28 and the book *The Evolution of the Property Relation: Understanding Paradigms, Debates, and Prospects* (2015).

Pat Devine is an Honorary Research Fellow at the University of Manchester, UK. He is the author, co-author or editor of five books, including *Democracy and Economic Planning: The Political Economy of a Self-governing Society* (1988/2010), and many papers, including 'Participatory Planning Through Negotiated Coordination', *Science and Society* (66:1, 2002); 'The Continuing Relevance of Marxism' in Sandra Moog and Rob Stones (eds.), *Nature, Social Relations and Human Needs: Essays in Honour of Ted Benton* (2009); 'Democracy, Participation and Social Planning' (with Fikret Adaman) in Clive Spash (ed.), *Routledge Handbook of Ecological Economics* (2017); and 'Planning for Freedom' in Michael Brie and Claus Thomasberger (eds.), (forthcoming). He is the Convener of the UK-based Red Green Study Group and joint author of its founding booklet, *What On Earth Is to Be Done?* (available on request).

Barbara E. Hopkins is Associate Professor of Economics at Wright State University in Dayton, Ohio, USA. She teaches courses in comparative capitalism, comparative systems of the Global South, political economy, and gender and public policy at Wright State University. She is a feminist economist focusing on the interplay between gender and economic systems. She has published in *Feminist Economics*, *Feminist Studies*, the *Review of Political Economy, Journal of Economic Issues*, and in several edited volumes. Her most recent publication is "Gender and Provisioning under different Capitalisms" in the *Handbook of Research on Gender and Economic Life* (2013).

Gui-yeon Jang is Research Professor in the Institute of Social Science, Gyeongsang National University, Korea. She received her Ph.D. in Sociology from Seoul National University, Korea. She has conducted research on labor issues, including labor relations, labor process, labor movement and class analysis, and published many papers.

Seongjin Jeong is Professor of Economics at Gyeongsang National University in Jinju, Republic of Korea. He is currently the President of the Korean Association of Political Economy and the Editor of *MARXISM 21*. His publications in English include "Marx's Crisis Theory as a Theory of World Market Crisis","Lenin's Economics: A Marxian Critique", *Research in Political Economy* (Vol.27, 2011); "The Chimera of Prosperity in Post-IMF South Korea and the Alter-globalization Movement" (co-authored with Richard Westra), in Richard Westra ed. *Confronting Global Neoliberalism* (2010); "Marx in South Korea", *Socialism and Democracy* (Vol.24, No.3, 2010); "Korean Left Debates on Alternatives to Neoliberalism", in Alfredo-Saad Filho and Galip Yalman eds. *Economic Transitions to Neoliberalism in Middle-Income Countries* (2010); "The Korean Developmental State: From Dirigisme to Neo-Liberalism", *Historical Materialism* (Vol.17, No.3, 2009); "Karl Marx in Beijing", *International Socialism* (No.123, 2009); *Marxist Perspectives on South Korea in the Global Economy* (co-edited with Martin Hart-Landsberg and Richard Westra, 2007); "Debates on the Economic Crisis within the Korean Left" (co-authored with Jo-Young Shin), *Rethinking Marxism* (Vol.11, No.2, 1999); "The Social Structure of Accumulation in South Korea", *Review of Radical Political Economics* (Vol.29, No.4, 1997).

Christine M. Klapeer is a political theorist with a strong emphasis on Queer, Feminist, Postcolonial and Critical Development Studies. She received her doctorate from the University of Innsbruck, Austria, and has worked at several universities, including the University of Vienna and the Central European University in Budapest. Christine currently holds a research position in Gender/Queer Studies at the University of Bayreuth, Germany, and is concerned with articulations and theories of (sexual) citizen-ship, (transnational) sexual politics and LGBTIQ-movements as well as with posthuman and eco-queer concepts of political subjectivity and agency. Her publication record includes a monograph entitled *Perverse Bürgerinnen. Staatsbürgerschaft und lesbische (Existenz Perverse Citizens: Citizenship and lesbian existence* (2014), as well as several articles on heter-onormativity, transnational LGBTIQ politics, and on queer/ing citizenship and self-ownership.

Saeed Rahnema is an award-winning retired Professor of Political Science and Public Policy, Department of Equity Studies at York University, Canada, and was the founding Director of York's School of Public Policy and Administration. In his homeland of Iran, Rahnema taught and worked at the Industrial Management Institute in Tehran, and was involved in the Left and Workers/Employees' Council movement during the revolution of 1979. He has also served as a Director of the Middle East Economic Association (MEEA) and as a member of the editorial boards of several journals. His recent book (ed.) is *Transition from Capitalism: Marxist Perspectives* (2016).

Karin Schönpflug is an economist with a degree from the University of Vienna, Austria. She has worked in the Austrian Ministry of Finance and is now a researcher of applied economics at Vienna's Institute for Higher Studies. She has taught economics and transdisciplinary studies at universities in Austria, the US and New Zealand. Her work focuses on the socio-economic inclusion and exclusion of queer and marginalized people, connecting feminist economics with utopian approaches. She published the book *Feminism, Economics, and Utopia: Time travelling through paradigms* (2008) and more recently contributed to *Global Justice and Desire: Queering Economy* (eds. Dhawan, Engel, Holzhey, and Woltersdorff, 2014).

Richard Westra is Designated Professor in the Graduate School of Law, Nagoya University, Japan. He is author or editor of 15 books. Among his most recent single-authored books are *Unleashing Usury: How Finance Opened the Door to Capitalism Then Swallowed It Whole* (2016) and *Exit from Globalization* (2014). His work has been published in numerous international peer-reviewed journals. He is coeditor of *Journal of Contemporary Asia*. He received his Ph.D. from Queen's University, Canada, in 2001.

Preface

This book is the third in a set published by Routledge in its Frontiers of Political Economy Series. The first volume, published in 2015, is Richard Westra, Dennis Badeen and Robert Albritton (eds.) *The Future of Capitalism After the Financial Crisis: The Varieties of Capitalism Debate in the Age of Austerity*. The second, published in 2017, is Richard Westra (ed.) *The Political Economy of Emerging Markets: Varieties of BRICS in the Age of Global Crises and Austerity*. The current volume moves beyond critique of the global neoliberal order to the proposing of alternatives.

What animates contributions to his volume is the disconcerting fact that in the present age of overlapping and mutually reinforcing deep global crises (financial convulsions, global warming, mass migrations, militarism, inequality, nation-states that can focus only on their immediate self-interests, and so forth) there is not more realistic dialogue focusing on the sort of radical alternatives that humanity needs to move forward, if it is to have a future that is not barbaric in the extreme. Most literature produced heretofore has focused on the causes of these crises and their long-term horrible consequences without much attention given to the sorts of major societal changes needed in order to advance both in the short term and long term: changes that would be difficult in the short term, and yet in the long term would bring to the fore and strongly manifest the best that humanity is capable of. We need much more thought and debate that goes beyond negative criticisms to positive alternatives that deal with what might be called "practical utopias". The tension between these terms is meant to bring out the tension between radical changes that may be very desirable, but also are possible if humanity can redirect its energies in serious ways in the near or distant (but not too distant) future.

To be sure, earlier writings that have received much attention on the Left conference circuit framed the question in terms of "real utopias". The problem we detected with this genre is that while the proposed "utopias" may have appeared "real", they were not very utopian and never offered a genuine alternative economic model. Rather, they elided the question of the "kind" of economy and "kinds" of economic principles the new utopias would be constructed around. Instead, they treated ways the current economy might be reconfigured to produce progressive outcomes. Unfortunately, the perilous state of human degeneration and multiplex social, financial and environmental forces bearing down on us has outstripped such Band-Aid solutions. This book intends to open discussion anew into utopias whose building may be practically commenced in the here and now.

The Editors 2016:
Japan
Canada
South Korea

Acknowledgements

The editors wish to acknowledge that editorial contribution by Richard Westra and Seongjin Jeong, as well as chapter contributions of Richard Westra, Seongjin Jeong, Gui Yeon Jang and Patrick Bond, received financial support from the National Research Foundation of South Korea Grant Number NRF-2013S1A5B8A01055117 for a three-year research project on Alternative Economic Systems. Editors also wish to acknowledge all the contributors for their courage in putting forward carefully thought-out proposals for change during such a trying period for humanity and in the current intellectual climate suppressive of critical thought and creative alternative visions.

1   Introduction to practical utopias

Robert Albritton and Richard Westra

The term "practical utopia" may seem to suffer from an inoperable inner tension. Is it an oxymoron? It could be, but whether it is or is not depends on its meaning. The meaning of "practical" taken from the New Shorter Oxford Dictionary (Brown 1993, 2317) that is most suitable to this volume is "inclined or suited to action". We live in a period of history that may turn out to be more destructive than the medieval period referred to as "The Black Death". Between 1346 and 1353 this particular plague has been estimated to have killed as many as two-thirds of the European population. Europeans did try to act practically to contain the Black Death, but their practical actions were largely ineffective because they were not informed by causal knowledge. The Black Death appeared to be passed from person to person, but no one knew that rats were significant movers of the disease.

Sir Thomas More's (1477–1535) *Utopia* (short form of title), first published in Latin in 1516, has played an important role in giving this word its English denotations and connotations. One connotation is that it refers to a society that is so ideal, that mere humans will never be able to act in ways that will even come close to bringing it about. In this connotation it means something like a "heaven on earth" fully realizing all the highest ethical and moral norms of human beings. In another connotation it may refer to a more just and sustainable society than any existing society, and to one that our actions could or should strive to attain, even if this should take several generations, or would constitute a set of ideals that we may approach but never quite reach. In this connotation a utopia is not simply an ideal blueprint to be copied in detail; rather, it is a set of norms and practices that may only be possible to put into practice partially and only after many mobilizations that ultimately are able to bring about a series of radical changes[1].

Thus in this collection of essays "practical" and "utopia" may overlap one another, but not always easily. Some essays will be more utopian and some more practical; all of them, however, will represent the particular author's efforts to think about a different future world, in which citizens of the world care for one another and for nature, are to a large extent equal and peace-loving, and attempt to promote global sustainability. Some essays will focus more on one of these ideals and some more on another, and while the depths and breadths of change advocated may vary from essay to essay, all of them advocate changes that no matter how difficult are in principle possible even if they may never be fully realized. But if one thing brings all the authors in this collection together, it is the acceptance that the human future demands an alternative economic system to capitalism.

Many books and articles have been written about the crises we face and how they are connected in ways that feed into one another. Unlike the era of the Black Death, we have a powerful stock of science, both social and natural science, to help us deal with these crises effectively. Despite these sciences, however, our practical actions have so far been extremely weak. Are we simply so overwhelmed that we lack the willpower to act? Do we not trust our very powerful sciences? What is our excuse?

We do have a limited excuse, for we have to deal with something that is far more deeply entrenched than the Black Death. To put it clearly and definitively, that something is capitalism. Capitalist corporations are reluctant to give up fossil fuel operations because they are so profitable, and nation-states are reluctant to give them up because they are their main energy source and sometimes their main source of economic growth. So year after year the CO_2 in the atmosphere increases while many capitalists pay enormous sums on propaganda against environmentalism. Also, they lobby governments to their point of view, while governments fail to do much, either because they are largely controlled by capitalist corporations or because they fear the unemployment and decline of GDP should fossil fuel production be diminished or shut down – even though there are alternative ways of dealing with unemployment, and all of us need to reject the growth fetish. In other words, we face a capitalism that is so deeply entrenched that anti-capitalist forces are reduced to nibbling at the edges of capitalist economic and political power. We hope that this book will feed into the debate that will ultimately contribute to an ability to take big bites rather than small nibbles out of capitalism, for it is a very powerful but declining capitalism that is the primary cause that sends us deeper into a future of global crises.

This is reflected in the world of books and articles. A lot is being written that is critical of capitalism for its ecological "know-nothingism"[2], but unfortunately, right-wing attacks on environmentalism, at least in the US, have much better access to the mass media that enter almost every home. Much is also being written about capitalism concerning its crises-ridden trajectory, particularly since the 2008 global meltdown. In fact, within broader Left circles such writing has become a cottage industry of late. This critical spate of writing has in turn widened appeal of future-directed thinking about non-capitalist alternatives. Yet, unfortunately, major influencers of progressives and radical youth, while talking about socialism as the solution to the raft of problems society faces, still find it difficult to sketch out in much detail what the proposed socialist or alternative economic system will look like or how it will work (Hedges 2015). Where the essays in this book make their major contribution to a desperately needed dialogue is precisely in the alternative economic systems as practical utopias that offer schemas for the future.

Some will argue that stronger forms of social democracy (e.g., Scandinavia, Germany) already offer alternative institutional arrangements that can move beyond capitalism. There is a grain of truth to this, and in early 20th-century discussions of socialism there was widespread belief that if committed working-class parties gained political power, they could begin to institute social democracy and gradually steer their societies toward socialism in a far less disruptive manner than the "orthodox" Marxist call for revolutionary rupture. However, in practice, even strong social democracy tended to crystallize around state interventions in the economies it managed that supported capitalism and capitalist institutions. One of the earliest attempts to synthesize debate over things like state intervention and economic planning as such that manifested itself in social democratic capitalist economies and in socialist economies is the work of Karl William Kapp. In his view social democratic economic management could proceed to only a certain point and maintain compatibility with capitalism, and an economy would be deemed socialist if that point was passed (Kapp 1939). Social democracies in practice, even strong ones, have never gone beyond that point.

The perceived failures of both socialist experiments that commenced with the Soviet Union – and of even strong social democracy moving that step further toward socialism, as its early radical proponents had hoped – has, at this point in history, made the task of designing practical utopias ever more urgent. Such urgency is grounded in the gathering acceptance that the existing multidimensional ecological crisis is the most serious set of crises ever confronted by humans. And, there is little doubt that the existential threat to humanity presented by the specter of climate change and environmental destruction is intimately intertwined with the operating system of the capitalist economy. Thus humanity is in effect saddled with a momentous choice of human life or capitalism. It is in the making of this choice for human life on the planet that calls have arisen for what is referred to as ecosocialism (Smith 2016). In other words, continuing critique of capitalism is important, but we also need thought that strongly argues for the sort of radical change required in the 21st century that cultivates strong interconnections amongst the best of socialist thought, feminist thought, anti-racist thought, anti-imperialist thought, anti-militarist thought, ecological thought, and the movements that attempt to advance these modes of thought in practice.

This book does precisely that. If we want to avoid a future that finds humanity groping in the dark trough of economic depression and natural catastrophe, we need to discuss and ultimately find degrees of unity around the positive features of post-capitalist alternative economic orders. Emphasizing positive alternative economic systems fires up the imagination and brings people together in order to get closer to or even reach these alternatives. There are thousands of movements around the world that are to some degree anti-capitalist, and with ongoing discussion may eventually reach a high degree of solidarity. But this will require work and patience. Also it will require an avoidance of sectarianism and the sort of infighting that can be so destructive of solidarity on the Left. A real citizenship of the world, a citizenship that is generally accepting of people's cultural differences and is built on a real caring for people and nature, needs to be central to an ethic of solidarity amongst global movements.

It is surprising that, in this age of overlapping and mutually reinforcing deep global crises, there is not greater breadth and depth of dialogue focusing on positive alternatives. This situation is beginning to change, and we hope this book collection will be read as part of this change.

Capitalism in crisis

Though we have argued that the most important task for the Left and all progressives today is to begin sketching the contours of a non-capitalist future realizable in the here and now, it is still worth setting out some of our own critiques of the multiplex crises of capitalism that foreground the discussion of change which follows.

Global warming

Global warming plays a role in many crises, and yet leading American capitalists (many are leading in the world) connected to the fossil fuel industry do their best to spread false propaganda about the nature of global warming. We watched with dismay the Republican Party candidate for Vice President of the US refer to "the war against coal". Many people who make a living directly or indirectly from coal are no doubt experiencing the necessity of reducing our dependence on coal as impacting our lives negatively. But this sort of use of the word "war" stimulates only anger and hate. Contrary to, and far more serious than, the "war against coal" is the do-nothing "war against all future generations of humans", a war that will endanger the future of life on earth. Surely we do not want to use the word "war" in either of these contexts, but we do want to radically reduce our dependence for so much of our energy on coal. For significant increases in global warming will have huge destructive consequences for life on earth. There is no war against coal, but there is a growing struggle to cut back sharply on coal and other fossil fuels as our main sources of energy and main causes of global warming.

Were the American government to offer a basic income (enough to lead a decent life) to coal workers, there would not be such a reaction to cutting back on coal usage. And if this were combined with retraining and guaranteed future good jobs, there would be even less reaction. Otherwise, closing down most coal mines will seem like a war on coal to all those who lose their incomes and have little likelihood of finding even precarious employment.

The energy derived from coal is the single greatest contributor to greenhouse gases. In principle a socialist government could provide a guaranteed decent income to all, could reduce the hours of the work week; mobilize and train, where necessary, former coal workers to meet any of the enormous needs of their fellow citizens who have new jobs, opt for early retirement, or work part-time. But in a capitalist society, when industries cut back or shut down, workers have to face the disasters of unemployment, and, to the extent that their former incomes are not replaced by some sort of unemployment insurance (this is basically a socialist policy, but is adopted by some capitalist countries to varying extents to stave off uprisings), they face lives of poverty and emptiness.

Global warming together with capitalism are important causes, if not the root causes, of many crises we face. Many books could be written on this, and certainly this book with its focus on the need for urgent radical changes is one.

Refugees

We are witnessing increasing numbers of refugees, numbers that have increased to over 65 million, including 100,000 unaccompanied children by the end of 2015, according to the United Nations High Commission on Refugees (UNHCR 2016). Refugees move primarily because of extreme inse-curities stemming from lack of basic necessities, systemic violence, or war. Rather than aiding suffering refugees, many European countries have shut down their borders and turned their backs on the growth of racist or fascist movements that oppose allowing refugees into their countries. For capitalism is fundamentally a highly competitive system such that those who have riches or good jobs can easily feel their jobs, their positions of wealth, or their cul-ture are threatened by "uncivilized have-nots".

While refugees may move for all sorts of reasons, climate refugees alone according to the UN Development Program could reach 200 million by 2050 (UNDP 2015). It is very likely that global warming will make food and water less available and stimulate more severe droughts and floods in the coming years. Along with these changes will come a massive increase in the number of climate refugees and fights over the decreasing supply of food and water. We need to learn as a world community how to cope with this, either by support-ing refugees in ways that are equitable, and/or by stopping the global warming that is behind the extreme climates that will increasingly destroy homes and crops thus forcing people to become refugees.

Unemployment and precarious work

Unemployment and underemployment, particularly as experienced by the world's youth, are deeply serious problems, but recently a new concept has emerged: "precarious employment", marking an increasingly widespread type of employment (Wikipedia). "Precarious" refers to work that is held at the pleasure of another. Hence, such work is typically low-paid, without benefits, and radically insecure. It is as if whoever is doing the hiring is doing a great favor for the hired, who should therefore be thankful for whatever low wage and insecure employment received. Must the youth of the world be thankful for living in poverty? According to the International Labor Organization (ILO 2016) 40 percent of the world's youth are living in poverty, either because they are unemployed, underemployed, or have precarious employment (Grossman 2016).

Often precarious work is accepted by those who are desperate even for the smallest of incomes, such as farmers who have been pushed off the land by land grabs or by rural poverty due to climate change. According to the UNDP (UNDP 2015) 80 percent of the world's food is produced by 500 million family farms, 72 percent of which are less than one hectare. This implies an extremely precarious livelihood. But as Frey and Osbourne point out in their 2013 study, even those who currently have fairly good manufacturing jobs in the US, the world's hegemonic capitalist country, face a bleak future. They argue that in the near future digital technologies will lead to the loss of 47 percent of all jobs in the US, and many of the jobs left will be precarious (Godrej 2016, 13–14).

Digital technologies will not only produce a radically altered job structure, but also are now and will increasingly in the future create enormous waste problems that are currently dealt with by shipping most of the IT waste to poor and developing countries (Frey and Osbourne 2013, 14). Besides having to deal with toxic wastes, these countries also have to deal with toxic mining operations, given that most of the mineral and metal materials needed to produce and expand computer technology are mined in developing countries that lack the wherewithal to deal effectively with the environmental destruction and toxicity of mining.

Global labor trends indicate that in a capitalist world, only those in the middle class or higher with steady well-paid jobs can expect incomes that will support a decent life in the near future.

Economic desolation

Forces euphemized as "globalization" and "financialization" involve a concatenating of processes where, simultaneously with integrated production systems of major economies being disintegrated and their pieces disarticulated across the globe to low-wage areas, commanding heights financial systems with governments in tow reorganized economies as casino-like entities. Bracketing here the ongoing debate over what the ultimate cause of this transformation was, from the late 1970s it worked like this: The outsourcing of production-centered activities to low-wage areas lowered business bottom lines to increase profits. However, in tandem with the disarticulation of production, the evolution of a new measure of business worth dubbed "shareholder value" compelled the newly freed funds into money games such as businesses buying and selling their own stock and engaging in mergers and acquisitions that miraculously increased the public value of companies, or their top line, with scant investment in the actual making of things for sale on the market.

In turn, the spreading economic desolation drove more and more people into debt to maintain the lifestyles that had been promised to them in the post–World War II period of mass consumption economies as the metric for political legitimacy. Expanding debt demanded significant change in financial systems which large financial institutions, with the support of governments, met through the promulgation of myriad newfangled financial debt instruments. Management of both the new corporate shareholder gamesmanship and "financialization" of the day-to-day lives of average working people impelled the wholesale reconfiguring and repurposing of banking systems nationally and globally away from their traditional capitalist role in intermediating real economic activity and toward casino arbitraging and expropriation of wealth. Governments were drawn into this by withdrawing policy support for the social democracy which underpinned the real economy where the mass public had been making their lives and instead lending it to maintain an economy of money games and exorbitant incomes for the few (Westra 2016).

Even in the advanced capitalist economies, the impact of this has been to decouple growth from development and industrialization which engendered what prosperity and rising incomes and life chances capitalism had gradually offered from the late 19th century. Degenerate philosophies like neoliberalism mandated harsh austerity for the growing ranks of disenfranchised workers and even the once-proud middle class, as if this whole process was the fault of their individual shortcomings. In the face of growing social discontent it is no surprise to see capitalist democracies flirt with more authoritarian and social control solutions.

Mass incarceration

The US has the highest incarceration rate of any major country in the world. With only 4.4 percent of the world's people, it has 22 percent of the world's prisoners[3]. What does this have to do with capitalism? To put it most simply, by itself (without state intervention as in the welfare state) capitalism breeds inequality. Generally we can say that the more capitalist the country, the greater the inequality and the weaker the welfare state. For example, it is generally cheaper to throw into prison those whose crimes stem from mental-health issues (about 50 percent of prisoners) than it is to give them a course of treatment and a job. Furthermore, people who are poor and hungry may find that they can make a living by selling drugs when they can't find other jobs. For example, African-American men between the ages of 20 and 24 and without a high school diploma or equivalent have a greater chance of being incarcerated than being employed (World Economic Forum, 2016). In some circumstances even non-violent crimes can add up to sentences of life imprisonment. Finally, it is worth noting that since 1990, spending on prisons has increased three times faster than spending on schools (ibid.).

The US has the most capitalist culture of any major country in the world, and this makes it extremely important for Americans to be rich in order to be admired and have power. As long as the criminality that wealth may be based on is covered up, no one will notice that it may be based upon tax avoidance, pyramid schemes, stock manipulations, insider trading, or many other ways of getting and/or hiding ill-gotten gains.

Wilkinson and Pickett (2010, 135–6) show that there is a correspondence between degree of inequality in a country and the murder rate. For example, the US has a higher degree of inequality than Japan, and the murder rate in the US is 64 per million while in Japan it is 5.2 per million. While there are no doubt other reasons for this divergence (e.g., gun laws and militarism), Wilkinson and Pickett show that there is a tendency across the board for there to be a correspondence between inequality and the murder rate. As they put it (2010, 139), "In more unequal societies children experience more bullying, fights, and conflict. And there is no better predictor of later violence than childhood violence".

Militarism

A study reported in *Business Insider* magazine in 2011 claims that there are one million American war veterans in prison (Morris 2011). Furthermore, 64 percent of crimes committed by war veterans are violent crimes, whereas in the non-vet population it is 48 percent (Bronson 2015). "The Lethal Warriors" was the name of the Second Army Battalion 12th Infantry that served 15 months in Iraq. David Philipps (2010) in his book *Lethal Warriors* shows that as returned veterans their murder rate was 100 times the national average, arguably due largely to post-traumatic stress disorder and other mental illnesses.

This would suggest that it is not only childhood violence that is a "predictor of later violence." Violence experienced in warfare helps to explain both violence to others and violence to self, for there is a very high suicide rate amongst returned war veterans. According to a study discussed in the *Military Times* (Shane and Kime 2016), on average 20 veterans commit suicide every day in the US, and this accounts for 18 percent of all suicides, while only 9 percent of the population are veterans.

Militarism not only spurs on violence throughout society, but also it plays a central role in the capitalist US economy. Take the recent US Air Force program to build the F-35 Joint Strike Fighter aircraft: almost every state gets part of the action to build the F-35, which is estimated to cost over $1.5 trillion over the 55-year life of the program (this estimate is likely low). This spreading of the money to every state assures the support of Congress. At this point not only is the production of this fighter way behind schedule, but also the costs have dramatically increased. The cost of one navy version (short take-off and landing) of the jet has now increased to $337 million (Wheeler 2014). Think about all the constructive things that could be done with this money were it to be used to increase human and environmental flourishing.

But, of course, the air force points out amongst other things the great benefits of their F-35 program. For example, they point out all the jobs that have been and will be created, particularly in Texas where its final assembly line is located. In this day and age, when capitalist manufacturing jobs seem to be declining everywhere except in some poor or middle-income countries (few regulations, few taxes, low wages, and various incentives), are we to increasingly rely of military spending to create the lion's share of capitalist manufacturing jobs that maintain "growth"?

The US military now has an active recruiting program aimed at high school students, particularly those who otherwise have a bleak future. Joining the US Army offers various sorts of training and discipline, a steady income, possible hero status, and a variety of post-military opportunities. All this is offered in an age of high youth unemployment and precarious employment, when for many the choice may come down to a life of crime or a life in the military.

Fundamentalism

"Fundamentalism" was first used to refer to Protestants who took the most fundamental beliefs of the *New Testament* as the literal truth: virgin birth, physical resurrection, infallibility of scriptures, the second coming of Christ, etc. Now the term is used more widely to refer to those who hold fanatical religious beliefs, beliefs that often lead them to look down upon and even hate all those who do not hold the same beliefs as they do. When fundamentalism takes on its more extreme forms, it can add fuel to the fires of violence by labelling non-believers in particular dogma as enemies who should not be tolerated. It is then that killing one's fellow human beings may open a pathway to heaven to the believers.

Sadly, in today's world "fundamentalism" has taken on wider usages. Almost any ideology can spur fundamentalist behavior to the extent that it uses rhetoric to stimulate intolerance, hatred, and violence. For example, extreme forms of nationalism, racism, sexism, and a general intolerance of the "other" can take on forms not unlike some of the extreme forms of religious fundamentalism. Because of its rigid clinging to religious dogma even in the face of a science that proves the dogma to be false, fundamentalism often leads people to accept dark and destructive courses of action.

People who are desperate because of poverty, or who are filled with anger and hatred because imperialist warfare has killed their loved ones, are in great need of making the world a better place, and fundamentalism can sometimes feed their needs by advocating very simple beliefs and courses of action that promise rewards in heaven. Our current world is a very complicated and violent place, where youth in particular have difficulty finding a path towards a decent life. The resulting feelings of emptiness have to be filled with something that promises a better life, even if the promise requires that one expose oneself to likely death. Those who have invaded their countries and killed hundreds of thousands of civilians are particularly opened to being considered infidels.

Land grabs

While it is possible that a poor country could benefit from selling or leasing large parcels of its land, so far the vast majority of land grabs have had disastrous effects on the people living on the land and on the long term ecological well-being of the globe. Often people who have farmed the land for generations or even centuries are unceremoniously pushed off the land that is the very basis of their identities.

Neocolonial land grabs go back in history as far as capitalism (e.g., enclosures), but these earlier forms may differ greatly in their nature, size, and impact. Even the Israeli land grabs of Palestine that continue to this day have a strong religious basis, as opposed to the more environmental and capitalist-profit-oriented land grabs of the last 15 years.

Today many rapidly developing countries lack the arable land and water to feed their people, and this becomes particularly problematic when the global prices of food rise sharply, as they have done from time to time since 2008. This will likely worsen in the future because of global warming, desertification, the pollution of land, the operation of commodity markets, the use of arable land to grow bio-fuels rather than food, and in general the use of agriculture for capitalist crops other than food (cotton, tobacco, bio-fuels, etc.).

For example, Saudi Arabia has pumped the water from very deep aquifers to irrigate the desert in order to grow food, but these aquifers are too deep to be replenished and are likely to run dry within ten years (Pearce 2012, 31). It is essential, then, for the Saudis to find secure sources of food elsewhere. A close and promising location is Ethiopia, where Al Amoudi's company Saudi Star is in the process of leasing 620,000 acres of rich farmland in order to grow corn and sunflowers. Corn is a very thirsty crop, but it is also versatile. Besides being food for humans, corn can be converted into ethanol bio-fuel for cars, into high-fructose corn syrup which currently sweetens foods (mostly junk foods) that are to a large extent the cause of a global obesity epidemic, into feed for animals that largely supply the world with meat; but all of this is at high ecological costs (corn is a thirsty crop that relies on pesticides and large mechanical inputs, giant animal feed lots are very polluting, etc.). In short, there is no guarantee that the corn produced will become nutritious food for humans. It all depends on the needs of Saudi Arabia and which capitalist markets are most profitable. People may be starving because of droughts and high food prices in Ethiopia, but since they would likely be too poor to afford corn, they simply face the enormous pain and hunger of starvation[4]. Saudi Arabia eats well while Ethiopia starves.

India also faces problems of enough nutritious food and water for its large and growing population, but usually profits come first. For example, Karuturi Global Corporation built the world's largest rose-growing greenhouse in Ethiopia with an output of 650 million stems a year (Pearce 2012, 6–8). While significant profits can be made by the Indian corporation, this does little to feed the millions of Ethiopians starving from a massive drought. In fact, it has been estimated that over one-third of the recent land grab crops globally are for the production of bio-fuels for internal combustion engines and not for human food consumption at all. Bio-fuels are primarily produced from corn and sugar, and much of the sugar that we consume comes from high-fructose corn syrup. It is not surprising, then, that in the US corn is not only by far the largest crop, but the most subsidized crop as well, as over 40 percent of the crop is converted into ethanol, not to provide nutritious food for people, but to feed cars. This occurs despite the fact that many studies show that by the time you consider all the inputs into producing ethanol from corn, the ecological and human costs (e.g., by raising the global costs of grains and other important foods) exceed those of the same amount of energy from fossil fuels. Thus some so-called renewable fuels may ultimately not only be ecologically costly, but just plain costly.

Sadly, many land grabs involve deforestation to cut valuable lumber, grow crops, and/or graze animals. Because forests and particularly rain forests absorb large amounts of CO_2 and give off large amounts of moisture, they play an important role in the world's weather and in reducing greenhouse gases. Thus the long-term results of cutting down and/or burning rainforests is an increasing desertification of the world: more droughts and weather so hot that most vegetation and animals will not survive. The result will be massive species extinction and an ever-increasing desertification of the world. Despite these consequences, huge swaths of rainforest in South Asia are being cut down for lumber or to grow bio-fuel crops for cars. For example, in Papua New Guinea 25 percent of the land (mostly rain forest) has taken the form of logging concessions (i.e., land grabs), and one logging corporation alone removes on average one million tons a year of rainforest logs (Pearce 2012, 181).

Here we see the extremely painful unfolding of a future shaped by short-term capitalist profit maximization and not by long-term ecological considerations. This must come to an end sooner rather than later, if we are to avoid an earth on fire.[5]

Socialism and environmentalism

Modern dialogues about socialism (not always with this name) go back as far as the 16th century, and ancient dialogues go back as far as Greece and Rome. Other than small utopian communities that often did not last long, real experimentation with modern socialism began in the 20th century with the Russian October Revolution of 1917. Since then, there has been a rich literature dealing with both the advantages and disadvantages of various forms of socialism. There are those who think socialism has proven to be a failure; there are many more, however, who think that if we learn from past failures, and find ways of moving towards democratic socialism, we can stop being trodden underfoot by a capitalism that always tends to put profit maximization first in its line of thought and action, even at the cost of impoverishing us and the nature that we depend on.

The above examples are the briefest of indications that show some of the ways capitalism ties in with the enormous problems of sustainability we have to deal with. The theoretical/practical problem that we face now is how to integrate ecological thought and action most effectively with socialist thought and action (Hedges 2015). For while socialists focus primarily on how to advance the flourishing of humans, environmentalists have sometimes focused first of all on the flourishing of nature. Now we are learning rather painfully how deeply the flourishing of humans depends on the flourishing of nature, and hence the necessity of creating new concepts such as ecosocialism. While all the contributors to this volume are aware of this connection, some focus mainly on the socialist side, while others on the ecological side. This is not because they think one side is necessarily more important, but rather it is because they have simply chosen to focus primarily on one side at this time.

As the reader will readily appreciate, this volume begins the task of achieving greater integration of the socialist and environmentalist sides of future-directed thinking. It also suggests that there may be many sides that are important and that need to be considered in relation to one another. For example, many feminists may also be socialists and environmentalists, but of course there are many versions of feminism, socialism, and environmentalism. Focusing on the local may be complemented by focusing on the global, and vice versa. Focusing on failures of past socialist experiments can help us avoid those failures in the future. At this point in history we need to avoid sectarianism and instead find ways of integrating as many progressive points of view as possible, for the construction of a better future will ultimately depend upon creating a high degree of mass solidarity in thought and action from the local level to the global.

Notes

1 See Panitch and Leys eds. (1999).
2 The "Know-Nothing" party was a "nativist" party active in American politics roughly from 1845 to 1855. Among other things, they wanted to restrict the holding of political positions to native-born Americans and require a residency of twenty-five years before citizenship applications would be accepted.
3 See Wikipedia, "US Incarceration Rate."
4 See Albritton (2009).
5 Already there is a large increase in forest fires in many parts of the world.

References

Albritton, R. (2009) *Let Them Eat Junk: How Capitalism Creates Hunger and Obesity*. London: Pluto Press.
Bronson, J. (2015) *Veterans in Prison and Jail*, US Department of Justice, NCJ 249144. www.bjs.gov/content/pub/pdf/vpj1112.pdf
Brown, L. ed. (1993) *The New Shorter Oxford-English Dictionary: Thumb Index Edition*. Oxford: Clarendon Press.
Frey, C. B. and Osbourne, M. A. (2013) *The Future of Employment: How Susceptible Are Jobs to Computerization?* Oxford Martin School of the University of Oxford.

Godrej, D. (2016) "Technology as if People Mattered", *New Internationalist 492*, pp. 13–14.

Grossman, E. (2016) "New UN Report Shows Just How Awful Globalization and Informal Employment Are for Workers", http://inthesetimes.com/working/entry/19577/new_u.n._report_shows_just_how_awful_globalization_and_informal_employment

Hedges, C. (2015) "What It Means to Be a Socialist", *Truthdig*, http://www.truthdig.com/report/item/what_it_means_to_be_a_socialist_20150920.

ILO (International Labor Organization) (2016) *World Employment Social Outlook: Trends for Youth*. Geneva: International Labor Organization.

Kapp, K. W. (1939) "Regulation and Economic Planning", *American Economic Review*, 29, 4, pp. 760–773.

Morris, D. (2011) "One Million US Vets in Prison", www.businessinsider.com/brad-eifert-18-veterans.

Panitch, L. and Leys, C. eds. (1999) *Socialist Register 2000, Necessary and Unnecessary Utopias*. Suffolk: Merlin Press.

Pearce, F. (2012) *The Land Grabbers: The New Fight over Who Owns the Earth*. Boston: Beacon Press.

Phillips, D. (2010) *Lethal Warriors: When the New Band of Brothers Came Home*. Houndmills, Basingstoke, Palgrave Macmillan.

Shane, L. and Kime, P. (2016) "New VA Study: Eighteen Percent of All Suicides", www.militarytimes.com/story/veterans/2016/07/07

Smith, R. (2016) "Degrowth, green capitalism and the promise of ecosocialism", *Links International Journal of Socialist Renewal*, http://links.org.au/degrowth-green-capitalism-ecosocialism-richard-smith.

United Nations High Commission on Refugees (UNHCR) (2016) www.unhcr.org/figures-at-a-glance.html

United Nations Development Program (UNDP) (2015) *Human Development Report 2015*, nin.tl/hdr2015UNDP

US Department of Education (July, 2016) *State and Local Expenditures on Corrections and Education*. Washington, DC: US Department of Education.

Westra, R. (2016) *Unleashing Usury: How Finance Opened the Door to Capitalism Then Swallowed It Whole*. Atlanta, GA: Clarity Press.

Wheeler, W. (July 27, 2014) "How Much Does an F-35 Actually Cost?" warisboring.com/how-much-does-an-f-35-actually-cost/21f95d239398

Wikipedia, "US Incarceration Rate," en.wikipedia/wiki/United_States_incarceration_rate

Wikipedia, "Precarious Work" https://en.wikipedia.org/wiki/Precarious_work

Wilkinson, R. and Pickett, K. (2010) *The Spirit Level: Why Equality Is Better for Everyone*. London: Penguin.

World Economic Forum (2016) "Department of Education Report", www.weforum.org/agenda/2016/07/us-spending-is-rising-much-faster-on-prisons

Part I
Socialism and ecology

2 Radical social democracy

A phase of transition to democratic socialism

Saeed Rahnema

Two key questions continue to confront anti-capitalist thinkers and activists: specifically, *what* kind of alternative society are we hoping to replace capitalism with, and *how* are we to achieve this goal? These are challenging questions particularly for those pursuing practical and achievable strategies.

For some, the responses to these questions are simple and short. That is, the alternative society to capitalism is socialism to be achieved though revolution, without clarifying either the kind of socialism or type of revolution that they have in mind. For the more pragmatic, a post-capitalist society is simply achievable through gradual reforms. But the struggles of the past hundred years, in different parts of the world, have demonstrated that the responses to these questions are far more complicated than originally imagined. The two questions are very much intertwined and need to be addressed concurrently, and the responses need to be continuously modified and adapted to changing conditions. Focusing on solving only one question and leaving the other for later is problematic. Eduard Bernstein famously said that the final goal of socialism is itself nothing, while progress towards that goal is everything. There are other theorists who argue the reverse, suggesting that the most important task is to clearly define what a post-capitalist society will look like. What is needed, however, is both a clear idea of the goal (not a blueprint, of course) and a clear identification of the practical means needed for achieving it. No doubt, there will be variances of the models and paths, determined by the specific conditions of each society within the globalized economy.

We learned this reality the hard way through the Iranian Revolution of 1979. Among all the contemporary upheavals in different parts of the world, the events that led to the downfall of the Shah's regime in Iran can be considered a true revolution – a revolution with the significant role of the left in its inception, along with its miserable failure in orienting it to the desired direction, and worse yet, paving the way for a most reactionary populist religious regime to come to power, rolling back almost a century of attempts at social progress.

In what follows, I will briefly provide a sketch of the different dimensions of this complex and interrelated totality[1]. Learning from the past experiences of both revolutionary and reformist strategies, it is argued here that a post-capitalist society is only possible when a counter-hegemony at different national and global levels is established to replace capitalism with a superior socio-economic system. The long and protracted process of transition to socialism involves a preparatory and transitional phase during the capitalist era, what I call *radical social democracy*[2], and involves new forms of mobilization, education and organization. The new strategies, aiming at a clear and workable goal, will meld aspects of militancy of the revolutionary approach with the pragmatism of incremental reform, towards establishing democratic socialism.

Post-capitalist society

Despite valuable attempts by writers like Peter Hudis to clarify Marx's concept of the post-capitalist society (Hudis 2012), Marx's vision in this regard remains unclear, limited, and in a sense utopian. In the *Critique of the Gotha Program*, Marx brilliantly argued that the new society that has "just" emerged from capitalist society is in "every respect, economically, morally, and intellectually, still stamped with the birth marks of the old society", and thus he envisaged two "phases" for moving to communist society. However, even his first phase seems to be too idealistic. In this phase, wage labour is supposed to be abolished immediately. Instead of wage, individual producers receive back from society what they give to it by "quantum of labour". Individual producers are remunerated on this basis and receive a certificate or a voucher, to draw from the "social stock of means of consumption as much as costs the same amount of labour". This idea sounds like jumping from one social formation to another. In the second or "higher phase", all distinctions are eliminated and people are expected to be free of any competition in a classless and stateless society, enjoying the "abundance" of goods and services based on their "needs" and not their "abilities." And "the enslaving subordination of the individual to the division of labour, and therewith also the antithesis between mental and physical labour" will supposedly "vanish" (Marx 1989a, 87). This ideal is so remote from actual reality that it cannot be put on any serious agenda of any credible left organization. Thus, we need to focus on the so-called first phase. Maybe because of being too idealistic, German and Russian socialists, particularly the latter, modified Marx's "two phases" and distinguished between "socialism" in the lower phase and "communism" in the higher phase, a model that became the blueprint for socialist movements in different parts of the world.

Lenin, in his *State and Revolution*, elaborated the distinction between the two phases, and Bolsheviks followed a relatively more practical conception, particularly during the NEP (New Economic Policy) period. However, as will be discussed below, their ultra-radical strategy in the October Revolution, the ensuing reaction of the right, along with the intrigues of the imperialist powers and the civil war, had already sealed their fate.

As for the Leninist's "first" or "lower phase", we have the experiences of the Soviet-type "actually existing socialism". Preoccupied with the main issue of "public ownership of the means of production", the most immediate socialist task for Russian socialists was "socialization" of the means of production, predominantly through state ownership. Another form of socialization, particularly in the agricultural sector, was collectivization. In certain cases, also some forms of worker control and self-management were introduced, though these were short-lived. State ownership included a total central planning system, producing a huge bureaucratic structure, and proved to be technically impossible in a large economy that involved correlation of tens of millions of items in a gigantic input/output model. The collectivization process carried out by force led to the disastrous decline of agricultural and food production. The whole process, amidst a bloody civil war, involved suppression of dissent, and the emergence of an outright authoritarian and tyrannical political system.

What was missing from the inception was a most important aspect of socialism, namely democracy and civil society's involvement in the decision-making processes. The so-called dictatorship of the proletariat turned into the dictatorship of a single party, and then the dictatorship of a single leader who would oversee a gigantic bureaucracy. Private property was eliminated, but the old capitalist class was replaced with a new bureaucratic elite. The "workers state" could not even tolerate workers' councils in factories. During the Revolution, "factory committees", acting as workers' councils, were organs of control and administration of their respective factories. In 1918 they were transformed into state-controlled trade union branches, and later became part of the factory troika, consisting of the plant manager, the Communist Party cell secretary, and the head of the union local. Under Stalin, even this troika was eliminated and the control of factories was handed over to the manager of the plant. Suppression of dissent and infringements of civil liberties widened the gap between the rulers and the ruled. Rosa Luxemburg was among the first to criticize this brand of socialism.

The most widespread criticism of the "actually existing socialism", concentrates on centralized bureaucratic state control. Some of these criticisms are put forward by those who are against the institution of the state itself, demanding its total abolition, an argument going back to the 1st International. While Bakunin's words sound prophetic in relation to the type of state that eventually emerged in the Soviet Union, his and his followers' expectation of the complete elimination of the state cannot be taken seriously. In 1872, in his arguments against Marx and German Social Democrats' policy of the conquest of political power as a precondition to economic emancipation, he wrote: "In the People's State of Marx ... [the government] will also administer the masses economically, concentrating in the hands of the state the production and division of wealth, the cultivation of land, the establishment and development of factories, the organization and direction of commerce ... the application of capital to production by the only banker ... There will be a new class, a new hierarchy ..." (Bakunin 1972, 31–19). This scenario did happen, but instead of calling for the elimination of the state, we need organizational mechanisms to prevent bureaucratization. No society can possibly be run without a state, or just through a "federation of self-governing workplaces and communes", as Bakunin was suggesting. Marx's brilliant notes on Bakunin's *Statism and Anarchy* are as valid today as they were then (Marx 1874).

Critical of state ownership and control, some socialists, along with most anarchists, advocate "self-management", "workers control", and "direct democracy". Still, no clear explanation is provided as to what exactly workers' control means. During the 1979 Iranian Revolution, when we established workers/employees councils (*Showras*) in the large- and medium-sized state-owned and newly nationalized industries, and in all major institutions, we were exerting full control for a while before realizing quickly that this was only temporary and reliant on a complex set of economic and political factors at different levels of decision-making (Rahnema 1992, 88). Very small units with few workers may have worker control and ownership, but this is not possible for large, particularly national institutions. As for "direct democracy", it is possible to introduce a system in which some specific issues in small towns or districts can be decided collectively, or use referenda on some national issues. But surely not all decisions can be made through these mechanisms, as most organizational decisions need typical professional and hierarchical structures, including different levels of government and governance. The question is, can monetary or fiscal policies be decided through direct democracy? Even the notion of "smashing" the old state machinery advanced by Marx is problematic. What exactly does it mean? Does it include closing all state institutions and firing the existing employees, or does it mean smashing the *relations* of power and changing policies? Instead of calling for the abolition of the state, we need a democratic, decentralized state with participative management.

A different socialism

Rather than simply brushing aside the experiences of Soviet-type socialism and declaring that it was not socialism, as many on the left do, lessons are to be learned from these extensive experiences. The same is true of the experience of the Paris Commune of 1871, which for some on the left is still a model for establishing the "dictatorship of the proletariat". The latter was of course just a short-lived "uprising of one city", and its most prominent supporter, Karl Marx, changed his views about it later, saying that "the majority of the commune was in no way socialist, nor could it have been", and a "compromise" with Versailles would have been more beneficial to the people (Marx 1992, 66). All the experiences of the past, including the Chinese, Cuban, Nicaraguan, and Iranian revolutions, provide us with valuable inputs, and they at least tell us what should be avoided, and what is not practical or attainable in short term.

The most significant aspect of the desired socialism is that, while maintaining the grand ideals that Marx articulated, it should be practicable and attainable, or "feasible", as Alec Nove has suggested (Nove 1983). In the realm of politics – unlike in literature and arts, where the sky is the limit – what is not attainable is not useful. The second aspect is that if socialism is not democratic, and if the majority does not embrace it, it will end up being a suppressive and authoritarian system and will inevitably fail. In a sense society should become socialist first and then elect a socialist state, otherwise a minority has to impose its will on the majority. A reading of Gramsci rightly points to this conclusion. Many other theorists, from Karl Polanyi to Alec Nove and Ellen Meiksins Wood, have brilliantly elaborated on the crucial importance of democracy for socialism. We also need to incorporate aspects of other ideologies that are conducive to the ideals of socialism – features related to individual and civil liberties and rights from liberalism, and decentralization and anti-authoritarianism from anarchism. Social Democratic movements in Europe incorporated democratic features in their brand of socialism, but as will be discussed later, they went off track in a different way.

The desired socialist system must deal with different dimensions of national development. I categorized these in four interrelated and at times perhaps contradictory pillars "economic growth", "social justice", "political democracy", and "ecological balance". Maximizing one dimension may at times minimize another one. Capitalist systems have maximized economic growth, and minimized social justice and ecology. Soviet-type socialist systems maximized certain elements of social justice at the cost of economic growth and ecology. What is needed is the optimization of all these dimensions. The pillar of political democracy and true representation of the public, which itself is reliant on the other three pillars, particularly social justice, is the most important factor in this process.

A most complicated issue to be tackled in this "attainable democratic socialism" is the question of public ownership of the means of production, and along with it the questions related to degrees of socialization, and the fate of private property. These issues that are central to the foundation of Marxian socialism present a serious dilemma. On the one hand, the immediate and complete elimination of private property was a major source of economic stagnation in the countries that exercised this policy. On the other, its prevalence would perpetuate class dominance, which is anathema to Marxian socialism. The critical Russian Marxist economist David Epstein has provided a workable solution in this regard. Instead of "public ownership", he suggests "public *control* of the means of production" (Epstein 2011, 95–109). Through public control, some degrees of private property persist but they are socially and democratically regulated. Other major issues to tackle relate to wages and compensations. The desired socialism of the future, at least for a long time, cannot possibly eliminate wage labour, and must even deal with wage differentiations and compensation of valuable contributions, inventions and initiatives. A "minimum guaranteed income" (Stern 2016), along with comprehensive training and education programs, constantly help prepare the workforce for new professional and occupational opportunities.

This system obviously needs a national governing structure which, unlike centralized states of the Soviet-type socialism, is democratic, decentralized, less hierarchical and participative, and has independent branches of government. A major function of such a state is to develop a dynamic national strategic *vision* through a participative mechanism of all levels of society, and which, unlike the central planning systems of the past, indicates some preferred directions and policies, based on which the autonomous economic, social and cultural institutions, corporations, and cooperatives would design their strategies. This same structure is also responsible for the development of infrastructure, communication, transportation, education, welfare systems, and housing, with the help of regional and local institutions. It runs the banking system and manages fiscal and monetary policies. It also provides oversight for the protection of the environment and citizen rights and liberties.

The socialist participative management system is based on a network of representation of work councils at different organizational and geographic levels. Each autonomous institution or corporation is led by the elected workers/employees' councils, with the representation of immediate stakeholders. Each level of decision-making has representation from both the lower organizational level and the higher one.

Needless to say, the attainment of the goal of socialism in post-capitalist society, which is the direct continuation of the long course of struggles during the capitalist era, is a protracted developmental cumulative process. This is particularly the case in the era of globalization, which has made the question of socialism in one country even more complicated than it ever was.

Modes of transition

Democratic socialism is the ultimate goal for the future, but the question of the present is how to prepare for a transition to such a social formation. From its inception, the question of strategy divided socialists, radical revolutionaries and moderate reformists following different paths and bitterly fighting one another. This has been the case in almost all socialist movements around the world, from the 1848 Revolutions in Europe, through the 1st, 2nd, and 3rd Internationals, and thereafter. In her powerful historical account of the 1848 Revolutions, Priscilla Robertson writes, "After the middle classes had won most of what they wanted, they often voluntarily gave up some of their new privileges so that the lower classes would not have to be given liberties". She compares this to the situation in the captivating story of a man who was asked "what he would like best in the world, provided his worst enemy could have the same thing in double measure – and he answered *one blind eye*". She then contrasts the policies advocated by Marx in that period who emphasized "do not minimize class conflict, exaggerate it", with the moderating reformist policies of Louis Blanc (Robertson 1971, 415–16). Two decades later, in the International Workingmen's Association (IWA), the same differences emerged among the socialists, ranging from the Owenites and Proudhon, to

Blanqui and Marx, as well as the eventual confrontations between Marxists and anarchists. Later, during the 2nd International, there were divisions between nationalist and anti-war Social Democrats; during the two Russian Revolutions of 1917, the bloody conflicts between the Mensheviks and the Bolsheviks; and during the German Revolution of 1918–19, between Ebert's Social Democrats and the Liebknecht/Luxemburg Spartacists. In the 1979 Iranian Revolution, we had the conflicts between the pro-Soviet Tudeh party along with the Aksariat section of the Fedayeen organization, and the "16th Azar" Fedayeen, different sections of the Minority Fedayeen, Workers Path and a multitude of Maoist organizations on the other. Examples in other movements abound.

The sad point is that both the revolutionary and reformist strategies failed in achieving socialism, and eventually changed course to the pursuit of capitalism. The present proponents of revolution and reform, while rejecting each other's strategies, do not clarify what kind of revolution or reform they have in mind. Marx's notion of the social revolution was that it would come about through a "self-conscious, independent movement of the immense majority" (Marx and Engels 1998, 250). Marx differentiated between this "radical revolution" which involves "general human emancipation" and a "political" or "partial" "revolution" which "leaves the pillars of the house standing" (Marx 1988a, 184). Yet, in practice, and despite his disagreements with August Blanqui over his belief in a revolution of a minority leading the unprepared masses, Marx was influenced by him, as reflected in his excitement about the 1848 revolution in France and later the Paris Commune of 1871. All other ensuing revolutions that carried Marx's name, despite mass involvement of the people, were actually Blanquist and not Marxian revolutions.

A major problem faced by revolutionaries in almost all revolutions was how to cope with the pent-up expectations and demands of the public who supported them. With all promises made during the revolutionary phase, once confronted with the stark realities, they realized that they had to downplay expectations, revise promises made, and possibly even resort to suppressing the demands. Examples are numerous: in the 1848 Revolution in France, when the government under the pressure of the Paris workers advertised "the guarantee of the right to work", some 100,000 people from the provinces were "lured" to Paris, overwhelming the authorities, and leading to the abandonment of the right and even dissolution of the national workshops (Robertson 1971, 69–70). Similar cases were revealed in the Russian Revolution, particularly in relation to the question of land and peasantry, or in the Chinese Revolution, particularly after "The Great Leap" and its failure, as well as the so-called Cultural Revolution and its disastrous consequences. Again, during the Iranian Revolution, the workers/employees' councils in the factories would come up with all sorts of resolutions without consideration for the resources needed for their fulfillment. To mention an example, in a jute-making factory of about 800 workers affiliated with the IDRO Workers/Employees Union[3], the council decided to bring back over 1,500 workers who had been laid off from that factory in prior years. When the new CEO of the plant, who was selected with the support of the council, could not convince the council members that the plant could not even maintain the existing number of workers, the council asked for the support of the union. When their request was turned down, they were extremely upset and threatened to leave the union. Later they had to face even further cuts.

All political revolutions of the past failed their objectives because of both their internal contradictions and weaknesses, as well as intrigues of the capitalist/imperialist forces. The main question, however, is whether a progressive revolution that does not have the backing of the conscious majority can have any chance of success in attaining its ultimate goals. Only a socialist revolution that is based on the "independent movement of a conscious majority", with belief in the socialist alternative, is capable of moving towards the final goal of transcending social relations, and that requires enormous preparation.

As for the reformist strategies, they also faced and had to deal with different types of contradictions. They tried to work for a gradual peaceful transition rather than violent revolutions. Marx and Engels, particularly in the latter part of their lives, had also postulated such a possibility. In 1872, in his *La Liberté Speech* after the Hague Congress of the First International, when Marx succeeded in getting the Anarchist Bakunin expelled from the International, he said "we do not deny that there are countries – such as America, England … perhaps … Holland … where the workers can attain their goal by peaceful means." But as for most countries of Europe, he stressed that "the lever of our revolution must be force" (Marx 1988b, 255). On many other occasions, Marx emphasized peaceful means for transition (Rahnema 2017, 9–12).

The main problem faced by the reformist social democrats, however, was that they had to follow policies that were appealing to different social classes, and had to enter into coalitions with other parties and constantly make cross-class compromises. Instead of incrementally moving towards socialist policies and goals, they followed the strategy of reform while trying to curtail the excesses of capitalism (Lavelle 2008). Both the German Social Democratic Party (SPD) and the Swedish Social Democratic Party (SAP) represented such a vision. They gradually distanced themselves from the goal of socialism and turned into liberal democrats. The shifts in social democratic parties also led to the more radical elements splitting off and forming new left parties like Die Linke in Germany, which, along with other left organizations – like the Left Party in Sweden, Syriza in Greece, Podemos in Spain, and the Left coalition in Portugal – tried to push for more radical reforms.

It is important to note, however, that despite their shift to the right, Social Democrats' many contributions to the improvement of the status of working people, and to democracy, should not be ignored. The same is the case with the contributions of the socialist experiences of the Soviets; their mere existence forced capitalist systems to give many concessions to social democratic and labour movements around the world.

In other parts of the world, some major attempts at political and economic transformations occurred through the electoral process. Guatemala under Arbenz, Chile under Allende – both of which were defeated following US interventions – come to mind. Also in Venezuela under Chavez and Maduro, and Bolivia under Morales, despite serious setbacks in part instigated by the right-wing and US imperialist interventions, some progressive policies were adopted including land reform, expansion of social safety nets, increased educational opportunities and housing, and worker-management which continue to exist. However, operating in the neo-liberal global capitalism, these progressive governments have been faced with enormous setbacks.

Moreover, the same electoral opportunities, have also given rise to reactionary political movements. In several Muslim-majority societies, beginning with the Iranian Revolution of 1979, Shi'a and Sunni Islamists have taken advantage of the genuine grievances and discontent of the deprived majority and their religious beliefs, gaining majority votes and establishing Sharia-based Islamist states. The misguided foreign policies of the US and its allies in the Middle East have assisted these conservative intransigent forces who have become a major obstacle to social development.

In brief, following tactics and strategies that were either too radical or void of needed radicalism at specific junctures, has contributed to the failures of both the revolutionary and the reformist camps. A most significant issue is that the level of radicalism needs to be *optimized* based on the actual and specific subjective and objective conditions. When radical advances are not carefully calculated and executed, failure is inevitable. Historical experiences of past revolutionary and reformist movements show that when they are not radical enough, they invariably lose to reactionary forces. On the other hand, radicalism beyond the optimum level leads to adventurism, impeding progress towards the goals of social transformation in a different way. The socialist revolutions and reformisms of the past universally were unsuccessful in envisioning and achieving, or embracing, this optimum.

Agents of transformation

A major issue in the discussion of the transition to post-capitalist society that remains unresolved is the agents and social forces who would make such transformations possible. For Marx, analyzing the capitalist system of his time, the revolutionary working class was the sole agent of transformation to socialism. He believed that parallel to constant expansion of capitalist accumulation and centralization, "grows the mass of misery, oppression, slavery, degradation, and exploitation; but with this grows the revolt of the working class, a class always increasing in numbers, and disciplined, united, organized" (Marx 1983, 715). However, along with many other features of the capitalist system, the working class also went through major transformations. The nature of the working class and its relation to capital obviously did not change, but its relative size, configuration, and revolutionary potentials have transformed significantly.

The working class, in a long process, became highly segmented and differentiated. Marx's focus was on the industrial workers who were working in large numbers in the labour-intensive factories of the time. Today, this section of the working class is a minority within the working population. Moreover, a growing number of these workers are now engaged in processing information (mental labour) as opposed to processing material (manual labour). The nature of work is constantly changing as a result of the practical emergence of new technologies. Consequently, we have many different strata of the working class. Corporate organizational changes and the breakdown of production processes have created scattered clusters of smaller production units, with much smaller numbers of workers, putting an end to the large concentrated factories that Lenin called "the proletarian fortresses". The "Cybertariat"[4], operating in the global network of the "gig economy", is working in totally different conditions controlled and managed not by humans, but by algorithms. In terms of class consciousness, "revolt" of the working class against capitalism did not occur in the manner anticipated. Some questioned the revolutionary role of the working class (Bernstein), and some argued that the consciousness should be introduced to the working class "from outside" by revolutionary socialists (Lenin).

Another major change in the configuration of the working class is the growing number of service and salaried workers resulting from the growth of state and corporate bureaucracies. This sizable and significant group of the working population, identified as the "new middle class", is no doubt a major political player in all countries. The traditional left, however, while romanticizing and exaggerating the role of workers, often denigrates or at least downplays the role of this section of the working population. The ambiguous status of the new middle class, including the fact that a section of it is ideologically on the side of capital, makes it difficult to identify its position in the class struggle. At the same time, the vast majority of progressive forces, the supporters of anti-capitalist, environmentalist, feminist, LGBTQ, anti-war, and labour movements belong to the middle class. It is true that in relation to capital, both wage workers and salaried employees belong to the same category of the working class, but in terms of social status and demands, they are different from each other. In the middle of the nineteenth century, when this class was almost non-existent or very small, Marx, quoting James Mill, implicitly recognized the importance of this class. Mill, while referring to a section of the capitalist class, had also mentioned social elements that are now identified as the new middle class, including "judges, administrators, teachers, inventors in all the arts, and superintendents in all the more important works, by which the dominion of the human species is extended over the powers of nature" (Marx 1989b, 287). Their scientific, administrative, and artistic contributions aside, in today's world the political role played by the new middle classes is quite significant.

Another important factor in the changing condition of the working class is that a sizable number of today's workforce is the so-called contingent labour; that is, workers "with no long-term, year-round, full-time employment with a single employer". According to a 2015 report by the International Labour Organization (ILO), "fully 75 percent of the world's workforce ... is employed in temporary jobs, on short term contract, or in informal jobs without contract". Many of these employments are based on free-agency or freelance. In the United States, "34 percent of the ... workforce is freelance" (Stern 2016, 76, 77).

Precariousness has created massive insecure employment, along with unemployment and underemployment, and has contributed to the expansion of the underclass. This is particularly the case in much of the developing world. Some aspects of Bakunin's argument with Marx in relation to the working class may have some relevance to the condition of today's working class. Criticizing Marx for focusing only on the "upper layer" of the working class and brushing aside others as lumpen-proletariat, Bakunin argued that the upper layers who are "the most cultured" and "live more comfortably than other workers", have a "semi bourgeois position", and are "the least social and the most individualistic". In contrast, he argued that "the flower of the proletariat ... that great mass, those millions of uncultivated, the disinherited, the miserable, the illiterates ... that great rabble of people ... almost unpolluted by bourgeois civilization ... which carries ... the seeds of the socialism of the future ... [is] alone ... powerful enough today to inaugurate and bring to triumph the Social Revolution" (Bakunin 1972, 294). Without agreeing with his conclusion, and while questioning the merit of Bakunin's total rejection of the "upper layer" of the working class as "semi bourgeois" or the identification of any specific section of the working class as the "flower of the proletariat", his reference to the underclass, which now forms such a widespread category, including many millions of slum-dwellers in big cities around the world, is noteworthy.

All these transformations point to the highly heterogeneous nature of today's working class. Furthermore, despite their significance and great potentials for confronting capitalism, the working class can no longer be considered as the sole agents of social transformation. The majority of the new middle class, particularly its progressive elements, and the masses of the unemployed and precariat are also important catalysts of transformations and potential agents of change. The sizable peasantry in less-developed societies can also be mobilized in the transition process, even though a good part of this population has turned into agricultural workers.

Under the dominance of neoliberal capitalism, aside from workers and salaried employees, we have other conceivable agents of change who are affected by the cruel policies of neo-liberalism, namely environmentalists, racialized minorities, women, students, some religious and ethnic minorities and anti-war activists. That is to say, in addition to the working class and the new middle class, the so-called "identitarian" social movements fighting for equity, tolerance, secularism, peace and the environment are an integral part of the anti-capitalist movement. The combined struggle of the working class, the progressive elements of the new middle class, along with the identitarian movements have the great potential of creating a progressive bloc against the dominant class. They constitute the majority of the population in almost all countries. An appropriate strategy, based on specific and achievable goals, can mobilize and attract them to the socialist cause. The stronger the social base and public support, the more progressive and radical an agenda can take shape and be put in place.

Preparing for the transition

As mentioned earlier, transition from capitalism to democratic socialism is possible only when anti-capitalist forces and a large segment of the agents of social transformation can establish a counter-hegemony at the national and global levels. Marx's two "phases" of social development dealt with the post-capitalist society, and he did not elaborate the process of the transition to the "first phase" of such society. Logically, and in the same manner that some "economic, moral and intellectual" aspects of the "old society" continue in the new one as Marx argued (Marx 1989a, 85), some aspects of the new society must also have at least begun to germinate in the old society. In other words, some elements of socialism will also need to start within the capitalist era.

This means that a preparatory phase needs to take place within the capitalist era, which involves an incessant and steady struggle towards economic, moral, intellectual and political change. The intent of this phase would be the overall strengthening of the position of labor vis-à-vis capital; advancements in gender, sexual and racial equity, ecological balance; and moving closer and closer to the "first" phase of post-capitalist society. I call this phase *radical social democracy* to differentiate it from today's social democracies, or socialism, which is the ultimate future objective. I don't call it democratic socialism, as has been suggested, because it is taking place when capitalism is still the dominant social formation.

Considering the problems and unworkability of abrupt political revolutionary strategies, discussed earlier, this process is gradualist. At the same time, having in mind the ineffectiveness of reformist strategies of the past in moving towards socialism, it involves an increased, though optimized, radical approach. Taking state power in this strategy is not with the aim of "smashing" its apparatuses, but changing its relations of power and policies. There is no question that the capitalist state, capitalists and conservative forces would do whatever they can to prevent progressive forces from advancing. That is why the strategy of radical social democracy, while peaceful and reform-oriented, may also be forced to adopt confrontational tactics and direct action to mobilize civil society. This was a policy adopted by reformist socialists as early as the mid-1920s, when Otto Bauer of the Austrian Social

Democratic Party coined the term "defensive violence". The policy included strikes, general strikes, even insurrection, as a last resort, in response to the violence of the capitalist class. The level of radicalism always needs to be optimized based on subjective and objective factors at the national and the global levels.

The overall political action model for the preparatory phase of transition to post-capitalist society includes a set of interrelated *actions* in different *domains*. It can be envisaged in a matrix correlating "socio-cultural", "political", "economic", and "ecological" *domains* on one axis, with *actions* that include "education", "organization", and "deployment" on the other.

The focus is first on the cultural domain which includes challenging the dominant ideology and creating a countercultural hegemony. It involves refuting the state's "moral and intellectual" works and its ideological apparatuses, the mainstream media, right-wing think-tanks, religious fundamentalists, and other institutions whose functions are misinformation and keeping the public ignorant of the realities of the capitalist system. Raising socialist consciousness and mobilizing working people to articulate higher aspirations is one of the main goals of political action in this phase.

When the "conscious" support of the "immense majority" is gained, the focus then will shift to the political domain, aiming at taking political power through democratic peaceful means and direct actions. Changes in the political domain consist of reforming the existing political system, including transforming the electoral process "from an instrument of deception to an instrument of emancipation" (Marx 1989b, 85). It also includes reforming and democratizing institutions of the state at the national, regional, and municipal levels, and guaranteeing political liberties and freedoms, and ultimately, transforming relations of power. The introduction of participatory management at all levels, from neighbourhoods and work place bodies to the highest levels of decision-making, is an integral part of changes in the political domain.

With the new political power in place changes in economic, social, and environmental polices follow. Economic transformation combines aspects of socialist strategic vision-building and capitalist market economy with the gradual dominance of the former over the latter. Radical reforms consist of socialization of the finance and banking systems, increasing regulations by democratic bodies of industry, business, foreign trade, price control, progressive taxation systems, working conditions, fair wage systems, a guaranteed minimum income, along with universal education, healthcare, pensions, affordable housing, and other reforms. Ecological and environmental regulations are an integral part of these reforms. The extent of these reforms is obviously linked not only to the subjective and objective conditions at the national level, but also to the global situation and social-political movements in other countries in their respective progress towards socialism. Needless to say, some of these reforms can be gained even before taking political power; as the progressive movement expands and gathers more support, it imposes progressive legislations, compelling the existing government to give more and more concessions.

Throughout this process, public education and dissemination of information about the social and economic malaise of the capitalist system, on the one hand, and the benefits of the socialist alternative, on the other, are of utmost importance. The creation of attractive, progressive and informative news and information media targeting different sections and strata of the population are crucial steps in the information war against the established regime.

Pivotal to the success of this process, however, is organization at different levels, from workplaces to neighbourhood, city, regional and national levels. Learning from the bureaucratic structures of the past on the one hand, and from the latest developments in organization theory and design, all organizations would be democratic, participative, flexible, agile and adaptable to changing circumstances.

As for workplace organizations, in countries that genuine independent labour unions and civil society organizations are legal and active, the goal should be to democratize and radicalize them. In countries where genuine unions do not exist, establishing such unions should be a most urgent item on the agenda.

In addition to unions, there should be a push for industrial democracy and increasing worker/employee participations in management. Work councils, or other forms of organizations, would act as the participatory arm of the unions and not as "worker control" organizations. Industrial democracy is certainly a relative concept and different degrees of its attainment, ranging from "information sharing" by management, to "consultation" with workers, and "co-determination" at different organizational levels – from the shop floor to the level of the firm – are directly related to the strength of organized labour. Considering the conflictual nature of labour-capital relations, the more powerful, better organized and more advanced the workers in each society, the higher the degree or level of industrial democracy that can be achieved, and vice versa.

As industrial and business workplaces become smaller and smaller and the number of full-time workers shrink, creating organizations in working-class neighbourhoods becomes more important for mobilizing workers, the unemployed and their friends and families. This can be done by creating neighbourhood cells for the purpose of mobilizing their community, organizing events, information dissemination sessions, and direct actions. Each cell would connect with other neighbourhood cells to coordinate actions at the broader community level, and elect representation to higher (ward, city, province, and national) levels.

All these activities are parallel to the formation of a left political party or parties. Unlike Leninist-type parties of "professional revolutionaries", based on "democratic centralism" and "non-factions", the new left political party would be democratic, least-hierarchical and participative. It would embrace all agents of transformation, from different strata of the working class and the middle class, along with identitarian groups, feminists, LGBTQ, anti-racists, peace activists and environmentalists. There is no illusion that the creation of a party that represents diverse and at times conflicting demands of these social classes and groups would be extremely complicated. However, without such an organization bringing together all those who are suffering under capitalism, it would be impossible to move to a post-capitalist society. This party would always remain outside the state, and even when the new transitory state is formed, will continue as an opposition force and push the state towards more radical reforms and changes.

With this sort of organization and ongoing educational undertakings, a growing number of people will be mobilized, in support of a radical social democracy at the national level, with the goal of the eventual move towards post-capitalist democratic socialism. Needless to say, socialism cannot be established in one country alone. No socialist economy can survive in a globalized capitalist economy, dominated by big imperialist countries and their international economic and financial institutions like the IMF, World Bank and WTO. The success of socialist systems at the global level is dependent on socialist transformations in the powerful capitalist states and the transformation of international institutions. This relies on progressive states coming to power in a growing number of countries, particularly in advanced industrial societies, which at present have the strongest influences on global economic institutions. Such a development rests on progressive voters who can elect such states, which itself is contingent on the success of left and progressive forces in mobilizing public support in favor of progressive candidates.

This will no doubt be a protracted and very difficult process. However, while it may seem utopian, it is a "practical utopia" and has a far better chance of success as compared to the fantastical alternative of toppling capitalist systems through political revolutions of avant-garde minorities, or the naïve optimism of gradual reforms leading to true socialism.

Notes

1 I have used part of the arguments I put forward in the introduction of my edited book, Rahnema, S. (2017).
2 The term "radical social democracy" has been in use in different languages by different writers, and there are political organizations like Chile's Partido Radical Socialdemocrata. My usage of the term, however, denotes a socialist-oriented movement during a capitalist era, and a preparatory phase for transition to post-capitalist society.
3 Industrial Development and Renovation Organization of Iran (IDRO), was the largest industrial conglomerate in Iran, with over 120 large- and medium-sized heavy and light industries and projects.
4 The term "cybertariat" was coined by Ursula Huws, referring to workers operating in the "gig economy".

References

Bakunin, M. (1972), *Bakunin on Anarchy*, translated and edited by S. Dolgoff, New York: Alfred A. Knopf.

Epstein, D. (2011), "Socialism, Private Property and Democracy", *Svobdnaya mysl*, 11.

Hudis, P. (2012), *Marx's Concept of the Alternative to Capitalism*, Chicago, IL: Haymarket Books.

Lavelle, A. (2008), *The Death of Social Democracy: Political Consequences in the 21st Century*, New York: International Publishers.

Marx, K. (1874), "Conspectus of Bakunin's Statism and Anarchy," *Marxist Internet Archive*, http://www.marxists.org/archive/marx/works/1874/04/bakunin-notes.htm

Marx, K. (1983), *Capital* Vol. 1, Ch. 32, Moscow: Progress Publishers.

Marx, K. (1988a), "Contribution to the Critique of Hegel's Philosophy of Law," in *Karl Marx, Frederick Engels: Collected Works, vol. 3, Marx and Engels: 1843–1844*. Translated by Jack Cohen, et al. New York: International Publishers.

Marx, K. (1988b), "On The Hague Congress: A Correspondent's Report of a Speech made at a Meeting in Amsterdam on September 8, 1872, in *Karl Marx, Frederick Engels: Collected Works, vol. 23, Marx and Engels: 1871–1874*. New York: International Publishers.

Marx, K. (1989a), "Critique of the Gotha Programme", in Karl Marx, Frederick Engels: Collected Works, vol. 24, Marx and Engels: *1874–1873*. Translated by David Forgacs et al., New York: International Publishers.

Marx, K. (1989b), "Parliamentary Debate on the Anti-Socialist Law," in *Karl Marx, Frederick Engels: Collected Works, vol. 24*, New York: International Publishers.

Marx, K. (1992), "Marx to Ferdinand Domela Nieuwenhuis," in *Karl Marx, Frederick Engels: Collected Works, vol. 46, Marx and Engels: 1880–1883*. Translated by Rodney Livingstone et al. New York: International Publishers.

Marx, K. and Friedrich Engels (1998), "Communist Manifesto," in *Socialist Register 1998: The Communist Manifesto Now*, ed. Leo Panitch, Colin Leys, London: Merlin Press.

Nove, A. (1983), *The Economics of Feasible Socialism*, London: Routledge.

Rahnema, S. (1992), "Work Councils in Iran: The Illusion of Worker Control," *Economic and Industrial Democracy: International Journal* 13, no. 1 (February).

Rahnema, S. (2017), *The Transition from Capitalism; Marxist Perspectives*, New York, London: Palgrave Macmillan.

Robertson, P. (1971), *Revolutions of 1848: A Social History*, Princeton, NJ: Princeton University Press.

Stern, A. (2016), *Raising the Floor*, New York: Public Affairs.

3   Ecosocialism for a new era

Pat Devine

We may be entering a new era. Multiple interlocking crises are calling into question the continuing viability of capitalism, re-posing Rosa Luxemburg's warning: "(Eco)socialism or barbarism". The global economy is experiencing major structural change and displaying signs of relative stagnation. Social cohesion is increasingly undermined as inequality reaches new levels. Failed states, terrorism and large-scale refugee movements are creating widespread human tragedy and social disruption. Democracy is under threat and authoritarian tendencies are gaining strength. And perhaps above all, in the long run, climate change and declining biodiversity pose unprecedented challenges that capitalism is intrinsically incapable of meeting

A new era?

Capitalism can be periodized in many different ways: rural agricultural and urban industrial; competitive and monopoly; national and imperialist; craft-based and industrial-scientific; Fordist and post-Fordist; and, after Karl Polanyi (1944/2001), the "peaceful" nineteenth century and, after Eric Hobsbawm (2004), the "extreme" twentieth century, or at least the first three-quarters of it. A start to thinking about the present conjuncture and possible future trajectories may be Polanyi's concept of the "double movement". He argued in his magnum opus, *The Great Transformation*, that the transformation from eighteenth-century rural agricultural capitalism to nineteenth-century urban industrial capitalism ushered in "a hundred years of peace" based on the four institutions of the nineteenth century: the balance of power, the international gold standard, the self-regulating market, and the liberal state (Polanyi 1944 / 2001). Peace did not mean the absence of war but the avoidance of major European-wide conflict for most of the century.

Of the four institutions, the attempt to create a self-regulating market was the dominant one that shaped the history of the century and ultimately brought about the downfall of the nineteenth-century settlement. The self-regulating market, or the market system, was Polanyi's term for capitalism, defined by the creation of the three "fictitious commodities" – labor, land and money. Fictitious, because they are not produced for sale in a market;

commodities, because they are nevertheless sold and bought in markets. This is effectively the same as Marx's definition of capitalism, when all the inputs into the production process have become commodities. Polanyi, although rejecting Marx's objective labor theory of value in favor of the subjective marginalist theory, basically accepted Marx's analysis of the underlying dynamic of the capitalist mode of production – "Accumulate, accumulate! That is the law of Moses and the prophets" – but he argued that the attempt to create a fully self-regulating market was "utopian", in the sense of being impossible to fully achieve.

The first moment of Polanyi's double movement, based on his analysis of nineteenth-century England, was the creation and consolidation of the markets for labor, land and money, the institutions of the self-regulating market, establishing the economy as separate and distinct from the rest of society and non-human nature, with its own dynamic and laws of motion. However, the disastrous consequences – the degrading impact of unregulated capitalism on labor, land and money – undermined the conditions on which capitalism depended for its continuous reproduction. It called forth the second moment of the double movement, a counter-movement of social protection consisting of various forms of resistance: Chartism, the growth of trade unions, the Factory Acts, urban planning, food safety legislation, pressure from the landed gentry and agricultural laborers to protect the countryside, financial regulations, limited liability, and so on.

However, regulatory interference with the laws of motion of the capitalist mode of production, together with its intrinsic cyclical instability and the inter-imperialist rivalry caused by the uneven geographic development of its underlying expansive dynamic, ushered in the extreme twentieth century. The nineteenth-century world was shattered by the First World War, Bolshevism, the Great Depression, Fascism, and the Second World War. Bolshevism and Fascism were both, in their very different ways, seen by Polanyi as manifestations of the countermovement against the destructive effects of the self-regulating market, his term for Marx's "anarchy of production" or today's "market forces". What emerged from the Second World War, in different ways in the different countries of the developed capitalist world, was a version of the Social Democratic, Keynesian Welfare State, enshrined in a replacement of the gold standard by the fixed exchange rates of the Bretton Woods institutions of the IMF and the World Bank, perhaps the apogee of the second moment of the double movement.

It seemed at the time as if a new era of stable capitalism had been established, sometimes referred to in retrospect as a "Golden Age" (Marglin and Schor 1992). Unemployment was at an historically unprecedented low level and growth at an unprecedentedly high level, and in the 1950s the conditions of working-class life were transformed through mass production and its accompanying mass consumption. As the British Conservative Prime Minister, Harold Macmillan, put it in the late 1950s, "You've never had it so good", and it was true. Yet all was not well. As Michal Kalecki had argued in

1943, unemployment is not a "market failure" but is actually functional for capitalism; full employment would cause problems for the system (Kalecki 1943). And so it proved. By the mid-1970s capitalism had begun to seize up: inflation was out of control, reaching 25% in the UK in 1975, and the rate of profit was falling, at bottom both due to the increased strength of labor in the labor market and in the workplace. Furthermore, welcome as the welfare state had been in slaying, or at least seriously weakening, Beveridge's five "Giant Evils" in society – "squalor, ignorance, want, idleness, and disease" – its structure was paternalistic, which slowly began to create dissatisfaction as the era of deference waned.

In the UK, the post-war settlement that had underpinned the Golden Age was a consensus across the political spectrum, primarily between the culturally conservative laborist Labor Party and the culturally conservative one-nation Conservative Party. By the 1970s this settlement had run into the sand, resulting in a Gramscian organic crisis, with the ruling class no longer able to rule in the old way, and a Gramscian war of maneuver, a struggle between two opposing trajectories over a resolution to the crisis. The outcome of the struggle had been determined by the preceding Gramscian war of position, the slow contest to build up ideological and institutional support for alternative hegemonic historical blocs. Radical change was needed, but the left's response to the accumulating problems as the post-war settlement unraveled had been defensively conservative, defending the paternalist collectivist gains of the welfare state rather than promoting a radical extension of participatory democracy extending to a challenge to the power of capital in the economy. The right, on the other hand, had been predominantly radically creative, developing an individualist, anti-collectivist, pro-market, residual-state trajectory that recognized the need for radical change. The radical right won the war of maneuver, and the result was neoliberalism.

Initially, the main focus of neoliberalism was on undermining the social forces and institutions that underpinned the post-war social democratic settlement: trade unions, public ownership, local government, social housing, social security, financial regulation, the professions. The guiding principle was to extend ever wider the domain of the market, to restore and strengthen market forces as the dominant driving force in the economy; as Andrew Glyn put it, *Capitalism Unleashed* (2006). Then, with the new configuration of social forces and the deepening ideological hegemony of "the market knows best" as the new common sense of the age, market principles were gradually introduced into the heart of the welfare state, education and health; while solidarity, national insurance-based, social security was gradually replaced by safety net welfare for losers. In the advanced capitalist countries, neoliberalism was supported and promoted by parties and governments of both the center right and increasingly also the center left; in the less developed countries it was imposed by the International Monetary Fund and the World Bank in the form of the "Washington Consensus".

Running in tandem with these developments was the rapid intensification of globalization as a result of technical change and political decisions by national governments and the international institutions created by them. The main technical development was the digital information revolution; the main political decision was the abolition of controls over capital movements and the deregulation of financial institutions and markets. The evolution of the European Union, which the UK joined in 1973 and decided to leave in 2016, is perhaps the most dramatic example of this, but it is paralleled across the globe, most recently in the various TTIP-type treaties. The result has been the creation of a global industrial reserve army, deindustrialization in most developed capitalist countries as production was moved to low-wage economies, and the undermining of the strength of labor, creating a deregulated low-wage race to the bottom and a new social group, the "precariat" (Standing 2011, 16).

The social protection regulations against the adverse consequences of the free market that had been achieved by Polanyi's counter-movement, the second moment of his double movement, had caused capitalism to seize up. The neoliberal attacks on and partial reversal of these regulations gave capitalism a new lease of life, but the fundamental dysfunctional contradictions of the system remained and resulted in the build-up of new fault lines. The inexorable dynamic for new sources of accumulation led to the invasion by capital of new domains for investment, commodifying ever more aspects of social existence and of non-human nature, and creating new arcane financial "products" which nobody fully understood through the process of financialization. The result was the systemic crisis starting in 2007–8 which showed no signs of ending ten years later as relative stagnation seemed to have become endemic in the advanced capitalist countries along with slower rates of growth in China and the other BRICSs.

The main policy objective of neoliberal governments and the international economic and financial institutions in response to the crisis has been to promote a renewal of economic growth, although ironically this has been pursued through the counterproductive policy of austerity, which actually inhibits growth. However, at a deeper level growth largely nullifies the second policy objective which has come to the fore with increasing urgency – the imperative of coming to terms with climate change. Recognition of the growing ecological crisis has been mounting for at least half a century, starting perhaps with Rachel Carson's 1962 *Silent Spring*, followed by the Club of Rome's 1972 *Limits to Growth*, the 1992 Rio Earth Summit, the 1997 Kyoto Protocol, and most recently the 2015 Paris Agreement. While the emphasis has primarily been on climate change, the wider issues of biodiversity loss and finite resource depletion are increasingly accepted as of pressing importance. And while the dominant mainstream response to the ecological crisis has been to advocate ecological modernization, fossil-free energy, and business-as-usual "green capitalism", there is growing recognition that ecological sustainability is incompatible with continued economic growth in the rich countries, if not yet acceptance that zero-growth or de-growth are incompatible with capitalism (Sustainable Development Commission 2009; Royal Society 2012).

We are confronted with four interlocking crises: economic, ecological, social, and political. Globalization, together with neoliberal austerity policies, has created levels of inequality not seen for a hundred years. Deindustrialization, the relative stagnation of the economy, and the effects of climate change have largely affected the poor and powerless in both the rich and the poor countries. Western so-called humanitarian interventions, together with widespread arms sales by military-industrial complexes around the world, have created failed states and civil wars which in turn have given rise to terrorism, a refugee crisis, population displacement and mass migration. In most of the developed capitalist countries this mixture has created discontent, feelings of lost community and identity, and widespread mistrust of the establishment and political elites. The result is a deep crisis of democratic legitimacy, with the rise of chauvinistic, ultra-nationalist, sometimes neo-fascist, parties of the far right, together with a parallel response on the left with the rise of anti-austerity, socialist and green parties, as Syriza in Greece, Podemos in Spain, Bernie Sanders in the US, and Jeremy Corbyn in the UK. We seem to be entering a new era. As Antonio Gramsci put it (1971), "The crisis consists precisely in the fact that *the old is dying and the new cannot be born*; in this interregnum a great variety of morbid symptoms appear".

A new organic crisis?

As already noted, neoliberal globalization has been orchestrated and presided over by the political parties of the right and the center left, supported and promoted by the think tanks of the right and center left, the international economic and financial institutions, and the media, together constituting the prevailing establishment. It is against this establishment that the anger of the increasing number of people adversely affected in different ways by global market forces has been directed. In many countries deindustrialization has destroyed local communities; real wages have stagnated since the 2008 crisis; rising inequality has undermined social cohesion; traditional values have been eroded; and immigration, refugees and terrorism have resulted in a growing reaction against "foreigners". A sense of powerlessness, a feeling that "they" never listen to "us", has developed.

Not surprisingly, the adverse consequences of globalization, and perhaps globalization itself, are increasingly under attack. Although the G20 countries meeting in 2008 resolved not to respond to the financial crisis by resorting to protectionism, by contrast with what happened in the 1930s Great Depression, in fact they have undertaken hundreds of protective measures, led by the US, Germany and the UK. Within the European Union the Schengen agreement allowing free movement of people without border checks in the adhering countries has effectively been abandoned, and the EU-wide principle of the right to live and work in any member country is under severe pressure. Attempts to share the humanitarian need to accommodate millions of refugees have been unsuccessful, and worryingly nasty chauvinistic and xenophobic right-wing nationalist movements and governments have come increasingly to the fore.

Yet there are also many encouraging signs of worldwide progressive resistance and prefigurative action. These range from defensive actions to preserve jobs and protect the environment to attempts to live in new non-hierarchical and ecologically sustainable ways. Examples include the development of plans for alternative uses of productive capacity, including workers' skills, in place of socially useless or damaging production like weapons or fossil fuels; Occupy Wall Street and UK Uncut; Reclaim the Streets, initially a feminist movement, subsequently anti-car; self-provisioning, guerrilla gardening, seed swapping, Community Assisted Agriculture, Via Campesina; LETs, Credit Unions, social entrepreneurs; Cooperatives; and Transition Towns. There have also been widespread heart-warming examples of grass roots popular actions of solidarity and support for refugees, in stark contrast to the repressive responses of many governments.

However, although many of these movements have subscribed to the mobilizing slogan of "another world is possible", what is largely missing from them is a credible vision of a post-capitalist ecosocialist world and a political strategy for moving towards it. Drawing on the historical experience of the failed Soviet model and the theoretical insights of Karl Marx and Karl Polanyi, the rest of this chapter outlines the author's view of what an ecosocialist society might look and feel like, the institutional architecture and processes on which such a society might be based – social ownership, subsidiarity and negotiated coordination, and a strategy for transition built around Gramsci's concept of hegemony. The present conjuncture, as we have seen, contains many "morbid symptoms", but it also contains possibilities for progressive movement towards the full realization of Enlightenment values and Marx's vision of the end of prehistory and the liberation of human kind.

An ecosocialist society: sketch of a future utopia

The argument of this chapter is that capitalism is incapable of creating the conditions necessary for the flourishing of human and non-human nature or, to put it another way, for social and ecological sustainability. The central lesson to be drawn from the Soviet, East European, Chinese and Latin American experiences is that socialism cannot be imposed from above; it must emerge from and be created by the collective and individual self-activation and organization of people in civil society. Although neoliberal hegemony is under increasing pressure, the prevailing zeitgeist still makes it difficult to present a convincing argument for a fundamentally different society, conducive to the flourishing of both human and non-human nature. This section attempts to do just that. It first outlines the principles on which an ecosocialist society might be based and the implications of those principles for different aspects of social life, and then suggests a possible set of institutions and processes that might enable these principles to be realized.

Principles and their implications

Two possible guiding principles for imagining an ecosocialist society are *the abolition of the metabolic rift* (Foster 1999) and *the abolition of the social division of labor* (Devine 1998, 2010, Ch. 7). Historically these two principles can be traced back to the work of Marx and have subsequently been developed by the left wing of the green movement and the more forward-looking wing of the socialist movement. More recently they have come together under the banner of ecosocialism. The metabolic rift refers to the impact of capitalism on non-human nature, undermining the ecosystems on which capitalism depends for its continuous reproduction and more generally degrading non-human nature, most notably at present through greenhouse gas emissions bringing about climate change and the threat to biodiversity from the impact of capitalist production on species habitats. The abolition of the social division of labor is a generalization of Marx's concept of the abolition of the distinction between mental and manual labor. By abolishing the alienating and distorting consequences of narrow specialization and the inequality inherent in a hierarchical ordering of people within the labor process, and in society more generally, it creates the conditions for human flourishing, for people to develop their full, all-around potentialities. The two principles are equally important and mutually interdependent. The achievement of one at the expense of the other would be morally unacceptable and is in any case impossible in practice.

The implications of these two principles for an ecosocialist society are inevitably extremely far-reaching, involving fundamental changes in society, in ourselves, and in future generations. It is the scale of the changes likely to be involved which makes it so difficult for us to engage in the thought experiment necessary. I start from Marx's characterization of the higher stage of communism in his brief discussion of a post-capitalist society in the *Critique of the Gotha Programme*: "from each according to his ability, to each according to his needs" (Marx 1875 / 1938)! It is important to note that this involves equality in terms of the satisfaction of people's needs, taking account of the fact that needs will differ for various reasons – life stage, health, geography, and climate. Marx also envisaged the higher stage of communism as being attainable only once abundance, the ability to satisfy everyone's needs, had been achieved. This has usually been interpreted on the supply side, as being brought about by the development of society's productive forces, by increases in productivity; but there are two compelling reasons why today attention must also be given to the demand side.

There is now accumulating scientific evidence that further economic growth in the richer capitalist countries is incompatible with the pressing need to curb greenhouse gas emissions in order to avoid catastrophic climate change, and more generally with the achievement of ecological sustainability, as argued in the UK's Sustainable Development Commission's *Prosperity without Growth?* and the Royal Society's *People and the Planet*. The productive capacity of these societies is already more than enough to produce what is needed for human flourishing, although of course it is not currently being used for that purpose, since they are capitalist societies. In the less developed societies there is still a need for economic growth to enable the basic and higher needs of people to be met. The only morally acceptable approach is movement towards equal global per capita access to resource use and waste disposal which, given that the current global ecological footprint is roughly one-and-a-half times global ecological carrying capacity, necessarily involves massive redistribution from the richer to the poorer countries. Valuable as their work is, what the Sustainable Development Commission and the Royal Society do not recognize is that steady state zero growth, let alone de-growth, are incompatible with capitalism, whose law of motion is "accumulate, accumulate".

This brings us to the second reason why the demand side requires attention. Productive capacity in the developed capitalist countries, and increasingly in the developing countries, is not used primarily to meet what is needed for human flourishing. Resource use and waste disposal in all countries are unequally distributed, in many countries increasingly and grotesquely so. The competitive consumerist ethos of capitalism generates not satisfaction but discontent. The undermining of social solidarity by competitive individualism results in the corrosion of trust and a feeling of losing out as people compare their house, car, doctor, their children's school, exam performance, clothes and toys, their success in the sales, with those of others. As Ted Benton (Red Green Study Group, new edition, forthcoming) has argued, it is not so much that capitalism generates false needs, but that it offers false, primarily material, means of satisfying real needs. At the same time the rich 1% increasingly live in a bubble, cut off from the rest of society in gated communities and posh restaurants, on their superyachts and private aeroplanes, with second or third homes around the world, and their children at private schools.

Kate Soper (1990) has developed the concept of "alternative hedonism", emphasizing the qualitative sources of pleasure and the good life, as opposed to the quantitative false means of consumerism. Ecologically sustainable lifestyles do not have to be the ascetic "hairshirt" parodies of hostile characterizations. Increasing productivity can be used to increase the time available for creative emancipatory self-development rather that the production and consumption of more "stuff". Richard Layard, in his book *Happiness*, and Richard Wilkinson and Kate Pickett, in their book *The Spirit Level*, show that once a threshold level of income that enables basic human needs for food and shelter, health and education, to be met, increased human well-being depends not on further increases in real income but on the qualitative aspects of life associated with more equal societies – the quality of personal relationships with family and friends, the degree of job satisfaction, the level of security people enjoy, the extent of social cohesion, and a sense of contributing to a common good. There is also increasing evidence that human flourishing is enhanced by experience of and engagement with the non-human natural world (Barton and Pretty 2010; Maller et al. 2006; Pretty 2004; Pretty et al. 2004).

A central reason why economic growth and consumerism are so ideologically dominant is that capitalism depends on growth, and consumerism is a form of compensation for the lack of substantive control over their lives that most people experience. The anarchy of capitalist production, the allocation of resources by the impersonal operation of market forces in pursuit of profit, creates a sense of powerlessness as people have no control over what happens to their jobs and communities. This is reinforced by the fact that government policy is made by an out of touch political elite in bed with business, which in any case is relatively impotent when faced with an increasingly globalized world dominated by transnational corporations. It is not surprising that an anti-establishment "us and them" mentality has developed, giving rise to dangerously morbid right-wing responses as well as to opportunities for various forms of creative hegemonic left political developments.

An ecosocialist society would be a self-governing society based on a bottom-up structure of participatory democracy founded on the voluntary associations of civil society in which people learn to make decisions and participate in implementing them. The structure would be shaped by the principle of subsidiarity: decisions should be made and implemented at the most local level, consistent with all who will be affected by a decision being able to participate, directly or indirectly, in making it. Such a layered structure of decision-making, from the local to the global, necessarily involves both direct and representative democracy. Abolition of the social division of labor, the hierarchical stratification of society into social classes or groups in which people spend most of their lives and which shape their human characteristics, creating partial rather than fully rounded people, is a necessary condition for people to develop their full potential to become fully rounded human beings and be able to participate effectively at all levels of society.

Marx advocated the abolition of the distinction between mental and manual labor, but this can be extended to a finer classification of social activity. I have elsewhere (Devine 1998; 2010, Ch. 7) suggested five broad categories – unskilled and repetitive, skilled, nurturing, creative, and planning and running – but nothing turns on the categories I have chosen, and most particular tasks can be assigned to more than one category. The social division of labor must be distinguished from the functional division of labor, the particular detailed type of work undertaken within each given category of social activity, as in Adam Smith's pin-making example. Within each category of social activity there are many different functional activities, as set out below (see Table 3.1).

In the course of their lives people would expect to undertake activities within each category, possibly more than one, roughly in proportion to the amount of work socially necessary in the society in each category. They would not spend their working lives performing activities in only one category, although there would probably be agreed exceptions in the case of activities that require long periods of specialist training. In particular there would no longer be a

Table 3.1 Classifications of social activities

Category of social activity	Illustrative functional examples within category
Planning and running	Running bodies responsible for functional services
	Running enterprises and other workplaces
	Running voluntary self-governing groups
	Serving on representative bodies
Creative	Artistic, scientific
	Design
	Some higher education and research
	Some professional
Nurturing	Care of the young, the ill, the disabled and the old
	Personal support
	Primary education
Skilled	Secondary education
	Skilled craft and technical
	Skilled non-manual
	Some higher education and research
	Some professional
Unskilled and repetitive	Assembly line
	Cleaning and housework
	Copy typing and call centers
	Driving
	Laboring, refuse collection

Source: Devine 1988; 2010 171.

distinction between the social group who run things and the social groups who are run. People would have experience of activities in all social categories and so would gain the knowledge necessary to be able to cooperate creatively with one another in the different detailed activities in which they engage.

We can consider the implications of the two underlying principles of an ecosocialist society in more detail in relation to different aspects of social life: production and work; nurturing and the life cycle; land use and living arrangements; and collegiality and spirituality (Ted Benton, Red Green Study Group, Ch. 6, forthcoming). In line with the principle of subsidiarity, production is likely to be much more locally based than under global capitalism. However, the local and the global should be envisaged as interdependent processes; global processes always involve some degree of localisation, and local processes are part of a larger globalised web of networks. Based on these considerations, it seems likely that in an ecosocialist society, global industrial agriculture will be replaced by organic food produced locally or regionally, with diet shaped primarily by local seasonal availability. The design of manufactured products and their production technology "would be based on four fundamental criteria: durability, ease of repair, pleasantness of manufacture, and absence of polluting effects" (Gorz 1980, 45). Long-distance trade would be undertaken only in response to different climatic, ecological and topographic conditions.

Workplaces would become cooperative centers of enjoyable social activity with work no longer primarily a burden but a source of pleasurable, stimulating, psychologically productive experience. Organic farming, craft activity, and maintenance work would complement complex technology based production, bringing people into closer contact with non-human nature and contributing to the overcoming of the metabolic rift. With the abolition of the social division of labor, people would share in the management, the design, organization and administration, of the workplace. In order to be able to experience the different categories of social activity it is likely that people would move between several workplaces in the course of their lives. Unrewarding work that could not be replaced by automation would be equally shared. Although work in formal workplaces would be primarily rewarding, it is likely that, as productivity increases, it would take up a smaller proportion of people's time than at present, leaving more time for activities not necessarily organized in formal workplaces.

An important part of such activities is likely to be the nurturing and caring activity that people need at different stages in their life cycle. They are likely to be undertaken by a combination of communal collective caring institutions – kindergartens, schools, higher education institutions, clinics, hospitals, care homes, and hospices, together with households and local community-based groupings. With the abolition of the social division of labor, including the sexual or gendered division of labor, nurturing and caring activities would be shared equally between men and women, enabling both to experience the joys and sadnesses involved in cherishing, caring for, and losing others. This would extend to the sharing of housework and child care in the home, thus ending women's double burden. Time outside the formal workplace would of course also be available for a wide range of other enjoyable and self-developing activities such as socializing, hobbies, pastimes, gardening, allotments, art and music, sport and outdoor activities.

Changes on the scale implied by a new relationship between human and non-human nature, as the metabolic rift is overcome, and a new relationship between people, as the social division of labor is overcome, will inevitably involve major changes in land use and living arrangements. Reversing the catastrophic decline in biodiversity since the 1950s, containing the extent of climate change, and restoring the integrity of the biosphere will require careful management of habitats by local communities within a national and global framework of agreed principles respecting non-human nature, whether by assigning it virtual rights or assigning it status as a virtual stakeholder. The change from global industrial agriculture to local organic farming has already been discussed. This would replace the present sterile, polluting, monocultural character of much of the countryside by flourishing biodiverse habitats. Overcoming the metabolic rift will also involve significant changes in water management, mineral extraction, and waste production and recycling.

A central issue to be faced is the relationship between town and country, urban and rural. Marx envisaged the abolition of the distinction between them, thus ending "rural idiocy" or, in more recent translations, "the isolation of rural life". Alternative approaches emphasize the cultural dynamism of cities and focus on reworking the relationship between town and country rather that abolishing the distinction between them. At stake is the pattern of human settlement. Whether in town or country, communities need to be in control of their environment, collectively shaping how the want to live, again within a national and global framework of agreed principles relating to human and minority rights, the environment, including greenhouse gas emissions and energy policy, and developmental matters concerning the distribution of population and employment and the desired direction of technological change.

The pattern of daily life developing as a result of all these changes is likely to be community based, with households, workplaces, education, health and leisure centers largely planned to be within walking or cycling distance, while incorporating vehicular access for those who need it. Urban areas would be "greened" by the inclusion of gardens, allotments, parks, sports fields and wild places. Rural areas would be planned to enable adequate access to such facilities, including cultural venues, with a convenient local transport system. Transport in an ecosocialist society would be planned with human needs and non-human nature in mind. It is likely that air and motor vehicle travel and container ship traffic would be greatly reduced as production becomes more localized, with rail providing most of the necessary freight transport. It is also likely that the character of personal travel will change, with people engaging in their daily work and free-time activities mainly locally while having fewer but longer holidays further afield, travelling by train or boat.

The closing of the metabolic rift and the end of the social division of labor would greatly enhance human well-being, the quality of human life, as well of course as enhancing the quality of non-human nature. Human needs include the need for spiritual experience, which historically has taken the form of different religious and supernatural beliefs but increasingly in the future is likely to take a secular form. Cooperative and convivial time spent with family and friends; collective endeavor in worthwhile tasks; physical activity, craftwork, creative and artistic activity; exposure to the cultural achievements of humanity over the centuries – all can be spiritual experiences conveying a sense of elation, awe, even sacredness. Re-engaging with non-human nature as part of our daily lives would also be a spiritual experience, enhancing our sense of well-being. As we act upon and in non-human nature we not only change non-human nature, for better or worse, we also change ourselves, our own nature, and in an ecosocialist society the change would be for the better.

Institutional architecture and processes

Ecosocialism can be thought of as a self-governing society in which civil society exercises social control over the state and the economy and mediates its relationship with non-human nature. Civil society consists of voluntary self-governing associations organized around different interests and causes. Citizens elect representative assemblies to promote the general good, choosing between the different visions, values and priorities of the competing political parties. The associations are involved in decision-making and implementation in economic enterprises and in state institutions, together with representatives of the directly elected representative assemblies, at each subsidiarity-defined relevant level. Social control is thus exercised through a combination of associations with particular interests and assemblies representing the general interest. The metabolic rift between society and non-human nature is overcome, and people undertake their fair share of running the associations and economic and state institutions, and serving as representatives, in the layered structure of participatory democracy. The diagram below sets this out in schematic form (see Figure 3.1).

Social Control

Civil society exercises social control over the economy and consciously mediates its relationship with nature, directly through self-governing associations, and indirectly through its control over the state.

Key
Social control
Conscious mediation

Figure 3.1 Social control. (Source: adaptation from Adaman, Devine and Ozkaynak 2007, 98.)

Much productive activity will be undertaken locally, in the household or small enterprises in the community. However, some economic activity will need to be organized and undertaken at the regional, national or international level, where economies of scale in production are large or system networks are needed. The activities of different enterprises have to be coordinated. Under capitalism this occurs primarily through the operation of market forces as enterprises compete for profits. Private ownership means that enterprises make their decisions independently rather than collectively. Decisions are not coordinated in advance but only after resources have been committed, output is sold and enterprises discover how much profit has been made. Less profitable enterprises contract or close; more profitable enterprises invest and expand. The outcome is not planned but emerges through the operation of the invisible hand, market forces.

The socialist critique of capitalism as an economic system is that private ownership results in exploitation and unearned income, with atomistically made decisions resulting in what Marx called the anarchy of production. The alternative of common ownership abolishes exploitation and enables decisions to be planned and coordinated in advance, before resources are committed, assisted by the Internet and new communications technologies. Various forms of common ownership have been advocated, most commonly public- or state-owned enterprises, or cooperatives and not-for-profit enterprises. However, both these generic forms have disadvantages as well as advantages. Public ownership enables production to be planned in advance, but public enterprises tend to be organized on a top-down basis rather than being run by those who work in them and make use of what they produce. Cooperatives offer more scope for bottom-up participation, but they are a form of collective private ownership, engaging in atomistic decision-making and competing against each other, with their decisions coordinated through the operation of market forces – "market socialism".

What is needed instead is social ownership, defined as ownership by those who are affected by the enterprises' activities. Social participatory planning starts at the level of the individual enterprise which is socially owned by those affected by its activities: its workers, customers and suppliers, the communities in which it is located, environmental, equal opportunities and other relevant interest groups, its industry council, and the planning councils in whose jurisdiction it operates. The social owners negotiate over policy in relation to the use of the enterprise's existing capacity, and the policy decisions are implemented through a process of worker self-management. It is important to deconstruct the concept of "the market", distinguishing between market exchange, based on the use of existing productive capacity, and the operation of market forces, bringing about changes in capacity. The enterprise sells the output produced with its existing capacity by engaging in market exchange with its customers, in competition with other enterprises in the same industry, which generates information about how well the enterprise is using its assets to satisfy its users' needs.

Social planning retains market exchange but not market forces. Decisions over changes in an enterprise's capacity, through investment or disinvestment, affect a wider set of groups than decisions over the use of an enterprise's existing capacity, so it is this wider set that constitutes the social owners at the level of the industry. At this level, enterprises do not compete with one another; the social owners make the decisions on investment and disinvestment together in the industry council. The council includes all the enterprises in the industry, the communities in which they are located, the industry councils of the industries buying the output of the industry and supplying its inputs, relevant interest groups at the industry level, and the planning councils for the regions affected. In the industry council, the social owners negotiate a coordinated plan for investment and disinvestment for each enterprise in the industry as a whole. It is this process of negotiated coordination that replaces the operation of market forces in a system of social planning.

Industry councils may be at the city, regional, national, international or global level, informed by the principle of subsidiarity that decisions should be made at the most local level consistent with all groups affected by a decision being involved in making that decision. The relevant level will be determined by the importance of economies of scale in production, the need to minimize transport costs, the desirability of having balanced economies wherever possible, the ecological and topographical characteristics of different locations and activities, and so on. The social owners at each level have three types of information available when engaging in their negotiations: data generated by market exchange on the performance of each enterprise, the explicit and tacit knowledge provided by the representatives of the different social owners of their particular experiences and needs, and the general societal-wide information provided by the representatives of the relevant planning councils. The process of negotiated coordination is a transformatory deliberative process of social learning. The social owners learn about the interests and concerns of others and the wider social objectives of the general assembly's at each level. It is not a process of aggregating pre-existing preferences but one in which people learn and preferences change.

Participatory planning through negotiated coordination in all aspects of social life would enable the two principles guiding ecosocialism, overcoming the metabolic rift and the social division of labor, to be realised, and a society conducive to the good life, to the flourishing of human and non-human nature, to be created, managed, and improved. Civil society would control the polity and the economy. Production and work, nurturing and the life cycle, land use and living arrangements, relationships with non-human nature would be shaped to meet human needs, the full development of human potential, spirituality and emancipation.

A political strategy for transformation

The transformations involved in moving from the present global capitalist system to a fundamentally different alternative system are enormous, and this presents us with a serious dilemma. The most urgent challenges facing the world are those of climate change and loss of biodiversity – most urgent only because if not tackled soon they are irreversible, which is not in any way to underestimate the challenges of poverty, inequality, and what Richard Sennett has called "ontological insecurity". Yet, the transformation needed can be realized only through a prolonged process of political struggle. The historical record shows that very rapid transformations impose what today would be regarded as unacceptable social and human cost, as in the case of early nineteenth-century industrialization in England and the Russian and Chinese revolutions that followed the first and second twentieth-century world wars.

Urgent though the pressing ecological challenges are, the only way forward is through popular struggle from below informed by a political strategy for transformation. Both are needed. Struggle against exploitation, oppression and injustice; threats to livelihood and settled ways of life; and environmental and ecological degradation will always occur, but unless they are related to a strategy for political power they are unable to bring about fundamental transformations in the system. Political strategies for transformation get nowhere unless they are related to struggles which challenge the existing power structure and change the balance of forces in society. The political strategy that does this that I find most compelling is that of the Italian Communist Party leader and Marxist, Antonio Gramsci, adapted to today's world.

Gramsci argued that the revolutions in Europe that followed the Bolshevik revolution after the First World War failed because the ruling class in those countries ruled not primarily through coercion, although they did, but primarily through consent based on the hegemonic dominance of their ideas embedded in the institutions of civil society. He argued that after a relatively settled period, the contradictions in capitalism give rise to a situation in which the ruling class can no longer rule in the old way, an organic crisis develops and a period of struggle follows, which he called a war of maneuver, in which the contending social forces seek to resolve the crisis in their favor. The outcome of this struggle, he argued, largely depends of the war of position undertaken in the preceding settled period, during which the contending forces seek to establish a hegemonic position in the institutions of civil society, articulated in terms of a hegemonic ideology. Following the first part of his well-known adage, "pessimism of the intellect", Gramsci thought that the most likely outcome of a war of maneuver would be a series of "passive revolutions" from above, taking account of and incorporating many of the demands of the opposing social forces in a new settlement that preserved the underlying capitalist class structure. However, following the second part of his adage, "optimism of the will", he hoped and worked for a political process through which each war of maneuver weakened the power of capital and created the conditions for the establishment of a new progressive hegemony in the next war of position, leading eventually to a transition to a post-capitalist and eventually (eco)socialist society.

In order to create a progressive hegemonic position in civil society, it is necessary to create what Gramsci called an "historic(al) bloc", consisting of an alliance of all the social forces adversely affected by the existing capitalist regime, and articulated in terms of a theoretically informed ideology that presents an alternative program seen as furthering the interests of the society as a whole. The social forces involved in such an alliance and character of the alternative program that it advances will obviously depend on the history of the society in question, its political system, the particular circumstances of the crises facing it, and the existing and developing institutions, movements and struggles existing in the country.

The 1945 post–Second World War settlement in the UK is a good example. Following the depression of the inter-war years and the experience of a more or less united country in the fight against Nazi Germany, a feeling of "never again" developed. The Labour Party led by Clement Attlee won the 1945 General Election and formed a government that introduced the Keynesian Social Democratic Welfare State, which had bipartisan support for full employment, the National Health Service, free education, a national insurance-based social security system, and public ownership of all the major utilities and the mining industry. The only major area of disagreement was over public ownership of the steel industry. The unraveling of this settlement was discussed earlier in this chapter.

The task in the present conjuncture is to develop the growing movement against globalization and austerity in favor of a new green deal. This will involve taking the aims of the 2015 Paris Agreement seriously and adopting measures to move beyond fossil fuels towards non-nuclear renewables, investing in green infrastructure, replacing free trade with managed trade as part of the move towards more local production of food and manufactured goods, abolishing tax havens and re-establishing controls over capital movements, implementing a progressive tax regime and a genuinely living wage that is enforced, as part of a movement towards tackling inequality and developing a humane policy towards immigration and asylum seekers. This will need major political changes within countries, together with fundamental reform of the international institutions.

The existing broken system of liberal representative democracy, in which competing elites have lost touch with those they are supposed to be representing, needs to be developed into a system of participatory democracy based on the principle of subsidiarity. The current competitive race to the bottom between countries needs to be replaced by cooperation between nations in order to deal with challenges that can be met only by collective regional and global action. These changes would create the basis for ending the disastrous wars destroying the countries of the Middle East and elsewhere, with the developed countries ending the present "humanitarian interventions", their arms sales and corrupt economic activities, and instead assisting the less developed countries to move to a situation in which the basic needs of their people are met. The forces on the ground pressing for such changes exist. What is missing is a theoretical and ideological framework unifying the diversity of these movements, developing a hegemonic discourse that challenges the existing elite neoliberal consensus, and promoting a solidaristic multicenter challenge to the prevailing capitalist power structures. Building such an alliance would in itself be prefigurative in that it could start the transformatory process throughout society more widely, as it would require people to negotiate and work together in ways that particular interest groups and traditional parties at the moment normally do not. As we act to change society, we change ourselves in ways that prepare us to act as citizens in a self-governing ecosocialist society.

Acknowledgements

This chapter has been greatly influenced by discussions in the Red Green Study Group since its formation in 1992. I should also like to thank Peter Dickens for helpful comments and Elena Lieven for continuous support, discussion and creative suggestions.

References

Adaman, Fikret, Pat Devine and Begum Ozkaynak, (2007) "Reinstituting the economic process: (re)embedding the economy in society and nature", in Mark Harvey, Ronnie Ramlogan and Sally Randles (eds), *Karl Polanyi: New Perspectives on the Place of the Economy in Society* (Manchester University Press, Manchester).

Barton, J. and J. Pretty (2010) "What is the best dose of nature and green exercise for mental health? A meta-study analysis", *Environmental Science and Technology*, 44: 3947–3955.

Devine, P. (1998 / 2010) *Democracy and Economic Planning: The Political Economy of a Self-Governing Society* (Polity Press, Cambridge).

Foster, John Bellamy (1999) "Marx's Theory of Metabolic Rift: Classical Foundations for Environmental Sociology", *American Journal of Sociology*, 105, 2: 366–405.

Glyn, Andrew (2006) *Capitalism Unleashed: Finance, Globalization, and Welfare* (Oxford University Press, Oxford).

Gorz, Andre (1980 / 82) *Farewell to the Working Class: An Essay on Post-Industrial Socialism* (Pluto, London).

Gramsci, Antonio (1971) *Selections from the Prison Notebooks* (Lawrence and Wishart, London).

Hobsbawm, Eric (2004) *Age of Extremes: The Short Twentieth Century, 1914–1991* (Michael Joseph, London).

Kalecki, Michal (1943) "Political Aspects of Full Employment", *Political Quarterly*, 14: 322–330.

Maller, Cecily, Mardie Townsend, Anita Pryor, Peter Brown and Lawrence St Leger (2006) "Healthy nature healthy people: 'Contact with nature' as an upstream health promotion intervention for populations", *Health Promotion International*, 21, 1: 45–54.

Marglin, Stephen and Juliet Schor (1992) *The Golden Age of Capitalism: Reinterpreting the Postwar Experience* (Clarendon Press, Oxford).

Marx, Karl (1875 / 1938) *Critique of the Gotha Programme* (International Publishers, New York).

Polanyi, Karl (1944 / 2001) *The Great Transformation: The Political and Economic Origins of Our Time* (Beacon Press, Boston).

Pretty, Jules (2004) "How Nature Contributes to Mental and Physical Health", *Spirituality & Health International*, 5: 68–78.

Pretty, Jules, M. Griffin and M. Sellens (2004) "Is Nature Good for You?", *Ecos*, 24: 2–9.

Red Green Study Group, *What On Earth Is To Be Done?* (new edition, forthcoming).

Royal Society, The (2012) *People and the Planet* (Royal Society, London).

Soper, Kate (1990) *Troubled Pleasures: Writings on Politics, Gender and Hedonism* (Verso, London).

Standing, Guy (2011) *The Precariat: The New Dangerous Class* (Bloomsbury Academic, London).

Sustainable Development Commission (2009) *Prosperity without Growth? The Transition to a Sustainable Economy* (Sustainable Development Commission, London).

4 The practical utopia of ecological community

Ann E. Davis

Introduction

Money is a "veil" in neoclassical economic thought, with no independent influence on "real" decision variables, such as capital, labor, and output. By contrast, in Keynesian economics, money influences the dynamics of the entire system. That is, there is no consensus on the nature of money in economic literature (Keynes 1964).

Perhaps there is a way to treat money as a veil in a different sense, which influences the way of seeing the world, like the proverbial rose-colored glasses. In this case, the glasses are green, providing a commercial cast to the way of seeing in modern industrial societies, a form of distortion. In this chapter, this latter meaning of the "veil" of money is more useful, shading common understanding of the purpose of life in financial terms. Think of the accountant's green eyeshades. The motive of "gain" has become the most important, in contrast to previous types of society (Polanyi 1944, 68). According to classical political economy, such rational self-interest will benefit both the people and the sovereign (Cardoso 2014, 585–588).

This importance of money to the entire society is related to the fiscal/ military state which emerged in the late seventeenth century (Neal 2000). The purpose of the state is to levy taxes to support war to conquer trade networks and territory, for the expansion of the state (Brewer 1988; Schumpeter 1991). In this context, money is the lifeblood flowing through the circulatory system; the substance which unifies a society based on individual private property and the autonomous individual, with the role of citizen as taxpayer and the role of the bondholder as *rentier*. Money is the ultimate purpose of economic activity and the metric of individual lifetimes, and the state's means of survival in a system of competing nation states.

As one specific example to be considered in this chapter, money influences the way in which land is viewed. Rather than a portion of a global ecosystem, a parcel of land is considered individual private property, and valued for its financial rate of return. Land is also the collateral for much of the financial system, the "material" substrate for financial contracts stretching into the future, the "real" of real estate. In this sense, land is the ultimate store of value for modern national currencies, which serve as the means of payment for settling contracts in a global financial system.

The premise of this chapter is the urgency, in the age of the "Anthropocene," to develop a new way of seeing land beyond money, to re-embed each parcel into the interdependent biogeochemical cycles which sustain all life on earth. By contrast, the financial system, which has its own imperative of compound annual growth, and which appears to have its own infinite time scale, presumes to be more important and more immediately practical.

Method: historical institutionalism

In order to develop a new understanding of land, it is useful to make use of the method of historical institutionalism (Davis 2015a). With this approach, one considers the concept of land, and the associated institutions and bodies of knowledge as an interrelated complex. For example, the concept of land changed from the feudal to the capitalist period, from a permanent residence with customary use rights to a commodity for resource extraction and sale. Land tenure systems changed dramatically with the economic transition, as well as the mediation of money (Polanyi 1944; North, Wallis, and Weingast 2009). As the real-estate market emerged, human settlement patterns changed, along with the development of new social and financial institutions. The body of knowledge of political economy also emerged and became a separate discipline in academic institutions (Poovey 1998; 2008). That is, viewing the entire complex of concept, institutions, and knowledge facilitates an analysis of the related institutions, along with their historical evolution. With this complex in mind, it is possible to envision a new set of institutions which could be possible. The specific parcel of land may still be identified by the same GPS coordinates, but the way in which it is incorporated into human life and work may change substantially.

In the civic republican tradition of ancient Greece, ownership of land was the foundation of autonomy and rationality, as well as political community (Pocock 1975). In the modern industrial economies, land is the prototype of "individual private property," and undergirds the notion of autonomous individuals. That is, one could conceivably be self-sufficient with a deed to a parcel of land, in terms of food, clothing, and shelter, even though the actual practices of the division of labor have long ago undermined the feasibility of such independence. In fact, the original myth of Robinson Crusoe was written by a man deeply engaged in the new financial economy of seventeenth century England (Goetzmann 2016, 322–327, 332–337; Poovey 2008, 93–110).

History

Land has functioned historically as the territory of empires and nation states. The system of sovereign, mutually exclusive nation states emerged from the long institutional development in the transition from feudalism to capitalism

(Ruggie 1993; Sassen 2006). The system of co-respective territories was a resolution of the competing claims of the universal entities of papacy and empire, finally resolved with the war of independence of the Dutch Republic in 1648, with the Peace of Westphalia. The global exploration of European states beginning in the late fifteenth and sixteenth centuries provided the impetus for commercial expansion and colonization of much of the "new world." The trade in slaves and exotic commodities, such as spices and hallucinogens, provided much of the foundation for monopoly merchant corporations and the rise of financial instruments and markets based on their projected returns (Goetzmann 2016). The land acquired from merchant trading posts and colonies became the foundation for the public domain with the successful war of independence for the United States in 1776. The distribution of this land to settlers with the homesteading movement and with suburbanization in the post-World War II period provided the basis again for economic stimulus and growth. Ultimately the yeoman's independence as well as the suburban homeowner's American Dream may have been undermined by the burden of debt (Levy 2012).

The allocation of public lands to private property, protected by the state and from the state by Constitutional provisions, provided the foundation for real estate, labor, and financial markets. Private property was a privileged form for financial accumulation, protected from the state, while also taxed by the state. The individual property owner mirrored the absolute sovereignty of the ruler of the nation. The subsequent economic growth benefitted both state and private owners of real and financial assets. The irony of the double role of the state is evident in such issues as "takings," where the attempts by government to support commerce with powers of eminent domain and environmental regulation are resisted in the name of protecting private property from government (Purdy 2015, 218–227). This particular approach to law and economics seeks to protect the financial value of land by disallowing environmental regulations, even in the case of coastal property threatened by sea-level rise. In some states, the science of climate change is denied to avoid recognizing its impact on real-estate values and the need for state regulation.

Impact of financial vision

The entire notion of "growth" in financial terms is a metaphor based on natural primary production. That is, money itself does not grow. The apparent expansion of value in the financial circuit is due to the intermediation of commodity production, intertwined with human and natural life forms (Moore 2015). The financial terminology of "stock" and "flow" is drawn from the metaphor of cattle, quite literally, livestock, and flows of milk diverted from the domesticated nurture of the next generation (Goetzmann 2016, 37–40; Smith 1994, 302–305). In other words, the financial system abstracts from and replaces the "natural" system of human and ecological reproduction, which is no longer visible. Money appears to be the active, autonomous agent, what Marx calls a form of "fetishism" (Marx 1967).

Incentives based on the ideal ownership model presume to reward stewardship and a long-term perspective. On the other hand, there are many examples where financial incentives emphasize the short-term time perspective, and avoid accounting for externalities: strip mining in Appalachia or cattle ranching in the Amazon or palm oil groves in Indonesia. Put differently, there is a financial "opportunity cost" for extended turnover time, which reduces the rate of profit. Speeding turnover of property, or "flipping" real estate, can lead to higher profitability, as in the cliché "time is money."

For some economists, markets are everywhere and constitute a universal aid to optimal decision making. For others, the tendency for "commodification" is resisted, as undermining intrinsic values and fragmenting community (Polanyi 1944; Marglin 2008). In other words, markets are not appropriate for all decisions, and some objects are "priceless," not adequately exchanged or valued in money terms.

Periodization

With this historical institutional methodology, one can view the *longue duree*, or the "long twentieth century" (Arrighi 1994; Moore 2015), to see institutional changes more clearly. For example, Marx discusses different forms of capital, such as "usurer's capital" and "merchant's capital," and other historians have identified the slave trade as a distinctive period in the eighteenth century (Beckert 2014; Baucom 2005), as well as the "industrial revolution" of the nineteenth century and the consumer-based growth model in the twentieth century (Cohen 2003). Across these very different periods, the tendency for capitalist development has been to increase productivity and substitute capital for labor, using "capitalist technology" and fossil fuel energy. In spite of appearances to the contrary, the capitalist economy is based on labor exchange, and the labor theory of value (Postone 1996), of which money is the symbolic representation. Using money as a convenient means of payment, store of value, and medium of circulation does not reveal to the lay citizen/consumer its foundation on the commodity labor power.

The interface of money and life developed historically, from annuities and dowry funds in Italian city-states in the early modern period, with the execution of counterfeiters and the imprisonment of debtors in the seventeenth century (Wennerlind 2011, 141–152). Treating labor as a commodity subordinated part of human life to the command of others. For example, the slave trade had a high mortality rate, and the social disruption caused by the emergence of the labor market was managed by Poor Law reforms in the nineteenth century and welfare in the twentieth century (Polanyi 1944). With the emergence of the industrial revolution, Marx discusses the requirement of living labor to add value to the "dead labor" embodied in machines, as well as the free gift from nature to industrial production (Marx 1967 Vol. I Ch. 8, 200, 206).

Capitalist production, therefore, develops technology, and the combining together of various processes into a social whole, only by sapping the original sources of all wealth – the soil and the laborer (Marx 1967 Vol. I Ch. 15, Section 10, 507).

The emergence of money and financial calculation was the product of institutional evolution over the last five hundred years. Money has become a dominant institution in modern life (Epstein 2005; Krippner 2005). This world view is not inevitable, or even necessarily progressive.

New vision: one earth

The dangers of CO_2 accumulation have been well documented and acknowledged, even by mainstream economists (Nordhaus 2013; Sachs 2015). For some, the cumulative impact of humans on earth ecosystems justifies a new term, the Anthropocene (Purdy 2015; Moore 2015).

Context of existing global compacts

Existing global compacts, such as the Kyoto Protocol and the European Exchange Trading System, are based on market mechanisms. Many economists recommend the use of financial metrics and incentives to protect the environment, even though this approach maintains the financial world view. Many economists view the market as a source of information, by means of price signals, to make optimal decisions regarding resource allocation (Mirowski 2013, 26, 51, 334). Existing systems of assessment estimate the ecological damage done by such externalities as global warming in money terms. But existing market signals are distorted by monopoly as well as skewed income distribution and externalities, with many critiques of indicators such as Gross National Product.

Existing economic techniques consider the environment as "externality," and rely on marginal decision-making and assumed zero cost of disposal. Price mechanisms would be modified to internalize the externalities, such as a carbon tax or cap-and-trade, according to Pigou's (1924) and Coase's (1960) recommendations. Marginal decision-making assumes that the macroeconomic context remains constant. When waste streams such as CO_2 accumulation in the atmosphere have already destabilized the global climate, this assumption no longer holds. A paradigm shift is needed, which incorporates industrial ecology, with new design assumptions such as "waste = food." With an integrated approach, "waste" in economics terms provides nutrients to another part of the ecosystem (McDonough and Braungart 2002; Stahel 2016).

Some economists recommend industrial policies to address the impact of climate change, such as supporting renewable energy and transition from fossil fuels, in addition to pricing carbon (Pollin 2015). The goal of reduction of the market of fossil fuels by 35% will be resisted, nonetheless, with a significant impact on some of the world's largest corporations, as well as oil-exporting nations. Job losses in those industries could be addressed by transitions to new employment, including jobs in renewable energy. In some cases like Saudi Arabia, the oil exporting nations are already considering industrial policies to expand renewable energy production. Although these techniques have long been advocated in the United States, political resistance has prevented any serious consideration and climate change denial is more pervasive (Mirowski 2013, 334–342).

Other economic tools, such as present discounted value, underestimate the impact of events occurring in the distant future, such as climate change. The choice of discount rate has become an issue, with Nicholas Stern preferring a low rate, and Nordhaus preferring the market rate (Nordhaus 213, 185–194). But this approach assumes an infinite financial market, that capital is "productive", and that consumption is the goal of all economic activity. These assumptions seem less compelling with a climate that is no longer stable or predictable, threatening to disrupt food production, much less global supply chains for consumer durables.

Further, CO_2 accumulation is only one environmental problem and carbon tax or carbon markets only one mechanism. There are other significant problems with waste streams, such as ocean acidification, eutrophication with nitrogen runoff, as well as accumulation of plastics in the ocean (Cressey 2016) and spent nuclear fuel overwhelming disposal capacity. There are invasive species introduced by climate shift and the threat of species extinction (Wilson 2016), as well as depletion and degradation of soil and water.

The approach in this chapter is for a more thorough, comprehensive re-visioning of economic activity. The technology exists to model and to assess global ecology and to map existing resources and human settlement patterns. Ecological knowledge exists to prioritize and restore arable land, forest cover, habitat, and species preservation, and to project the impact of sea level rise. Information technology capabilities exist to project new sustainable settlement patterns and to build new infrastructure to support renewable energies and technologies. The discussion which follows engages in an alternative perspective, a world without money as we know it. The recommendation here is to base metrics and decision-making systems directly on biogeochemical indicators, to more accurately measure the resilience of global ecosystems, to move entirely beyond money: that is, to return to the original sources of wealth: the soil and human labor.

Vision

The objective of this chapter is to see beyond capitalist imperatives for growth and financial rate of return, to view land without the distorting veil of money. This new view of nature has been called the "ecological imagination" (Purdy 2015), succeeding the earlier cultural conceptions of nature as a teacher, as a refuge, or as God's gift to humanity for its own utility.

The formulation of a new vision of the economy requires a comprehensive approach (Harvey 2010), which includes an analysis of the set of related institutions as well as its knowledge foundations. New visions can also seek models and insights from reflection on the long-term history of capitalist institutißns. Instead of the objectification of the economy, stressing functions performed by abstract impersonal agents, there would be a reflexive economics, integrating subject and object (Albritton 2001, 29–35). Instead of governance by the "invisible hand" of the market, there would be deliberate, democratic communities (Schor 2010, 2011; Graeber 2013; Alperovitz 2013).

Like the Physiocrats, the vision described further below is that all wealth is based on human communities living on the land. A new set of financial institutions can be constructed which express and preserve this value. In this twenty-first-century version, all sustainability and well-being is based on ecology and community. Environmental restoration is imperative to limit further disruptions in global climate and to restore fertility of the soil for food production and habitat restoration.

Design of ecological communities

Merchant "nations" were originally separate communities in major trading ports which were organized by birthplace of the resident merchants (Rothman 2012, 3, 198–210; Marx 1967 Vol. III, 900–907), diasporas which served as trade and financial networks. Although the unique appeal of one's birthplace remains palpable, the requirement of exclusive territorial boundaries for nation states may be no longer necessary or constructive for global governance.

Breaching the various institutional divides of modern capitalist society, land-based communities could be designed with regional borders associated with watersheds, or other ecological boundaries. Citizenship would be based on hereditary usufruct rights to the land, with responsibilities for preservation and restoration. The constitution would guarantee subsistence, health, and education, as well as universal political representation in regional and global governance structures. Communities and families would be based on voluntary associations and long-term mutual commitments, including kinship, marital ties, and regional restoration/residential/agricultural communities. Rather than individual private property, there would be collective management of the regional ecology.

New money, new financial institutions

Rather than national currencies, it is possible to design a single global ecological currency, managed by global level decision-making institutions based on biogeochemical quotas and limits. The management of the global currency would be public, with regional federations feeding into the formulation of global priorities. The ecosystems of the earth are the basic store of value.

Management of these interrelated resources would be the basis for use rights and for prioritizing common investments.

The land would be owned in common instead of real-estate parcels based on individual private property. The basic "money" supply would be based on permits for land use rights, such as agriculture, mining, residential, retail and industrial structures. There would be a global land bank, drawing upon earlier experiments (Goetzmann 2016, 351–354, 386–400; Wennerlind 2011, 73–75, 114–121), with these permits for reserves, and credit extended based on the initial allocation of permits to each region. Credits would be earned by achieving regional restoration goals, including cultural and historical as well as ecological, and could be used for international recreational travel, education, or trade.

Migration and relocation would be considered based on applications and review of ecological impact at the regional and global levels. Rather than a neo-serfdom with the population tied to the land, there would be a new view of "residence," which includes contributions to the local community and ecology, as well as integration of public and private. Rather than a re-enchantment of nature, there would be an enlightened recognition of interdependence. There would be a new view of "freedom" to integrate across all spheres, with a view of the whole based on global ecology, rather than individual private property in the so-called "private sphere," which has no geographical address. In the "Anthropocene" (Purdy 2015; Wilson 2016), there is a new urgency to coordinated global action.

Learning community

Rather than the abstract equal individual (Mirowski 2013, 93–155), there would be a personal, residential community. As with the cultural resonance of the term "nation," there would be an emphasis on the importance of birth place for personal identity and community connections. Instead of the "imagined community" of Benedict Anderson (1991), there would be a specific historical and geographical location, with awareness of continuity from the past into the future. Instead of a national mythic "origin story," there would be a personal, genealogical history. Rather than individual "identity" based on conspicuous consumption, there would be group cohesion and dedication to learning and personal development (Stiglitz and Greenwald 2014; Sen 1999; Nussbaum 2011). Rather than immediate gratification, there would be an appreciation of geological and ecological time spans.

The goal would be to integrate cyberspace with global ecologies, "grounding" the relationships among ecological regions. Instead of the Internet based on commerce and self-presentation, as well as pornography and terrorism, social networking would be location-specific. Instead of the abstract individual with equal rights based on property ownership, communities would form to protect human and ecological resources. Membership would be based on common identities, such as "of woman born" (Rich 1976) and residents of the planet earth.

Knowledge as a public good

Instead of use of information technology tools for control and surveillance, there would be "open source" collaboration and sharing, using "creative commons" licensing (Hess and Ostrom 2007; Lessig 2005). Competition for scientific discoveries and innovations would be recognized with world-wide renown, rather than the count of the world's richest men.

New model for "economic development"

Money in a capitalist economy establishes and requires institutional divisions, hierarchies, and imperatives. Money is a form of governance, which obscures the conception of the whole which is required for governance of the commons (Ostrom 1990). Instead of individual private property circulated by money with externalities defined as "outside" the system, the redesign of "property" would include integrated social and ecological units. Long-term relationships would be based on explicit, concrete human and ecological relationships, instead of financial "flows," with metrics beyond GDP to assess "present value" and future potential (Commission 2010). Calculations of cost/benefit analysis and "opportunity costs" are the outcome of the assumed perpetual infinite financial market, rather than existing in the "real world." But financial markets are social constructions, which create and reinforce their own appropriate behavior (MacKenzie 2006, 2009). Money is not a convenient convention which is simply in the interests of everyone (Searle 2010), but an obstacle to personal, human, and ecological development. Financial markets have become "fetters" on investment, welfare, and sustainability.

Money in a capitalist economy is for the purposes of abstraction, discipline of labor and extraction of surplus. Research and development is for invention of new "capitalist technology." Investment in a capitalist economy is for tools which improve labor productivity and achieve automation and control. Such a financial system based on labor time of commodity production is no longer necessary. Rather than the standard time of disciplined production or "expansion" of money (Postone 1996), there would be a new vision of time, based on seasons, the life cycle of human communities, and ecological and evolutionary time (Wilson 2016).

Instead of a public/private divide, there would be a new meaning of "public." This would be an integrated relationship of community to global governance, for the purposes of ecological resilience and human development (Nussbaum 2011; Sen 1999). Instead of a population divided into sectors and spheres, there would be an integrated human community, existing for its own purposes rather than for production for profit. The already-public institutions, like joint stock corporations and credit (Marx 1967 Vol. III Ch. 27, 436–441) would be repurposed, along with knowledge (Hess and Ostrom 2007). The globe-spanning Internet would be the foundation of political deliberation and assessment of progress, rather than commercial and consumer-driven.

The view of the earth and its climate would be newly integrated, apart from the separable real-estate parcels, national territories, and boundaries of parks and preserves (Wilson 2016).

New model for the state

A new model of the economy would return to the meaning of "eco" derived from the Greek *oikos* (Purdy 2015, 17). A new form of money on a local or regional basis would be based on land use permits, backed by an ecological index. There would be a new form of the state, a fiscal/ecological state (in contrast with fiscal/military state; Brewer 1988), which can issue regional currencies that are collectively managed by a global governance association of ecological regions. This contrasts with existing currencies which are based on public debt, used for defending the national boundaries and competing national economies. Rather than competition among nation states, it is possible to develop cooperation to maintain and support the earth's ecosystems.

A comprehensive ecological index based on carbon sinks, net primary production, water purification, and species diversity can be developed by communities of scientists and applied consistently across all regional communities. Satellite surveillance shared by global mapping is already capable of providing such comprehensive ecological assessment techniques (Tollefson 2016).

Rather than technology designed to replace and control labor in the production and realization of private commodities, or "capitalist technology," there would be a new "ecological technology." Research and development would focus on ever-improving ecological science and modeling, and reflexive human understanding. Based on these regional currencies and tax/expenditure policies at the state level, public goods would be provided, such as education, ecological restoration, artificial intelligence, transportation and communication, renewable energy, and advanced manufacturing (3D printing and robots; Ford 2015). With advanced "ecological technology" offered as a public good, consumer and producer goods can provide for high productivity of labor in commodity production, as well as ecological restoration. The labor intensive sectors are small scale agriculture consistent with the regional ecology, and human development institutions (health, education, training, care of dependents). Wages denominated in regional currencies would be weighted for priority sectors, determined by the regional and global governance institutions.

Branded consumer products marketed on a global scale could be replaced by products unique to each culture, community, and regional ecology. Instead of an abstract Euclidian plane with homogeneous house and yard based on the suburban "American Dream" (Groffman et al. 2014), land would be differentiated, with unique ecological niches nurtured with specialized labor. Exposure to diverse cuisines, arts and cultures would enhance the appreciation of each community's history and world view.

62   *Ann E. Davis*

New communities, new values

There would be a new form of "collective intentionality" (Searle 2010), with deliberation on shared purposes and methods, in communities located in geography, ecology, and history. Instead of the "labor supply function" which considers employment in the home or in the factory, there would be no longer such distinctive "private spheres." Instead of a calculus of production and profits, for the purposes of M – M′, there would be a new governance system based on production for human needs and ecological restoration. Rather than facilitate such decision-making, existing market prices distort measures of value by omitting externalities, household labor, and the effects of monopoly market power. Rather than production for profit that would "trickle down" to households and communities, production would simply be for provisioning and ecological resilience, as envisioned by feminist economists (Power 2004).

There would be an annual and five-year global and regional production plan, produced with universal citizenship. Labor would be managed by sector, with ecological restoration, as well as cultural and historical, as the primary commitment in each region, coordinated by a global ecological plan. Production units would be managed at the regional level, based on the priority for the region. Recruitment and managerial responsibility would be based on skills, merit, and personal interests. For some priority projects, there might be recruitment and assignment, with coordination at the global level.

Reintegration of household, agriculture, and commodity production

Instead of the illusion of the household on a parcel of land treated as individual private property supported by individual wage earners, the land in this practical utopia would be inhabited and managed collectively. Instead of a household disciplined by financial flows (Davis 2015b), the household could be revalued, along with domestic labor, by reintegrating household production with agriculture and commodity production, as well as human reproduction. Such a reintegration of household, agricultural, and commodity production allows for intergenerational training by observing and supporting the process of production of food and commodities. An integrated kin/community residential pattern may also improve the opportunities of simple division of labor without mechanization. Further, with the treatment of land and advanced technology and artificial intelligence as a public good, the ownership of instruments of production is no longer a bargaining chip for gaining access to the surplus. With incentives for environmental restoration, improved knowledge of ecology can enhance productivity in the agricultural sector as well.

Human development would become the product of a gender and generational, as well as sector, integration, providing for more holistic personal and community development. The artificial divide between workplace and home is no longer bounded by a gender division of labor (Davis CJE forthcoming).

Instead of "individual" personalities based on property ownership, there would be personal investments in community. Instead of production of sexuality to underscore differentiated individual identities (Foucault 1978; Hewitson 2013), there would be communal cohesion based on shared work in the preservation of intergenerational continuities and ecologies. Instead of religious or state control of human reproduction, children would represent the community's contribution, along with the ecology, seen as an integrated whole. Instead of prioritizing the human, there would be a vision of all species playing a role in an interdependent earth system (Falkowski 2015).

The organization of production of commodities and services can be reintegrated with local governance institutions, as was the practice prior to the modern public/private divide. Such local governance models include the medieval commune and guild, municipal socialism in the United Kingdom, as well as the Town and Village Enterprises (TVEs) in China. Following Ostrom's contributions, there is a large literature on case studies of the commons, compiled by the International Association for the Study of the Commons (IASC). Local utilities have a monopoly on the energy franchise, only as part of the political compromise that led to the private regulated utility model in the early twentieth century (Davis 2016). With advances in renewable energy, the production of energy in local settings can also be a source of public revenue while being more sustainable, drawing upon unique local resources, such as hydro, solar, geothermal, and wind. Methods of production, recycling, and reuse can also be integrated with the local ecology and geology.

Redesign of human settlement patterns

The need for new infrastructure for renewable energy and for advanced information technology provides the opportunity and capacity to redesign human settlement patterns, rather than simply perpetuate the legacy of previous development priorities. The existence of major population centers on coastal areas threatened by sea level rise makes such migration and relocation necessary.

Instead of suburban sprawl, new cities with an ecological design of transportation, communication, and water and waste infrastructure would be developed. Hyper-loop and high-speed rail with broadband Internet would facilitate connecting the globe. Instead of large single-family homes as status symbols, clustered "tiny houses" and coordinated land use and transportation access would improve personal mobility in ecological context.

New economic knowledge

Instead of "objective" knowledge based on a separation of natural and social (Latour 1993, 2013; Daston and Galison 2010), there would be reflexive, embedded awareness. Instead of information technology being guided by "capitalist technology" imperatives, a new possibility for collective self-determination exists as well as for ecological integration among scales and biospheres. Using techniques such as Geographic Information Systems (GIS), mapping can preserve the local unit, in context of global geological and atmospheric systems. The Internet and information technology can integrate both concrete and abstract, in terms of individual persons, landscapes, products. Instead of surveillance and control in production, there would be a third "industrial divide" for "customer-driven," participatory innovation (like "makers"; Piore and Sabel 1984; Hippel 2005; Dosi and Galambos 2013). Instead of marketing and display, there would be continual updates on information regarding innovations in production, consumption, health, education, and ecology. Instead of status and recognition based on "conspicuous" ownership of consumer goods, recognition would be based on capabilities, virtues, and skills. Instead of objective individual mediation by means of language and institutions (Searle 2010), there would be subjective communications in an integrated arts/science, "non-distorted" forms and media of communication (Habermas 1990). Instead of a politics based on the hoped-for convergence of *bourgeois* and *homme*, with an equitable distribution of property (Davis 2015a, 102–103), there would be a governance based on the person and her personal relationships, without the mediating infrastructure of individual private property and its representation.

New state forms and global governance

Existing global governance is based on the model of "free trade" (Mazower 2012) and international financial management institutions, such as the IMF and World Bank (Eichengreen 2011). The protection of property and markets at the national and international levels is the foundation for this current governance system. A new model for global governance can be extended from such efforts as the United Nations Intergovernmental Panel on Climate Change (UNIPCC), the Kyoto Protocol, and the Internet. One could imagine a new relationship among the IMF, the World Bank, and the WTO in collaboration with the United Nations Millennial Development Goals (UNMDG) and the UNIPCC, to integrate financial and ecological governance in the short term. Global governance could be based on a new knowledge foundation which integrates ecology and human sciences, and a new system of representation based on regional ecological communities. There would be a conversion of information technology from a "capitalist technology" to an "ecological technology," repurposed for interactive democracy.

Conclusion

At present there is an urgent challenge: to develop a vision of land beyond capitalism and the real-estate market towards a resilient global ecosystem.

Money and finance are "fetters" on the economy, serving to reify, abstract, and discipline labor, while also obscuring its centrality. Money divides the human community into both subject and object, making collective action more difficult to conceive and to coordinate. The embodiment of new technologies in investment is delayed with the sole focus on profit, while growth is reduced and instability increased. With this new vision, new knowledge, new culture, and new set of identities, the priorities for action would shift, and new institutions would form. Integration of the global community would provide tools for reflexivity and learning, to sustain a resilient earth, with peace and plenty.

The careful study of the critique of political economy can facilitate the development of alternative visions. The primacy of monetary flows emerged to finance war among competing nation states. The ecosystem and meaning of human life have been subordinated to that goal, the fight to the death for territory and profit. Now life on earth is at risk. The politics of transition remains daunting in an increasingly polarized and unstable world. Yet the political gridlock itself can be attributed to the separation of economics and politics (Polanyi 1944). There are abundant models of community and sustainability for study and improvement, once the politics of markets is allowed to be a topic for debate.

Money is more like a shroud than a veil, hiding the impact of life and death on planet earth. The articulation and critique of this financial vision is essential, for the sake of the future of real life on earth.

It is possible to see with a new shade of green, informed by ecology. For example, Robert J. Goldstein has re-envisioned property to include "green wood in the bundle of sticks," to provide courts with a new consideration for ecological resilience in all landed-property decisions (Goldstein 2005). That is, "nature" should be included in the bundle of rights that comprises the concept of property, with ownership invested in the global community, not the individual. The conceptual separation of natural and human considerations, whether in institutions like money or in property, is no longer viable for either.

References

Albritton, Robert. *Dialectics and Deconstruction in Political Economy*. New York: Palgrave, 2001.

Alperowitz, Gar. *What Then Must We Do? Straight Talk about the Next American Revolution*. White River Junction, VT: Chelsea Green Publishing, 2013.

Anderson, Benedict. *Imagined Communities: Reflections on the Origin and Spread of Nationalism*. New York: Verso, 1991.

Arrighi, Giovanni. *The Long Twentieth Century: Money, Power, and the Origins of Our Times*. London: Verson, 1994.

Baucom, Ian. *Specters of the Atlantic: Finance Capital, Slavery, and the Philosophy of History*. Durham, NC: Duke University Press, 2005.

Beckert, Sven. *Empire of Cotton: A Global History*. New York: Alfred A. Knopf, 2014.

Brewer, John. *The Sinews of Power: War, Money, and the English State 1688–1783*. Cambridge, MA: Harvard University Press, 1988.

Cardoso, Jose Luis. "The Political Economy of Rising Capitalism," in Larry Neal and Jeffrey G. Williamson (eds.). *The Cambridge History of Capitalism*. Volume I: *The Rise of Capitalism: From Ancient Origins to 1848*. New York: Cambridge University Press, 2014, 574–599.

Coase, Ronald H. "The Problem of Social Cost," *Journal of Law and Economics*, Vol. III, October 1960, 1–44.

Cohen, Lizabeth. *A Consumer's Republic: The Politics of Mass Consumption in Postwar America*. New York: Vintage, 2003.

Commission for the Measurement of Economic Performance and Social Progress. *Mismeasuring Our Lives: Why Doesn't GDP Add Up?* New York: New Press, 2010.

Cressey, Daniel. "The Plastic Ocean." *Nature*, Vol. 536, August 18, 2016, 263–265.

Daston, Lorraine and Peter L. Galison. *Objectivity*. New York: Zone Books, 2010.

Davis, Ann E. *The Evolution of the Property Relation: Understanding Paradigms, Debates, Prospects*. New York: Palgrave MacMillan, 2015a.

Davis, Ann E. 2016 "Contested Continuity: Competing Explanations of the Evolution of the Corporate Form." *Journal of Economic Issues*, Vol. 50, No. 2, June.

_____. "The Process of Provisioning: The Halter for the Workhorse." *Journal of Economic Issues*, Vol. XLIX, No. 2, June 2015b, 449–457.

_____. "Paradoxical Positions: The Methodological Contributions of Feminist Scholarship." *Cambridge Journal of Economics*, Vol. 41, No. 1, 2017, 181–201.

_____. "Contested Continuity: Competing Explanations of the Evolution of the Corporate Form." *Journal of Economic Issues*, Vol. 50, No. 2, June, 2016, 611–619.

_____.2017 "Paradoxical Positions: The Methodological Contributions of Feminist Scholarship," *Cambridge Journal of Economics*, Vol. 41, No. 1, 181–201.

Dosi, Giovanni and Louis Galambos (eds.). *The Third Industrial Revolution in Global Business*. New York: Cambridge University Press, 2013.

Eichengreen, Barry. *Exorbitant Privilege: The Rise and Fall of the Dollar and the Future of the International Monetary System*. New York: Oxford University Press, 2011.

Epstein, Gerald A. (ed.). *Financialization and the World Economy*. Cheltenham, UK: Edward Elgar, 2005.

Falkowski, Paul G. *Life's Engines: How Microbes Made Earth Habitable*. Princeton, NJ: Princeton University Press, 2015.

Ford, Martin. *The Rise of the Robots: Technology and the Threat of a Jobless Future*. New York: Basic Books, 2015.

Foucault, Michel. *The History of Sexuality*. New York: Pantheon, 1978.

Goetzmann, William N. *Money Changes Everything: How Finance Made Civilization Possible*. Princeton, NJ: Princeton University Press, 2016.

Goldstein, Robert J. *Ecology and Environmental Ethics: Green Wood in the Bundle of Sticks*. Aldershot: Ashgate, 2005.

Graeber, David. *The Democracy Project: A History, A Crisis, A Movement*. New York: Spiegel and Grau, 2013.

Groffman, Peter et al. "Ecological Homogenization of Urban USA." *Frontiers in Ecology*, Vol. 12, No. 1, 2014, 74–81.

Habermas, Jürgen. *Moral Consciousness and Communicative Action*. Cambridge, MA: MIT Press, 1990.

Harvey, David. *The Enigma of Capital and the Crisis of Capitalism*. New York: Oxford University Press, 2010.

Hess, Charlotte and Elinor Ostrom (eds.). *Understanding Knowledge as a Common: From Theory to Practice*. Cambridge, MA: MIT Press, 2007.

Hewitson, G. "Economics and the Family: A Postcolonial Perspective." *Cambridge Journal of Economics*, Vol. 37, 2013, 91–111.

Hippel, Eric von. *Democratizing Innovation*. Cambridge, MA: MIT Press, 2005.

Keynes, John Maynard. *The General Theory of Employment, Interest, and Money*. New York: Harcourt, Brace & World, Inc, 1964.

Krippner, Greta R. "The Financialization of the American Economy." *Socio-Economic Review*, Vol. 3, 2005, 173–208.

Latour, Bruno. *We Have Never Been Modern*. Cambridge, MA: Harvard University Press, 1993.

_____. *An Inquiry into Modes of Existence: An Anthropology of the Moderns.* Cambridge, MA: Harvard University Press, 2013.

Lessig, Lawrence. *Free Culture: The Nature and Future of Creativity.* New York: Penguin, 2005.

Levy, Jonathan. "The Mortgage Worked the Hardest," in Michael Zakim and Gary J. Kornblith (eds.). *Capitalism Takes Command: The Social Transformation of Nineteenth-Century America.* Chicago: University of Chicago Press, 2012, 39–68.

MacKenzie, Donald A. *An Engine Not a Camera: How Financial Models Shape Markets.* Cambridge, MA: MIT Press, 2006.

_____. *Material Markets: How Economic Agents Are Constructed.* New York: Oxford University Press, 2009.

Marglin, Stephen A. *The Dismal Science: How Thinking Like an Economist Undermines Community.* Cambridge, MA: Harvard University Press, 2008.

Marx, Karl. *Capital.* Vols. I, II, III. New York: International Publishers, 1967.

Mazower, Mark. *Governing the World: The History of an Idea.* New York: Penguin Press, 2012.

McDonough, William and Michael Braungart. *Cradle to Cradle: Remaking the Way We Make Things.* New York: North Point Press, 2002.

Mirowski, Philip. *Never Let a Serious Crisis Go to Waste: How Neoliberalism Survived the Financial Meltdown.* New York: Verso, 2013.

Moore, Jason W. *Capitalism in the Web of Life: Ecology and the Accumulation of Capital.* London: Verso, 2015.

Neal, Larry. "How It All Began: The Monetary and Financial Architecture of Europe During the First Global Capital Markets, 1648–1815." *Financial History Review,* 7, 2000, 117–140.

Nordhaus, William. *The Climate Casino: Risk, Uncertainty, and Economics for a Warming World.* New Haven, CT: Yale University Press, 2013.

North, Douglass C., John Joseph Wallis, and Barry R. Weingast. *Violence and Social Orders: A Conceptual Framework for Interpreting Recorded Human History.* New York: Cambridge University Press, 2009.

Nussbaum, Martha C. *Creating Capabilities: The Human Development Approach.* Cambridge, MA: Harvard University Press, 2011.

Ostrom, Elinor. *Governing the Commons: The Evolution of Institutions for Collective Action.* Cambridge: Cambridge University Press, 1990.

Pigou, A.C. *The Economics of Welfare.* London: MacMillan, 1924.

Piore, Michael J. and Charles F. Sabel. *The Second Industrial Divide.* New York: Basic Books, 1984.

Pocock, J.G.A. *The Machiavellian Moment: Florentine Political Thought and the Atlantic Republican Tradition.* Princeton, NJ: Princeton University Press, 1975.

Polanyi, Karl. *The Great Transformation: The Political and Economic Origins of Our Time.* Boston: Beacon Press, 1944.

Pollin, Robert. *Greening the Global Economy.* Cambridge, MA: MIT Press, 2015.

Poovey, Mary. *A History of the Modern Fact: Problems of Knowledge in the Sciences of Wealth and Society.* Chicago: University of Chicago Press, 1998.

_____. *Genres of the Credit Economy: Mediating Value in the Eighteenth- and Nineteenth-Century Britain.* Chicago: University of Chicago Press, 2008.

Postone, Moishe. *Time, Labor, and Social Domination: A Reinterpretation of Marx's Critical Theory.* New York: Cambridge University Press, 1996.

Power, Marilyn. "Social Provisioning as a Starting Point for Feminist Economics," *Feminist Economics,* Vol. 10, No. 3, 2004, 3–19.

_____. *After Nature: A Politics for the Anthropocene.* Cambridge, MA: Harvard University Press, 2015.

Rich, Adrienne. *Of Woman Born: Motherhood as Experience and Institution.* New York: W.W. Norton & Co., Inc., 1976.

Rothman, E. Natalie. *Brokering Empire: Trans-Imperial Subjects between Venice and Istanbul*. Ithaca: Cornell University Press, 2012.

Ruggie, John Gerard. "Territoriality and Beyond: Problematizing Modernity in International Relations," *International Organization*, Vol. 47, No. 1, Winter, 1993, 139–174.

Sassen, Saskia. *Territory, Authority, Rights: From Medieval to Global Assemblages*. Princeton, NJ: Princeton University Press, 2006.

Sachs, Jeffrey D. *The Age of Sustainable Development*. New York: Columbia University Press, 2015.

Schor, Juliet. *Plenitude: The New Economics of True Wealth*. New York: Penguin, 2010.

_____. *True Wealth: How and Why Millions of Americans Are Creating a Time-Rich, Ecological Light, Small-Scale, High Satisfaction Economy*. New York: Penguin, 2011.

Schumpeter, Joseph A. "The Crisis of the Tax State," in *The Economics and Sociology of Capitalism*. Richard Swedberg (ed.). Princeton, NJ: Princeton University Press, 1991, 99–140.

Searle, John R. *Making the Social World: The Structure of Human Civilization*. New York: Oxford University Press, 2010.

Sen, Amartya. *Development as Freedom*. New York: Alfred A. Knopf, 1999.

Smith, Adam. *An Inquiry into the Nature and Causes of the Wealth of Nations*. New York: Modern Library, 1994.

Stahel, Walter R. "Circular Economy." *Nature*, Vol. 531, March 24, 2016, 435–438.

Stiglitz, Joseph E. and Bruce C. Greenwald. *Creating a Learning Society: A New Approach to Growth, Development, and Social Progress*. New York: Columbia University Press, 2014.

Tollefson, Jeff. "Carbon-Sensing Satellite System Faces High Hurdles: Space Agencies Plan an Advanced Fleet, but Technical and Political Challenges Abound." *Nature*, Vol. 533, May 26, 2016, 446–447.

Wennerlind, Carl. *Casualties of Credit: The English Financial Revolution, 1620–1720*. Cambridge, MA: Harvard University Press, 2011.

Wilson, Edward O. *Half-Earth: Our Planet's Fight for Life*. New York: W.W. Norton & Co., 2016.

5 Soviet planning and the labor-time calculation model: implications for 21st-century socialism[1]

Seongjin Jeong

Introduction

The Marxian model of a communist economy, in its first phase, is characterized by "planning based on labor-time calculation" (hereafter abbreviated as PLTC). This chapter critically evaluates the history of Soviet experiences to explain why the Soviet economy of 1917–91 was not a labor-time planned economy. Although input-output tables were essential to the calculation of the total labor time needed to produce goods and services, and were available to Soviet planners, they never seriously considered using them and instead depended on material balances. This chapter explores the implications for Marxian PLTC for 21st-century socialism.

Marx's planning based on labor-time calculation

Marx assumed that in communism, the market would be abolished and replaced by PLTC using labor certificates. This is the crux of Marx's theory of an alternative society, repeated in his mature works, including *Grundrisse*, *Capital*, and *Critique of the Gotha Programme*. In *Grundrisse* Marx wrote:

> On the basis of communal production, the determination of time remains, of course, essential. ... Economy of time, to this all economy ultimately reduces itself. ... Thus, economy of time, along with the planned distribution of labor time among the various branches of production, remains the first economic law on the basis of the communal production. However, this is essentially different from a measurement of exchange values (labor or products) by labor time.
>
> (Marx, 1973 172–3)

In Marx's communism, economic life, including production, distribution and consumption, is not operated under external compulsion but autonomously controlled by the free will of human beings. Unlike capitalism where the "regulation of total production by value" (Marx, 1981: 1020) is the rule, associated individuals control production. In the *Grundrisse* Marx made it clear that a post-capitalist society, organized through the association of free individuals was incompatible with exchange value, money and markets (Marx, 1973: 158–9). In Marx's communism, the production process is under the "conscious and planned control" of "freely associated men" (Marx, 1976: 173), and "socialized man, the associated producers, govern the human metabolism with nature in a rational way, bring it under their collective control instead of being dominated by it as a blind power; accomplishing it with the least expenditure of energy and in conditions most worthy and appropriate for their human nature" (Marx, 1981: 959). In other words, planners are the direct producers themselves. Considering that the essence of Marxian planning is the conscious and autonomous control of production by free producers from below, the conventional assertion that Marx regarded the problem of socialist production mainly in terms of administration and technical methods is groundless. In *The Civil War in France*, Marx emphasized that "possible communism" is nothing else than the coordination and planned control of national production by cooperative associations (Marx, 1986: 335). The principle of economic coordination in Marx's communism is participatory planning, or planning from below, based on labor-time calculation. Marx sketched it in *Critique of the Gotha Programme* as follows:

> Within a collective society based on the common ownership of the means of production, the producers do not exchange their products; just as little does the labor employed on the products appear here as *the value* of these products, as a material quality possessed by them, since now, in contrast to capitalist society, individual labor no longer exists in an indirect fashion but directly as a component part of the total labor. The phrase 'proceeds of labor,' objectionable even today on account of its ambiguity, thus loses all meaning. What we are dealing with here is a communist society, not as it has *developed* on its own foundations, but on the contrary, just as it *emerges* from capitalist society, which is thus in every respect, economically, morally and intellectually, still stamped with the birth-marks of the old society from whose womb it emerges. Accordingly, the individual producer receives back from society – after the deductions have been made – exactly what he gives to it. What he has given to it is his individual quantum of labor. For example, the social working day consists of the sum of the individual hours of work; the individual labor time of the individual producer is the part of the social working day contributed by him, his share in it. He receives a certificate from society that he has furnished such and such an amount of labor (after deducting his labor for the common funds), and with this certificate he draws from the social stock of means of consumption as much as the same amount of labor costs. The same amount of labor which he has given to society in one form he receives back in another. (Marx, 1989a: 85–6, emphasis in original)

Lenin's Concept of Planning

Apart from his overemphasis on nationalization, accounting, and control in Soviet planning, Lenin did not contribute anything notable to the development of Marxian planning. Unlike Marx, Lenin distinguished the first phase of communism from its developed phase, identifying the former with socialism. He emphasized how "accounting and control ... is mainly what is needed for the 'smooth working', for the proper functioning, of the *first phase* of communism" (Lenin, 1964: 478, emphasis in original). In 1918 Lenin asserted that he had no Marxist precedent for the construction of a socialist economy, neglecting Marx's model of PLTC: "We know about socialism, but knowledge of organization on a scale of millions, knowledge of the organization and distribution of goods, etc. – this we do not have" (Lenin, 1965a: 296). Eventually, Lenin found a precedent in the contemporary German war-time state monopoly capitalist economy. In May 1918, he asserted: "Our task is to study the state capitalism of the Germans, to spare no effort in copying it and not shrink from adopting dictatorial methods to hasten the copying of it. Our task is to hasten this copying even more than Peter hastened the copying of Western culture by barbarian Russia, and we must not hesitate to use barbarous methods in fighting barbarism" (Lenin, 1965b: 340). Lenin believed that capitalism itself was creating the centralized accounting mechanism that could be used for Soviet planning (Barnett, 2004: 54–5).

However, Lenin's conception of communism and planning is problematic from a Marxian standpoint. There is no distinction between socialism and communism in Marx. For Marx, the two are synonymous. Unlike Lenin[2], Marx never imagined the existence of the state in communism (Marx, 1989b: 519). It is also obvious that Lenin's famous catchphrase, "Communism is Soviet power plus the electrification of the whole country" (Lenin, 1966: 419) is a far cry from Marx's view of communism, for the latter presupposes the "withering away" of any sort of state, not just a bourgeois one but also Soviet power even in its first phase. Lenin's approach to planning mainly in terms of control of the economy by the party-state, centered on the management of a state capitalist trust, is also opposite from Marx's conception of democratic planning from below. Above all, Lenin had no interest in PLTC, despite his repeated emphasis on the importance of accounting and calculation in planning[3].

Trial of labor-time calculation planning during War Communism

During the period of War Communism from 1918 to 1921, Lenin and the Bolsheviks attempted to nationalize industries and abolish the market economy. As the regime of War Communism was characterized by the nonexistence or non-functioning of a market economy, it is frequently regarded as a prototype of Marxian communism. In fact, War Communism was nothing else than a rationing economy, imposed by the extreme shortage and besieged situation of wartime. Indeed, the industrial production of Russia in 1920 fell to less than 15 percent of that of 1913. On the other hand, the supply of money doubled from 1913 to 1918, and quintupled by 1920. With galloping inflation, the distribution of the goods at the prices fixed by the Soviet government became virtually free. The calculation of equivalents was frequently made on the basis of amounts of grain or other products. Indeed, as Carr noted, "The financial characteristic of war communism was the virtual elimination of money from the economy. This was, however, in no sense the product either of doctrine or of deliberate design. ... the system was dictated not so much by theory as by urgent practical needs" (Carr, 1952: 246, 230). However, the Bolsheviks made virtue of necessity and even tried to accelerate the process by identifying specifically how the market economy would cease to function with the coming of communism. In 1918, the 2nd All-Russian Congress of Councils of the National Economy "express[ed] the desire to see the final elimination of any influence of money upon the relations of economic units" (Nove, 1992: 64). In 1919, Lenin trumpeted the abolition of money and the expansion of planning in the Draft Programme of the Russian Communist Party (RCP): "The RCP will strive as speedily as possible to introduce the most radical measures to pave the way for the abolition of money, first and foremost to replace it by savings-bank books, cheques, short-term notes" (Lenin, 1965c: 115–6).

In *The ABC of Communism* (1919), one of the representative works of War Communism, Bukharin and Preobrazhensky described communism as a system where workers collectively own the means of production and take the goods that they need from public warehouses. According to them, the communist economy was a planned administrative one managed by newly trained specialist recruited from the working class: "*one of the fundamental tasks of the Soviet Power was and is that of uniting all the economic activities of the country in accordance with a general plan of direction by the State ... The foundation of communist society is laid by the organization of industry, and first of all by a purposive unification of industry under State control*" (Bukharin and Preobrazhensky, 1966: 266, emphasis in original). During this period, the Bolsheviks seriously considered replacing money with natural units, including a "labor unit" (Nove, 1992: 65). Some Party members imagined that they would "come in the end to doing without any calculations in rubles, reckoning the energy used by number of days and hours" (quoted in Carr, 1952: 264). Reflecting the contemporary mood, in 1920 the 3rd All-Russian Congress of Councils of the National Economy decided to organize a seminar to study the "problems of a moneyless economy". At the seminar, Kreve suggested a "labor unit" (*trudovaya edinista, tred*) – that is, socially necessary labor – as the unit of account for the moneyless economy. Kreve's model seemed similar to Marxian PLTC, for it assumed that "the worker would receive units specifying the number of man-hours worked, and would draw from the 'distributive organs' various products up to this labor-value" (Nove, 1986: 56).

However, this construction did not progress beyond theory. In fact, the market economy was not abolished during War Communism. Indeed, the Soviet government introduced a new ruble, *chervonets*, in 1919, replacing the old ruble of the Czar. The so-called abolition of money during this period was nothing else than a clearance transaction on the books, similar to the practices of the banks of Western capitalism. Money functioned as accounting money during War Communism. Goods were distributed not only through rationing at fixed prices by the state agencies but also substantially through private commerce, including parcel businesses.

New Economic Policy and the struggle for planning

In 1921, the Soviet government ended the period of War Communism and adopted the New Economic Policy (NEP). The NEP allowed peasants to pay taxes – already lower than War Communism's requisitions – in kind and sell agricultural surpluses in local markets. It also permitted small scale private business. The Soviet economy revived; however, it was accompanied by severe contradictions, such as the "scissor crisis", food shortages in urban areas, and increasing inequality, which intensified Party debates about the economy's direction. Trotsky, the leader of the Left Opposition, regarded these problems as symptoms of the revival of capitalism and argued in response for the acceleration of industrialization and the strengthening of planning. Trotsky insisted on the empowerment of the State Planning Commission (Gosplan) as the center of economic planning: "The lack of a real economic centre to watch over economic activity, conduct experiments in that field, record and disseminate results and coordinate in practice all sides of economic activity and thus actually work at a coordinated economic plan … not only inflicts the severest of shocks on the economy, such as [the] fuel and food crisis, but also excludes the possibility of the planned and coordinated elaboration of new premises for economic policy" (quoted in Swain, 2014: 149, 141–2). In 1922, at the 11th Congress of the RCP, while the majority of Bolshevik leaders put the priority on finance, Trotsky argued that planning should take place through actual monitoring of large-scale state-owned industries. He argued that the imbalances between industry and agriculture could be corrected by planning. In 1932, Trotsky listed three conditions of a planned economy: "(1) special state departments, that is, the hierarchical system of *plan commissions*, in the center and locally; (2) *trade*, as a system of market regulation; (3) *Soviet democracy*, as a system for the living regulation by the masses of the structure of the economy … Only through the interaction of these three elements, state planning, the market, and Soviet democracy, can the correct direction of the economy of the transitional epoch be attained" (Trotsky, 1973: 273, 275, emphasis in original).

Trotsky was critical of Stalin and the Party's interference with economic management. For Trotsky, this was not planning; what the economy needed was the economic guidance of specialists. In 1923, Trotsky argued that the work of planning should be transferred from the Party to Gosplan

(Swain, 2014: 142–3, 147). Indeed, Trotsky's policies in the 1920s were oriented to a democratic socialist economy (Day, 1973). Trotsky's concept of planning was crucially different from a Stalinist command economy, in that it emphasized control by market and Soviet democracy as well as autonomy from the party. However, it is also true that Trotsky's concept of planning substantially deviated from that of Marx, in that it prioritized the roles of leadership of the party and the state sector. Indeed, Trotsky tended to equate planning with the issue of leadership, reverting to his militaristic approach to planning during War Communism. Above all, the Marxian idea of PLTC is totally missing from Trotsky's concept of planning.

Besides Trotsky and Left Opposition theorists, like Preobrazhensky, many prominent Russian economists, like Kondratiev, Chayanov, Milyutin, Kritsman, Smit, Groman, Popov, Strumilin and Varga, produced important works on planning during the NEP. For example, 30 percent of the articles published in a Soviet daily newspaper, *Economic Life*, and a Soviet monthly economic journal, *National Economy*, between October 1920 and February 1921 were about the issue of planning (Remington, 1982: 589). Based on these flourishing studies of planning, the Central Statistical Administration of Gosplan published *The Balance of the National Economy of the USSR, 1923–24* in 1926 (Davies, 1960: 289; Jasny, 1972: 104). It laid the basis for the control figures of 1925–26, consequently reborn as the first Five-Year Plan during 1926–27 (Davies, 1960: 290). It also provided a prototype of input-output tables (Leontief, 1960). However, under the NEP the PLTC, tried in the preceding period of War Communism, was no longer considered as a feasible option but instead was postponed to the distant future of developed communism. For example, Preobrazhensky, once a representative theoretician of War Communism, argued in his book *The New Economics* (1926) that only after the transition to socialism would the economy be coordinated "on the basis of direct calculation of labor-time" (Preobrazhensky, 1965: 20).

Suppression of Marxian planning under the Stalinist administrative command economy

All the debates on planning during the NEP suddenly stopped with Stalin's counterrevolution in 1929. In 1931 Stalin purged and executed most of the planning experts, such as Kondratiev, Chayanov, Groman, Ginzberg, Rubin et al., branding them as Menshevik counterrevolutionaries. Ginzberg was accused of lowering the target rate of growth of the first Five-Year Plan. *The Balance of the National Economy of the USSR, 1923–24* was denounced as based on the anti-Bolshevik philosophy of equilibrium advocated by Bogdanov (Remington, 1982: 589). Stalin himself discarded *The Balance of the National Economy of the USSR, 1923–24* as just "juggling with figures" (Stalin, 1954a: 178), signaling the physical termination of planning specialists. Ironically, the so-called Stalinist planned economy was born on the corpses of almost all the contemporary Marxist planners.

Stalin forcibly started and drove the first Five-Year Plan after the state capitalist counterrevolution in 1929. Seventeen hundred pages long, *The First Five-Year Plan of Building the Soviet National Economy* was authorized at the 15th Party Conference and published in 1929. This was the historically unprecedented attempt to administer the whole economic system. In 1931 Stalin announced that the purpose of the plan was to catch up with Western advanced capitalist countries: "We are fifty or a hundred years behind the advanced countries. We must make good this distance in ten years. Either we do it, or we shall go under" (Stalin, 1954c: 40–1). With the promulgation of the new constitution in 1936, Stalin declared that Soviet Russia had entered the first phase of communism[4]. In 1939, Stalin asserted that Soviet Russia was advancing towards the developed phase of communism by surpassing the advanced capitalist countries in terms of per capita product: "Only if we outstrip the principal capitalist countries economically can we reckon upon our country being fully saturated with consumer goods, on having an abundance of products, and on being able to make the transition from the first phase of Communism to its second phase" (Stalin, 1978b: 378–9). Stalin's words clearly show that the main purpose of Stalinist planning was to catch up with the advanced capitalist countries rather than to organize the allocation of resources in an egalitarian and non-market way (Ellman, 2014: 4, 15).

Stalinist planning was practiced as follows. Stalinist planners tried to resolve the problem of complexity inherent in a planned economy by concentrating on a limited number of sectors. Indeed, Gosplan planned only a few strategic industries, targeting the ministries and not individual companies. The party's top directive was transmitted through the ministries downward to the level of individual companies as the "control figures", preliminary production targets of the Five-Year Plans. These were computed only for a few strategically important products, such as corn and steel. In 1951, Gosplan's Five-Year Plan was compiled for 127 products, while material balances, the main tool of planning, were prepared for 60 products, although there were millions of products in contemporary Russia (Gregory, 2004: 117, 152). Then, the mandatory "technpromfinplan" (technical-industrial-financial plan), involving detailed directions for the operations of individual companies, including output, assortment, labor and finance for the following year, was determined. The plans were not prepared from scratch but revised and updated the performances of the previous year. Intense bargaining and conflicts through vertical and horizontal interactions among the plan units were also characteristic of Stalinist planning. Accurate techniques like input-output tables or optimal linear programming, which could balance supply and demand, were never applied to Stalinist planning. As Gosplan planned to produce goods or services on an aggregated, rather than disaggregated basis, balancing the national economy through consistent planning was impossible from the start. In fact, Stalinist planning was not meant to achieve a balanced national economy: unbalanced growth was not a problem to be avoided but tolerated and even promoted.

Far from being a Marxian planned economy, characterized by democratic control from below, the Stalinist economy was not planned in the technical sense of the word. Indeed, all the plans in Stalinist Russia were preliminary and subject to change by the party-state at any time. What actually executed the resource allocation in Stalinist Russia was not planning itself but the resource manager of the party-state. Resources were allocated by "feel and intuition," and planners had little idea about the technical coefficients of inputs and outputs (Gregory, 2004: 211): "They, not the plan, allocate resources" (Gregory and Stuart, 2014: 394). In Stalinist Russia, Five-Year Plans were never operational. Instead, they were composed of preliminary and always-changing plans of ministries, *glavks* and companies on an annual, quarterly and monthly basis (Gregory, 2004: 111). Thus, it would not be correct to describe Stalinist Russia as a planned economy. Rather, it was a kind of administrative command economy (Gregory, 2004). In 1930 Stalin himself argued as follows: "For us the five year plan, like every other, is merely a plan adopted as a first approximation, which has to be made more precise, altered and perfected in conformity with the experience gained in the localities, with the experience gained in carrying out the plan ... The drafting of a plan is only the *beginning of planning*. Real guidance in planning develops only after the plan has been drafted" (Stalin, 1954b: 357, emphasis in original). In Stalinist Russia, all the words of the plan played the role of ritual, propaganda, or vision, serving to justify the un-planned exploitative regime. What was fundamental to Stalinist Russia was not the plan but "the role of administrative hierarchies at all levels of decision making" and "the absence of control over decision making by the population" (Ellman, 2014: 14). The conventional wisdom that Stalin adopted Trotsky's project of Marxian planning after he purged both Trotskyists and Bukharinists in 1929 is far from the truth. In fact, the Stalinist planned economy emerged from the physical destruction of all the ideas of Marxian planning in the 1920s, including Trotsky's. Moreover, equating the developed phase of communism with outstripping the economic level of advanced capitalist countries or modernization is a cruel mockery of Marx's ideal of communism[5]. Stalinist Russia had nothing to do with Marx's idea of an emancipated society without exploitation and oppression. Just considering the facts, such as a rapid increase in the labor productivity despite decreasing or stagnant real wages in Stalinist Russia (Nove, 1992: 208, 210, 253, 253), is enough to confirm that Stalinist Russia was no less an exploitative regime than a Western capitalist one.

Practices of planning based on labor-time calculation: material balances and input-output tables

The above discussion shows that Stalinist Russia had nothing to do with Marx's PLTC. However, in technical respects, Soviet experiences after the revolution of 1917 witnessed two important developments in Marxian labor-time planning: material balances and input-output tables. Material balances were balance sheets, compiled for specific products in physical terms, in order to balance the demand for the products and their availability by comparing the products' supply and use schedules, in which prices played no role. Material balances were compiled and adjusted by the planners and were expected to be useful for balancing the supply and demand of the basic industrial goods, agricultural products, transportation goods, and others without resorting to market prices. Material balances were widely adopted as a major planning instrument in most Stalinist regimes; however, their planners were not able to compile balances for millions of products. At most, they could do that only for hundreds of products, which they considered to be the "commanding heights" of the economy (Ellman, 1973: 35). Moreover, material balances turned out to be less useful for their stated purpose, even for a few select items. Above all, it was very difficult to correctly determine the total quantities of the inputs that were required to produce the outputs, that is, total input coefficients, from material balances, for the latter could not take into consideration all the so-called second-round effects. The latter are the effects of changing one input or output to other inputs and outputs elsewhere in the balance, implying that changes in one part of material balances result in changes throughout the whole (Gregory and Stuart, 2014: 174–5). For example, when more steel is needed, more coal is also needed to produce more steel, which again necessitates more production of electricity, and so on. Algebraically, the second-round effects can be expressed as the sum of '$I + A + A^2 + A^3 + ...$' (refer to the notes below Equation 5.2 for the meaning of A). However, only the first two terms of the sum, $I + A$, can be captured in material balances. This means that constructing a balanced plan is beyond the latter's scope (Hatanaka, 1967: 143). Nemchinov, a leading Soviet planner in the 1960s, confessed as follows: "We have the rows of material balances but not the table – the row is balanced but the column is not" (quoted in Treml, 1967: 89)[6]. Moreover, Stalinist planners usually compiled the plan from the previous year, using the input coefficients of the previous year, without knowing whether they were optimal minimum quantities of inputs required to produce the unit output. From this, the repetition of existing technology, a fixation on the past pattern of resource allocation, and the dwindling dynamism of the economy were inevitable. Even if the consistent plan, which could balance supply with demand, was found through material balances, there was no guarantee that it would be optimal, maximizing the objectives of planners among all the feasible consistent plans. In fact, Popov, editor of *The Balance of the National Economy of the USSR, 1923–24*, cautioned as early as 1926 that material balances were just "a tool to study structural changes in the Soviet economy", rather than "a tool to implement directive planning of fast industrial development" (Akhabbar, 2014: 196).

As late as the late 1950s, when the malfunctioning of material balances planning became severe, Soviet planners began to seek an alternative in input-output tables. Nemchinov emphasized their merit, while emphasizing that input-output tables originated in Russia (Ellman, 1973: 3)[7]. In 1958, Leontief's seminal work on input-output tables, *The Structure of the American Economy*

(1941), was translated and published in the USSR (Tretyakova and Birman, 1976). Eventually in 1961, the Central Statistical Administration of Gosplan published *The Input-Output Tables of the USSR for 1959*. The main features of input-output tables can be summarized as Equations 5.1 and 5.2:

$$X = AX + Y \tag{5.1}$$

$$X = (I-A)^{-1}Y \tag{5.2}$$

[X: vector of X_i (total output of sector i); A: matrix of a_{ij} (direct input coefficient ($=X_{ij}/X_j$); X_{ij}: sale from sector i to sector j; in other words, input of sector i to sector j); Y: vector of Y_i (the final demand for X_i)]

By using Equation 5.2, planners can simulate the effects of an alternative mix of final demand, Y, on total output, X. Especially by considering all the second-round effects, $I + A + A^2 + A^3 + \ldots$, through the calculation of $(I-A)^{-1}$, input-output tables enables the planning of a consistent set of total outputs, which was not possible using material balances.

However, input-output tables were rarely used for Soviet planning, despite their significant merits. As Belkin, one of the leading planners in USSR, confessed in 1963, "input-output techniques have been sufficiently perfected but are not being used in actual planning" (quoted in Treml, 1967: 102). Even when input-output tables were compiled, they were regarded as just an experiment rather than as an actual planning tool (Treml, 1967: 101). Why were they not put to use? In planning using material balances, planners first set the target of total output, X, while final demand, Y, is determined as residual. In planning using input-output tables, the order is reversed. As Equation 5.2 shows, the direction of causation in planning using input-output tables runs from final demand, Y, to total output, X. Hence Soviet planners criticized input-output tables as a consumer oriented approach incongruent with a Marxian emphasis on production and accumulation. Paradoxically, the pursuit of consistency and equilibrium enabled by input-output tables was not what Soviet planners wanted. Their top priority was to maximize their discretionary power. Indeed, "fear of the abolition of the administrative system of intermediate goods supply lies at the core of the opposition [to the introduction of planning based on input-output tables]. The moment the demand for intermediate goods is derived from final demand in an activity model, the *raison d'etre* of the entire administrative supply system, comes into question" (Becker, 1967: 128).

But a grain of salt is needed when evaluating the relative advantage of input-output tables. First, it is not so comprehensive in its coverage of sectors compared to material balances. In fact, the number of sectors compiled in an input-output table was usually about 500 to 600, far short of comprehensive. Moreover, an input-output table is not free from the fallacy of the aggregation of material balances (Ellman, 1973: 32). On the contrary, from the perspective of Marxian communist planning, material balances may appear to be a better tool than input-output tables. For example, Green (2000) argued that material balances promote the communist ideal of diversity. Indeed, material balances apply different measures of a natural unit, like ton, meter, m², m³, etc., to different products rather than homogenizing them to a single unit, like money or labor-time, which differ only in their quantities. According to Green (2000), "both the Soviet version of 'material balances' and future communist planning required and will require, the use of not one, but many separate natural units. The experience of the method of 'material balances' verifies that there is no single natural unit of economic planning". However, considering that input-output tables can be compiled in terms of physical natural units as well as monetary or labor-time ones, the alleged merit of material balances evaporates. It is also not correct to regard material balances as a specifically communist method of resource allocation. Even in capitalism, variants of material balances have been frequently used to allocate some strategically crucial goods when the monetary economy does not work, like during war-time. Material balances may appear to be more true to the Marxian distinction between productive and unproductive labor, for they cover only material productive sectors. However, as Shaikh and Tonak (1994) show, input-output tables render possible an accurate empirical distinction between productive and unproductive labor.

It is impossible to achieve macroeconomic coordination and balance without adopting a single unit of measure that enables the calculation of social averages. Thus, while admitting the need for diversity and individuality, it is crucial to stick to planning using labor-time, at least in the first phase of Marxian communism. Planning without this single accounting unit is simply a contradiction in terms, tantamount to the rejection of planning altogether. From the Marxian perspective of PLTC, input-output tables are all the more indispensable in that only they can provide the necessary tools and data for that task. The main elements of this planning model can be summarized as follows. First, indicative prices of the products, expressed as labor-time directly and indirectly expended for the products, are calculated using Equations 5.3 and 5.4.

$$\lambda = A\lambda + 1 \tag{5.3}$$

$$\lambda = (I-A)^{-1}1 \tag{5.4}$$

[λ: vector of λ_j (labor-time directly and indirectly expended for the production of Xj; l: vector of l_j (labor-time directly expended for the production of X_j)]

It is also assumed that the producers are compensated by the labor certificates, which show how much time they worked (l_i), after deducting the tax for the common use of labor-time, such as investment, collective consumption, support for the disabled, and so on. People submit their consumption plan for each product before the beginning of the year, considering its indicative price as the labor-time embodied in it (λ_i) calculated by Equation 5.4, as well as their budget, based on the labor certificates they got through their work the previous year. People also submit their yearly labor plan (l_i) which shows their preferred workplace (industry and job) and scheduled labor-time for the next year. Producers also submit their production as well as procurement plans for the equipment, materials and labor before the beginning of the year, considering their announced indicative prices. If the total sums of planned supply and demand for all products and labor are balanced in the simulation, then the system is in equilibrium and labor, production, and consumption are executed as planned. If the planned demand does not equal the planned supply for any good, planners announce a new indicative price: a newly calculated labor-time socially necessary to produce it (λ_i), until the two measures become balanced. The planners raise it for goods with excess demand and lower it for goods with excess supply. When the consumption and production plans are balanced after a few iterations, people draw consumption goods from the social warehouse, obtaining the amount equal to their labor certificate in terms of labor-time. As the above procedure shows, PLTC implies the radical egalitarian principle of equal exchange in labor-time. That is why Soviet planners never attempted to practice this planning using input-output tables, although the tools were available then. Indeed, it conflicted with the interests of Soviet ruling class, including that of their planners (Cottrell and Cockshott, 1993).

Implications for socialism for the 21st century

PLTC is one of the essential components of Marx's communism. However, in Russia, it was tried just temporarily during War Communism, marginalized with the transition to the NEP, and eventually discarded after the establishment of the Stalinist administrative command economy in the 1930s. Nevertheless, Soviet experiences left us a valuable legacy for labor-time calculation planning, such as material balances and the input-output table. Despite its failure, the experiences of planning in Soviet Russia can be isolated and reconstructed as an alternative model for actualizing Marxian communism in the 21st century. For that, in addition to their history recounted above, some methodological conjectures are in order. First, it will be useful to clarify the meaning of labor-time for constructing a Marxian model of PLTC. Sometimes it is argued that it should not be social but actual or individual labor-time, for the category of socially necessary labor-time no longer exists in communism where the category of abstract labor or value, specific to capitalism, is abolished (Hudis, 2012). However, PLTC, as was suggested in *Critique of the Gotha Programme*, is unthinkable if the unit of calculation is actual or individual labor-time. In the first phase of communism, where the economy of time to cope with the state of scarcity is still needed, PLTC is unavoidable, and its unit should be social. If the main task of economic coordination in the first phase of communism is the *ex ante* equilibration of social demands and social production of goods and services for social individuals on a higher level, while recovering the metabolism between nature and humanity that has been broken in capitalism, then planning based on socially necessary labor time is imperative. Indeed, all the existing planning models, regardless of whether it is Stalinist or democratic participatory, adopt the average or socially necessary quantities as their yardstick for planning. It also needs to be noted that the category of "socially necessary labor-time" can exist even after the category of value is abolished. As Marx emphasized, not just labor-time, but *congealed* or *objectified* labor-time is value[8].

On the other hand, privileging of the labor-time planning model as a final or closed model of a post-capitalist alternative society conflicts with Marxian communism that pursues the eventual abolition of labor (Jeong, 2016). Indeed, the historical mission of PLTC expires with the transition to the developed phase of Marxian communism. According to Marx, PLTC, characterized by the exchange of equal quantities of labor using labor certificates, is not an absolute principle of communism that should be permanently observed and reproduced, but rather it is part of the remains or "defects" of capitalism that need to be overcome "from the outset" of the first phase of communism. What Marx called defects in *Critique of the Gotha Programme*[9] is nothing other than the principle of the exchange of equal quantities of labor, where "a given amount of one labor in one form is exchanged for an equal amount of labor in another form" (Marx, 1989a: 86). For Marx, actualizing the principle of the exchange of equal quantities of labor has nothing to do with the abolition of workers' exploitation, not to mention building communism. One of the essential contributions of Marx to a critique of political economy was to prove the existence of exploitation even on the basis of the exchange of equal quantities of labor. It would be alien to Marx to conceive of full-blown communism not as the abolition of value, abstract labor, and labor but as some sort of labor society where the principle of the exchange of equal quantities of labor, using a labor-time calculation planning model, predominates. Indeed, Marx assumed that even in the first phase of communism, the substantial part of the total social product will not be distributed to people according to the labor-time they perform but deducted for the common use "from the outset": "*Secondly, that which is intended for the common satisfaction of needs*, such as schools, health services, etc. [is deducted]. From the outset, this part grows considerably in comparison with present-day society and it grows in proportion as the new society develops" (Marx, 1989a: 85, emphasis in original). The fetishization of labor-time calculation should be avoided. Just replacing a market price-based coordination by a labor-time calculation is not sufficient to free the system from the law of value. Existing works on reverse transformation, which finds the total labor-time embodied in products, using the input-output tables in price units, mostly show that they are proportional to their prices and that the ratios of value to price, or surplus value to profit converge at '1' (Shaikh and Tonak, 1994). If the price of a product is proportional to the socially necessary time embodied in it, just converting the former to the latter by calculating the inverse matrix of input coefficients using an input-output table could neither reveal a novel fact nor produce a new reality. The Marxian communist model of PLTC is inherently contradictory, in that it tends to virtually simulate and reproduce the capitalist labor-value system. Moreover, the calculation of labor-time embodied in a product by solving Equation 5.4 might be accused of committing Adam Smith's dogma of 'v + s', as it was criticized by Marx (1978: 446–54), in that it reduces all the dead labor embodied in the means of production that was consumed to produce the product, or constant capital, to the sum of dated labor, and puts them on the same level as living labor, l in Equation 5.4.

It is also important not to forget that the diversity of individuals, with their cultural and aesthetic aspects, is abstracted from PLTC. As Marx noted, individuals "are regarded *only as workers* and nothing more is seen in them, everything else being ignored" (Marx, 1989a: 87, emphasis in original). Indeed, it is difficult for Marxian PLTC to take into consideration all the diversity of human life in an emancipated communist society or ecological issues. In addition, with the radical shortening of the working day thanks to the rapid development of artificial intelligence, machine learning, the internet of things, 3D printing and so on, the scope of PLTC would be substantially narrowed in the future. Admitting the limitations of the Marxian model of PLTC is as important as its application.

It also should be noted that PLTC cannot be equated with the developed phase of Marxian communism where labor is abolished, for it is still the model of the first phase of communism, which just "*emerges* from capitalist society" (Marx, 1989a: 85) and where the "economy of time" is still crucial. With the transition to the developed phase of communism, where abundance will become a reality, labor will also be transformed into activities. Considering that the essence of Marxian communism is not the domination of labor but its abolition, PLTC should be considered a tool for facilitating the tendency of the abolition of labor, rather than the best possible alternative post-capitalist model. It is necessary to promote and extend this tendency – already beginning to operate in the first phase of communism – towards the developed phase of communism through PLTC (Jeong, 2016). The abolition of labor as well as needs-based distribution should be considered a current task that must be tried "from the outset" of the first phase of communism rather than reserved for distant future objectives (Lebowitz, 2015).

However, the above qualifications should not be considered a rejection of PLTC. Far from being incongruent with the developed phase of communism, PLTC is indispensable to the advance of communism to its developed phase. Only by labor-time calculation can a radical shortening of labor-time, the expansion of free time, needs-based distribution, and the abolition of labor itself can be planned.

Notes

1 This chapter is supported by the National Research Foundation of Korea Grant funded by the Korean Government (NRF-2013S1A5B8A01055117). Author is thankful to Greg Sharzer for illuminating comments.
2 Lenin argued that the "bourgeois state" would remain in the first phase of communism: "under communism there remains for a time not only bourgeois law, but even the bourgeois state, without the bourgeoisie!" (Lenin, 1964: 476).
3 While extolling GOELRO (State Commission for Electrification of Russia), Lenin was disdainful of the "empty talk and word-spinning" of debates over planning (Barnett, 2004: 96).
4 "Our Soviet society has already, in the main, succeeded in achieving Socialism; it has created a Socialist system, i.e., it has brought about what Marxists in other words call the first, or lower, phase of Communism. Hence, in the main, we have already achieved the first phase of Communism. ... The fundamental principle of this phase of Communism is, as you know, the formula: 'From each according to his abilities, to each according to his work'" (Stalin, 1978a: 164).
5 Barnett (2004: 116) described the entire history of the USSR "as a giant category mistake", in that "the facts of Soviet history were represented as belonging to one logical type of category, 'planning', when actually they really belonged to another very different type, 'industrialization'".
6 The problem of inconsistency of material balances might not be so severe in the balance of the entire economy, as in *The Balance of the National Economy of the USSR, 1923–24* which attempted to cover the whole economy, because the former is only a truncated part of the latter. However, devoid of an inverse matrix of input coefficients, that is, $(I-A)^{-1}$ in Equation 5.4, even the balance of the entire economy could not handle the problem of inconsistency.
7 Leontief admitted that he hinted at the idea of input-output tables in 1925 while he worked for the production of *The Balance of the National Economy of the USSR, 1923–24* in Soviet Russia (Foley, 1998). In fact, the idea of inverse matrix of input coefficients, that is, $(I-A)^{-1}$ in Equation 5.4, which is the essence of input-output tables, can be dated back to the work of Dmitriev (1974), a prerevolutionary Russian economist, published in 1898–1902.
8 "Human labor-power in its fluid state, or human labor, creates value, but is not itself value. It becomes value in its coagulated state, in objective form. ... Labor is the substance, and the immanent measure of value, but it has no value itself" (Marx, 1976: 142, 677).
9 "But *these defects* are inevitable in the first phase of communist society as it is when it has just emerged after prolonged birth pangs from capitalist society" (Marx, 1989a: 87, emphasis added).

References

Akhabbar, A. 2014. Statistical Balances in Unbalanced Times. The Balance of the National Economy of the USSR, 1923–24." Pavel Illich Popov's contribution. *Research in the History of Economic Thought and Methodology*. Vol. 32: 167–216.

Barnett, V. 2004. *The Revolutionary Russian Economy, 1890–1940: Ideas, Debates and Alternatives*. Routledge.

Becker, A. 1967. "Comments". In J. Hardt ed. *Mathematics and Computers in Soviet Economic Planning*. Yale University Press.

Bukharin, N. and Preobrazhensky, E. 1966. *The ABC of Communism*. University of Michigan Press.

Carr, E. 1952. *The Bolshevik Revolution 1917–1923*. Vol. 2. Macmillan Press.

Cottrell, A. and Cockshott, W. 1993. "Socialist Planning after the Collapse of the Soviet Union". *Revue européenne des sciences sociales*. Vol. 31. No. 96: 167–185.

Davies, R. 1960. "Some Soviet Economic Controllers I". *Soviet Studies*. Vol. 11. No. 3: 286–306.

Day, R. 1973. *Leon Trotsky and the Politics of Economic Isolation*. Cambridge University Press.

Dmitriev, V. 1974. *Economic Essays on Value, Competition and Utility*. Cambridge University Press.

Ellman, M. 1973. *Planning Problems in the USSR*. Cambridge University Press.

Ellman, M. 2014. *Socialist Planning*. 3rd edition. Cambridge University Press.

Foley, D. 1998. "An Interview with Wassily Leontief". *Macroeconomic Dynamics*. Vol. 2: 116–140.

Green, J. 2000. "Labor-Money and Socialist Planning". *Communist Voice*. Nos. 25–27. http://www.communistvoice.org

Gregory, P. 2004. *The Political Economy of Stalinism: Evidence from the Soviet Secret Archives*. Cambridge University Press.

Gregory, P. and Stuart, R. 2014. *The Global Economy and its Economic Systems*. South-Western Cengage Learning.

Hatanaka, M. 1967. "Comments", in J. Hardt ed. *Mathematics and Computers in Soviet Economic Planning*. Yale University Press.

Hudis, P. 2012. *Marx's Concept of the Alternative to Capitalism*. Brill.

Jasny, N. 1972. *Soviet Economists of the Twenties: Names to Be Remembered*. Cambridge University Press.

Jeong, S. 2016. "Marx's Communism as Associations of Free Individuals: A Reappraisal". *Marx-Engels Jahrbuch*. 2015/16: 115–134.

Lebowitz, M. 2015. *The Socialist Imperative: From Gotha to Now*. Monthly Review Press.

Lenin, V. 1964. *The State and Revolution* (1918). *Collected Works*. Vol. 25. Progress Publishers.

Lenin, V. 1965a. "Session of the All-Russia C.E.C" (1918.4.29.). *Collected Works*. Vol. 27. Progress Publishers.

Lenin, V. 1965b. "'Left-Wing' Childishness and the Petty-Bourgeois Mentality" (1918.5.9.). *Collected Works*. Vol. 27. Progress Publishers.

Lenin, V. 1965c. "Draft Programme of the R.C.P.(B.)" (1919.3.). *Collected Works*. Vol. 29. Progress Publishers.

Lenin, V. 1966. "Our Foreign and Domestic Position and the Tasks of the Party". (1920.11.21.). *Collected Works*. Vol. 31. Progress Publishers.

Leontief, W. 1960. "The Decline and Rise of Soviet Economic Science". *Foreign Affairs*. January: 261–272.

Marx, K. 1973. *Grundrisse*. Penguin Books.

Marx, K. 1976. *Capital*. Vol. 1. Penguin Books.

Marx, K. 1978. *Capital*. Vol. 2. Penguin Books.

Marx, K. 1981. *Capital*. Vol. 3. Penguin Books.

Marx, K. 1986. *The Civil War in France*. in K. Marx and F. Engels. *Collected Works*. Vol. 22.

Marx, K. 1989a. "Critique of the Gotha Programme". in K. Marx and F. Engels. *Collected Works*. Vol. 24. Progress Publishers.

Marx, K. 1989b. "Notes on Bakunin's Book Statehood and Anarchy" (1875). in K. Marx and F. Engels. *Collected Works*. Vol. 24.Progress Publishers.

Nove, A. 1986. *Socialism, Economics and Development*. Allen & Unwin.

Nove, A. 1992. *An Economic History of the USSR 1917–1991*. Penguin Books.

Preobrazhensky, E. 1965. *The New Economics* (1926). Clarendon Press.

Remington, T. 1982. "Varga and the Foundation of Soviet Planning". *Soviet Studies*. Vol. 34. No. 4: 585–600.

Shaikh, A. and Tonak, E. 1994. *Measuring the Wealth of Nations*. Cambridge University Press.

Stalin, J. 1954a. "Concerning Questions of Agrarian Polocy in the U.S.S.R.", Speech Delivered at a Conference of Marxist Students of Agrarian Questions (1929.12.27.). *Works*. Vol. 12. Foreign Languages Publishing House.

Stalin, J. 1954b. "Political Report of the Central Committee to the Sixteenth Congress of the C.P.S.U. (B)" (1930.6.27). *Works*. Vol.12. Foreign Languages Publishing House.

Stalin, J. 1954c. "The Tasks of Business Executives". Speech Delivered at the First All-Union Conference of Leading Personnel of Socialist Industry (1931.2.4.). *Works*. Vol. 13. Foreign Languages Publishing House.

Stalin, J. 1978a. "On the Draft Constitution of the U.S.S.R.: Report delivered at the Extraordinary Eighth Congress of Soviets of the U.S.S.R." (1936.11.25.). *Works*. Vol. 14. Red Star Press Ltd.

Stalin, J. 1978b. "Report on the Work of the Central Committee to the Eighteenth Congress of the C.P.S.U.(B.)" (1939.3.10.), *Works*, Vol. 14, Red Star Press Ltd.

Swain, G. 2014. *Trotsky and the Russian Revolution*. Routledge.

Treml, V. 1967. "Input–output analysis and Soviet planning". In J. Hardt ed. *Mathematics and Computers in Soviet Economic Planning*. Yale University Press.

Tretyakova, A. and Birman, I. 1976. "Input-output analysis in the USSR", *Soviet Studies*, Vol. 28. No. 2: 157–186.

Trotsky, L. 1973. "The Soviet Economy in Danger" (1932.10.22.), *Writings of Leon Trotsky [1932]*. Pathfinder Press.

Part II
Positive practicalities

Leaping ahead

6 Provisioning under austerity

An evolutionary strategy for meeting human needs through the next millennium

Barbara E. Hopkins

We live in challenging times. The recent financial crisis has precipitated a reduction in social spending and an increase in need. According to the Organisation for Economic Co-operation and Development (OECD) (2014), "the proportion of people living in households with no income from work has gone up [since 2007] in most countries, doubling in Greece, Ireland, and Spain" (21). We also face an impending environmental crisis. Global climate change threatens current production levels. A research team at Berkeley has predicted that global incomes will fall by 23 percent by 2100, and that the losses will exacerbate inequalities (Burke et al. 2015). Loss of biodiversity further threatens sustainable development. A recent study estimates that 58.1 percent of the land surface, where 71.4 percent of the human population live, is beyond "safe limits" (Newbold et al. 2016).

Environmental concerns drive efforts to reduce population growth, but reductions in population growth spawn the social challenges of an aging population and a crisis in eldercare. Scientists question the capacity of our planet to continue to sustain a growing population (Gao 2015). While we have been successful at slowing population growth through reduced fertility, technological improvements in healthcare and expanded access to it have increased longevity. This has led to a population that is ageing. As the share of the population over 60 and over 80 continues to grow, we face a crisis in care for the elderly, because more work caring for the elderly will be required of fewer people[1]. Thus, we face a triple crisis, economic, ecological, and eldercare. It seems clear that we, the humans on this planet, need to work together to address these challenges. It seems equally clear to me that big changes are needed. Fundamental changes in the way we live our lives and satisfy our needs.

Of these three challenges, the crisis of eldercare receives the least attention in public discourse and the least attention in proposals for alternative economic arrangements. The United Nations predicts that by 2050, the share of Europe's population that is over 60 will increase from 24 to 34 percent. In North America, those over sixty will increase their share of the population from 21 to 28 percent. Already, in Europe and English-speaking North America the Potential Support Ratio (PSR), the number of people between

20 and 64 divided by those 65 or older, is only 4. In Japan, this measure is only 2.1. By 2050, the United Nations predicts that in seven Asian countries, 24 European countries, and four countries of Latin America and the Caribbean the PSRs are expected to fall below 2 (United Nations Department of Economic and Social Affairs Population Division 2015).

When potential support ratios are considered in public discourse, it is mainly to raise concerns about pay-as-you-go pension systems, in which current workers fund current pensioners (Worstall 2016). For those who want to prop up capitalist investment, the solution is a funding system in which each worker funds his or her own retirement by investing in capital (Kuné 2001). In this system each worker bears their own individual risk and is responsible for developing investment skills. For liberals, who defend the basic principle of pay-as-you-go, the solution to the problem of falling PSRs is to increase productivity. Pay-as-you-go is not just about the number of workers, but also about how much more each worker can produce, so greater productivity means that each worker would have the capacity to fund more dependents (Willmore 2004). The environmental crisis should make us somewhat wary of solutions involving increasing production. Nevertheless, even if this could solve the problem of the intergenerational flow of money, the care crisis is about intergenerational transfers of time with few opportunities for technological improvement.

Traditionally, women have taken on this work for their families unpaid, but more and more women are in full-time paid employment. Liz O'Donnell, writing in the *Atlantic*, highlights the crisis faced by the 44 million unpaid caregivers in the United States, mostly daughters, who receive little support from society to do that work (O'Donnell 2016). As the population continues to age, how are fewer workers, who are working longer hours, going to find the time to care for their parents and who is going to care for the elderly who either did not have children or who have lost their children to accidents, disease, or wars? Some of this work can be and is being done by paid workers, but this work reflects the inequalities of each society. In the United States, 90 percent of in-home care workers are women, and 56 percent are women of color (Hess 2013). This care is often difficult to afford for the pensioners receiving it, but it is poorly remunerated for those doing the work (Hess 2013). Despite recent work on robots doing care work in Japan that may be promising in the future (Muoio 2015), care work has not been able to generate the kind of productivity improvements that have justified increasing wages in manufacturing after World War II.

Since each of us hope to grow old and experience the likelihood that when we do we will need extensive care, provisioning for human needs requires developing a solution to the care crisis. Solving the care crisis without exacerbating the environmental crisis or further exploiting those most harmed by the economic crisis requires choosing a set of economic arrangements that redistribute the burden of care more equally. Emphasizing the universal need and obligation for care could help to transform the culture by reinforcing principles of mutual support over individualism and develop the human capacity for care. This requires changing our understanding of capitalism. We need to consider unpaid work in proposals for alternative economic arrangements. We need to rethink not only institutions engaged in formal production; we need to rethink the institution of family.

Care work as a necessary impurity in capitalism and post-capitalism

In a recent blog post, feminist economist, Nancy Folbre, wrote that "[the economic alternatives to capitalism project] presumes we agree on what 'capitalism' is. I don't think we do" (Folbre 2016). Coming from an explicitly institutionalist perspective, Geoffrey Hodgson (2006; 2015) agrees. Both Folbre and Hodgson agree that one of the problems with most descriptions of capitalism is the focus on capitalist market processes and the profit-maximizing decision-making mechanism. This ignores all of the economic activity outside the for-profit sector. The unpaid care sector is an example of the institutionalist concept of necessary impurities. From the vantage point of this concept, many of the proposals for alternatives to capitalism fail to account for major problems, such as the care crisis, and also ignore fruitful opportunities for evolutionary change.

Necessary impurities are subsystems that operate differently than the dominant system (Hodgson 2002). If the defining characteristic of capitalism is commodity exchange, then families and care provided within them are necessary impurities: impure, because they do not interact through commodity exchange; necessary, because the system cannot persist without them. The concept of necessary impurities suggests that there is no reason to expect, as Marx and Hayek did, that eventually capitalist forms would expand to encompass the entire economy. If childrearing were practiced as a capitalist process, then children would be property and eventually sold as slaves, which would, at that point, no longer be capitalist either and would violate antislavery laws (Hodgson 2002). Eldercare is also difficult to frame as a capitalist process. If eldercare is the production of the elderly, there is no market. Even if we view eldercare as a commodifiable service, it incorporates non-capitalist elements. Often the recipient of the service is not the economic agent engaged in the market exchange. A family member or the state might be engaging the service, implying a responsibility beyond commodity exchange.

There are three ways to incorporate necessary impurities in our understandings of post-capitalist systems. One is to assume that those institutions that are not strictly capitalist, would remain unchanged, but this seems unrealistic and undesirable. Institutionalists and post-structuralists in the tradition of Resnick and Wolff take change as a given. Even within capitalism, families as institutions have always been evolving. Over the 19th century in the United States, increased opportunities to access productive resources through government allocation, such as homesteading, and through the development of credit markets meant that marriage and inheritance ceased to be the primary mechanism for capital formation (Shammas 1994). Among the capitalist class, this weakened the hold that parents had over adult children whose financial security no longer depended on parental approval. In the 20th century women's employment became the norm, and women, as breadwinners, are less able to devote as much time to eldercare. Since families have gotten smaller, the burdens fall on a smaller number of children. As described above, the existing family system for providing intergenerational care is inadequate.

The second alternative is to consider that the mechanisms used to replace the market allocation in a post-capitalist society would also replace the impurities, in this case, the economic functions of families. In order to imagine how this would work, we need to consider commodified care under capitalism and examine whether post-capitalist alternatives would be different. Under capitalism, there are growing markets for services provided to the elderly and the disabled, such as meal preparation and more intimate care services such as bathing and helping to get a person out of bed and into a wheelchair. However, eldercare also implies making decisions for a relative or friend who can no longer make decisions for themselves. This last aspect is harder to envision being done by an impersonal market or market alternative.

Traditionally proposals for post-capitalist economies tend to focus on the problem of creating an alternative allocation mechanism, mostly variants on planning that, unlike the Soviet model, would involve some form of democratic control. Market socialist variants use markets as the basis for an allocation mechanism, but then manipulate outcomes by controlling prices or providing subsidies. Market socialist alternatives would be quite similar to state interventions in welfare capitalism. In both cases, we need to consider whether the different priorities implied by the different allocation systems solve the problems of commodification. We can evaluate these alternative mechanisms for provision of elder care based on three principles: the quality of the care; the fairness of the distribution, both in terms of the individuals receiving care and in terms of those assigned to perform the caring work; and finally in terms of providing adequate levels of care.

Evaluating the quality of care has four aspects: skill, motivation of workers, accountability of workers, and the autonomy of care-receivers. Commodification, whether allocated through markets or planning, compared to family provision, has the potential for increasing the skill level of caregivers through professionalization (Folbre and Nelson 2000). How well this works under post-capitalist mechanisms depends on the details of the system that are not apparent in the proposals, specifically the degree to which decision-makers value care and allocate resources to training programs and income to those who develop care skills.

Considering motivation does not lead to any clear conclusions about different systems for providing care. Motivation may be stronger under family provision, because the caregiver, theoretically, loves the person being cared for. Love is reinforced by social norms of obligation to one's parents.

Inheritance expectations can also create a financial incentive for family, but it represents a very vague contract and for a family member to admit that he or she, and especially she, is influenced by money in this way is generally considered crass and morally objectionable. Nevertheless, crass as it might be, since family members who are potential caregivers need to give up opportunities to generate income, money needs to be a considered. For families in which there are no other breadwinners and the family is not independently wealthy, the need to generate income for subsistence takes precedence. Furthermore, love cannot be taken for granted. Social relationships do not always generate positive emotions. Families can also create resentments and anger (Barrett and McIntosh 1982). Even when love is the dominant emotion, the frustrations of dealing with a relative with reduced cognitive capacity may be more intense when the caregiver is more emotionally engaged and when caregivers are dealing with the role reversal from care-receiving child to caregiver to an aging parent. Research shows that the growing problem of elder abuse is not limited to paid caregivers (Cooper et al. 2009).

Just as the motivations of family members are complex, the motivations of paid employees cannot be reduced to financial motivations. Workers generally report genuine concern for those they are caring for and are driven by moral considerations as well as financial remuneration (Folbre and Nelson 2000). Motivation can be affected by economic systems. Indeed, part of the critique of capitalism is that it encourages a pecuniary logic in which financial motivation takes precedence over moral concerns. However, this represents a vague promise. While planning proposals displace financial motivation, it is not clear how post-capitalist systems would cultivate moral responsibility or how the democratic processes might define moral responsibility within specific cultural contexts that would likely retain gender biases. There is no reason to assume that a post-capitalist allocation system will generate a set of motivations that is any less messy than the current process of marketization.

Irrespective of what motivates care workers in families or markets, establishing mechanisms for accountability is challenging in any system. Lack of accountability has traditionally been one of the drawbacks of a planned economy in which workers have job security. In their proposal for participatory planning, Albert and Hahnel (2002; 1992) address this problem by having each person's work be evaluated by his or her co-workers. This assumes that workplaces, like the traditional factory, have multiple workers who are in a position to evaluate each other's work. Unfortunately, a great deal of care work is done in isolation, in the home of those being cared for. Any effort to increase the visibility of work quality is likely to decrease the privacy of the person being cared for. This problem would apply to family, market, and post-capitalist systems. In formal work places like nursing homes, Albert and Hahnel's proposal might work if the work culture supports it and if the allocation of resources is adequate. In the U.S., regulatory monitoring has failed to guarantee minimum standards of quality. Many of these problems are the result of under provision of resources, specifically too few care workers (Eaton 2005).

Any mechanism for accountability would have to differ from the standard market model in which the buyer can refuse to do business with the seller. Paid care arrangements often involve third parties, either a family member or the state. In the United States, policy makers have not resolved how to address the related problem of Medicare fraud in which organizations claiming to provide care either do so unnecessarily, unethically, or fictitiously (Hyman 2001). Thus, the information problems generally attributed to central planning apply to all economic systems that provide care as a commodity.

Declining cognitive ability of the person receiving care can also make monitoring care workers difficult, reducing accountability. An elderly person who is beginning to lose short-term memory, for example, will have a hard time remembering details of an agreement on tasks, conditions, and pay and, perhaps, where a written agreement was placed. It becomes difficult to monitor whether tasks were completed or whether the hours claimed were actually worked. In extreme cases those receiving care may be unable to communicate problems with their care because they lack the skills or because they fear reprisal from those they depend on. When accountability is difficult, the importance of motivation and self-regulation become more important.

The final aspect of quality is the degree to which a system for providing care preserves the autonomy of adults receiving care. Freedom is a traditional criterion for evaluating economic systems, but it becomes more complicated in the context of care. Caregivers have a great deal of power over those needing care. For those who can afford market provision, it can increase the autonomy of care-receivers by making them less dependent on family members (Folbre and Nelson 2000). However, this autonomy is constrained by the ability for the care-receivers to control the purchase of care or to make their will known to the entity that controls the purchase of care. In the case of Sharon Kowalski, a lesbian whose guardianship was awarded to her parents who then denied access to her lover against Sharon's wishes, the fact that the family controlled care undermined autonomy, but the state's involvement simply reproduced cultural bias both against homosexuals and against those with disabilities (Griscom 2005). Thus, maximum autonomy is achieved by individuals with both cognitive and communicative capabilities and adequate resource capabilities to determine contracts for care provision with market actors[2]. How successfully state provision – whether under a market system or a post-capitalist system – would balance autonomy with other considerations such as safety or the efficiency of provision depends on the cultural norms surrounding the system of care provision.

In theory, a post-capitalist allocation would be more equitable. Ideally it would not discriminate in allocating care based on social status or class position, and it could provide reasonable rewards for care work. At best, this applies only to models of planning where a democratic process replaces markets in setting priorities. Worker ownership combined with markets, such as

Burczak's (2006) model, would suffer the same kinds of problems as capitalist markets. Relative to family care, market provision increases inequalities both among those receiving care and among those providing care (Folbre and Nelson 2000). Wealth inequality means that some people can afford high-quality care, while others are dependent on the state to provide basic care. Similarly, while markets release some women from the obligation of this work, women of color are concentrated among poorly paid care providers in the United States (Hess 2013). Thus, in the absence of significant state provisioning care markets produce and reproduce a highly classed culture in which those who earned enough – or inherited enough – are able to receive rents from assets and afford domestic help that is affordable because of significant differences in relative wages.

Unfortunately, while planned allocations that result from democratic decision-making appear inherently more equitable than market allocations, it is not clear that democratic decision-making will result in an equitable distribution of resources unless those participating in the process explicitly share that as a goal. Post-capitalist proposals that focus on democratic decision-making to set priorities fail to adequately address the patriarchal grounding of inequality in care work. Cultural values, such as attitudes and beliefs about women's proper role or racialized biases about domestic work, shape the market valuation of care work (Hirsh et al. 2013). There is no reason to assume that democratic processes would not simply reproduce these biases. This is part of the point of Albert and Hahnel's (1992) emphasis on specific rules such as making sure that jobs have equal levels of empowerment, which is unique to their proposal for participatory planning. Thus, equity would depend on specific policies aimed at making it so not post-capitalism per se.

Finally, providing adequate levels of care seems difficult in every system. Market failures lead to under-provision because care provides benefits to society as a whole beyond the benefits experienced by individuals who pay for care (Folbre and Nelson 2000). These external benefits are more obvious in the context of children, because children represent future workers and citizens in the society and the quality of care affects the kind of workers and citizens they will be. However, expecting full accounting of social benefits through democratic decision-making would require a different mind-set than is currently evident in many U.S. communities that have considered school bond issues (Tedin et al. 2001). Furthermore, the logic of consumer sovereignty does not hold in care markets. The problem is that the person being cared for may not be the best judge for determining the level of care needed and the quality expected. This principle is generally agreed upon for children, who might think eating nothing but french fries and cake for breakfast, lunch, and dinner and staying up late every night is a good idea. For the elderly, the gradual cognitive decline associated with Alzheimer's disease will also reduce their ability to satisfy the logic of consumer sovereignty. The complex information required to negotiate various medical conditions may further undermine consumer sovereignty. We might wonder how an individual with reduced short-term memory can manage differing advice coming from different medical professionals.

In the current market system, state resources are allocated for care. According to Scheil-Adlung (2015) public funding for long-term care in the U.S., Canada, and Europe ranges from a low of 136.8 dollars per person over 65 in Portugal to a high of 8,406 dollars in Norway, with the liberal market economies of the U.S., Canada, and the U.K. averaging 2,480 dollars. Scheil-Adlung argues that even when private markets use insurance schemes private market provision of long-term care is inadequate. Portugal and the other Southern European economies, Greece, Italy, and Spain, are among the lowest in government provision, and these are the same countries that have high expectations of family care. They are not economies in which a market allocation of care prevails. In the U.S., the government pays about 64 percent of the cost of formal paid long-term services and support for the elderly and disabled (O'Shaughnessy 2014). Among the chronically disabled elders living in the community rather than institutions, 64.6 percent relied exclusively on unpaid family care and of the others that received some paid care 42 percent used government programs to pay for it (U.S. Department of Health and Human Services 2012)[3].

The volatility of wealth complicates market provision. The financial crisis has eroded not just state support for care, but the ability for pensioners to pay for their own care. Between 2007 and 2009 the value of American families' real estate fell by $5.9 trillion or $52,900 per household (Swagel 2009). While retirees might not have found themselves owing on loans that were greater than the value of the house, the opportunities for reverse mortgages to generate income would have been reduced. Similarly, "the value of [American] families' equity holdings fell $10.4 trillion from the middle of 2007 to the end of March 2009 ..., $97,000 per household" (Swagel 2009, p. 14). Given that wealth is not equally distributed, for those who were lucky enough to have assets that could fund care in retirement, the losses would have been much greater. And, those losses would have been realized either if asset income represented the only way to afford care or because federal rules for minimum required distributions from IRAs and 401ks forced anyone over 70½ to sell shares.

In theory, post-capitalist democratic planning would place greater value on care work than a market allocation does. This could manifest as both increases in state support for care and as policies that promote work-family balance that would facilitate family care. As with questions of equity, we are expecting and hoping that a post-capitalist society having rejected commodification of human beings will value the human dignity of the elderly and, thus, will allocate resources to support their well-being. A U.S. electorate that would support planning would have to be very different from our current society, but it is not clear how democratic planning would effect a change in thinking. We cannot take for granted that greater dignity for workers will necessarily lead to greater dignity for retirees, much less that such respect would necessarily extend to women who devoted their lives to unpaid work. As with equity, the potential gender biases of democratic decision-making could easily reflect an expectation that women should be doing this work for free and only limited collective resources should be devoted to care. If we think about democratic decision-making as the realm in which distributional conflict takes place, outcomes are unpredictable. In Folbre's (1994) understanding of capitalism and intersectionality, the principle that we each belong to many different groups that are engaged in distributional conflicts leads to outcomes that are unpredictable. We are all part of struggles that go beyond the struggle between capital and labor, and sometimes we are allied to our class and other times we are allied to our gender or our race, ethnicity, etc. Thus, one might wonder what could prevent a democratic outcome that assigns women of color a greater responsibility for the burden of care work? What could prevent men in general from allocating too few resources to care, expecting that women just pick up the slack?

In summary, there is very little difference in the elder care that can be predicted between the broad categories of welfare capitalism, a democratically organized planned economy, and a worker owned market economy. The details of policy are what matter. The ability to select the best policies depend on the culture and the nature of the democratic institutions. Even with the best policies some form of care from family or friends will always be necessary. However, given that adequate provision from markets and welfare states is unlikely in the context of austerity, family and friends become even more important.

Provisioning and post-familialism

I have come to recognize that families as social institutions need to be reformed or replaced. In their current form, they are inadequate for meeting the growing care needs and will be even less so if human beings achieve zero population growth. The formal sector provides necessary care services under welfare capitalism and would still be necessary in a post-capitalist system, but it would be inadequate. Alternative nonbiological post-families could fill the void. They could distribute care work broadly and equitably, facilitate human connection based on shared responsibility, and develop care as a skill. They may even be able to address other aspects of risk-sharing, such as pooling resources during economic downturns.

The nuclear family based on marriage and children is not adequate for sharing risk or providing for the most basic intergenerational transfers. Nevertheless, government policies are based on the idea that families, which represent a euphemism for women's unpaid labor, have primary responsibility for elder care (Montgomery 1999). Parents are supposed to take care of children and children are supposed to take care of parents. In ten of the thirty-six OECD countries, poverty among children up to 17 years old is over 15 percent. Child poverty is below 9.8 percent in only nine countries

(OECD 2016). Taking care of parents is even more difficult. Women are increasingly in the labor force, in part because their earned income is more important to avoid poverty. Migration locates children far from their parents. And families have fewer children. The family responsibility model has become increasingly untenable. Rather than shifting away from family responsibility, however, many policy analysts have started to call for the enforcement of filial responsibility laws as a way to pay for the increasing burdens on the state (Edelstone 2002). In the United States these laws have not been used much, but in a recent case a nursing home was able to obtain a legal judgment against the son of a patient for an unpaid bill of $93,000, although a second appeal is still pending (Greene 2012). The judgment was deemed feasible because the son's annual income was $85,000. In 2011, according to the U.S. Census, median wealth excluding home equity was $16,942. For families in the fourth income quintile, median wealth excluding home equity was $45,331. In other words, most families would not have been able to pay that bill, and those that could would have had to clean out retirement accounts and college savings accounts. The idea that middle-class nuclear families if they followed the rules and saved for a rainy day could protect themselves from life's risks has always been a myth (Coontz 1992; 1988). The exact nature of that failure and the interplay with government provision have changed and evolved over time, but the idea that most nuclear families as economic institutions can provide financial or caring security has no basis.

The basic idea of risk sharing is that by cooperating and pooling resources each participant can be protected at a lower cost, because it is unlikely that all the pooling participants will need resources at the same moment in time. This is the principle behind insurance. Unfortunately, what seems to be clear is that collectively Americans have not been saving enough for the care needs of their retirement. In 2011, women aged 65 and older received a total income of $22,069 on average (Fischer and Hayes 2013). In a 2010 survey by the IWPR, 47 percent of elderly women in the United States were not confident that they had enough resources to last throughout their retirement (Hess et al. 2011). According to websites offering advice for seniors in the U.S., the absolute minimum cost of assisted living is $1,800 per month ($21,600 per year), which does not include all meals or any out-of-pocket medical costs or services like reminders to take one's medication. Additional services could raise the cost to as high as $4000 per month (Assisted Senior Living 2016). Given that calculations for living wages do not include saving for retirement or education and that the median household income is not much larger than the living wage for two working parents and two children in my relatively inexpensive city, it is not clear that most families can increase their savings to cover care needs in retirement without relying on state support. Clearly, the numbers are not adding up. Unless governments significantly increase funding, unpaid work has to be an important component of care into the future.

In addition to risk sharing, families are important for decision-making when an individual requiring care cannot make decisions for him- or herself. Assigning this role to someone who knows the individual needing care well and who cares for that individual, especially someone predesignated by the individual needing care, would be much more likely to represent the wishes of that individual than an objective third party. Furthermore, when individual professionals are making these decisions, those decisions might conflict. Negotiating the healthcare system seems to require an advocate. Thus, who can play the role of advocate and provide unpaid labor when this role can no longer be forced upon women?

Post-families could provide an equitable cooperative alternative to nuclear families. They need to be disconnected with the biological process of reproduction, so that they can allow for declines in fertility that are necessary for environmental sustainability, but they do not need to replace the relationship between parent and child. Post-families, like extended families, could absorb couples and parents with children. Post-families would be groups of individuals that include singles and couples, parents with children and childless adults, young and old. Post-family members may be diverse along other dimensions of identity as well, but would share values that allow members to imagine shared purposes and goals and promote social cohesion. These alternative families need the diversity of age in order to facilitate intergenerational transfers of wealth and care, but shared values may lead to greater homogeneity for other characteristics of identity.

Post-families can redistribute the care burden by shifting our understanding of the purpose of economic activity and developing principles that emphasize equity rather than efficiency. Introductory economics courses encourage students to focus on the efficient allocation of scarce resources. This implies a set of resources that should all be spent and the choice is to decide which uses are more important. The future tends to be heavily discounted. For feminists (Power 2004) and heterodox economists in general (Lee 2013), economics is about social provisioning. Instead of asking how we can use up the world's resources, thinking about social provisioning forces us to ask how can we satisfy our needs and how we will be able to do so into the future.

Post-families would allocate care based on the question of how they can meet the basic needs of its members. Equity could be built into decision-making by applying a principle that each post-family member must contribute care to others that is equivalent to the care an average individual would need over a lifetime. This emphasizes the basic truth that all members of a community need care at different points in their life. This care should be balanced between desirable tasks and undesirable tasks in proportion to needs. For childless adults, care should be balanced between care of children, the sick, and the elderly in proportion to needs. Parents, may place greater emphasis on care of children due to their special relationship to their children. Post-family members would choose an individual or group to be advocates should he or she become incapacitated. Given zero population growth this system should provide enough care.

Post-families, as the foundation of a post-capitalism, could strengthen post-family values, by which I mean the ethical principle that we are collectively responsible for the well-being of our fellow human beings. Post-families would represent an expansion of the sphere that economists like Gary Becker believe to be altruistic[4]. Family represents a sphere in which individuals are concerned about the well-being of others, and impersonal exchange and maximum gain are considered crass. Families are supposed to be communities of shared risk, where it is expected that the luck of one will be shared with all. As feminists have shown, this is a romanticized picture of families. In reality, family members do not always prioritize the well-being of other family members (Barrett and McIntosh 1982; Braunstein and Folbre 2001). Nevertheless, the ideal represents a kind of cultural foundation for developing imagined communities that share economic risks and mutual care, where shared responsibility for one another is the norm.

Finally, since post-families require care work from every member of society, they can contribute to the development of care as a skill that every member of society is expected to cultivate. Schools would develop courses that teach relevant skills and care ethics. As Nelson (2013), argues care represents a human capacity that is important for the functioning not just of families, but also for the ethical function of business. By making care work a responsibility of every human being and highlighting the fact that all human beings require care, post-families would contribute to the development of the human capacity for care.

There are precedents for institutions that provide care and support but are not based on biological relationships, legal contracts, or market exchange. Some of these institutions represent an alternative to traditional families and some represent cooperation between families. Religious orders provided an alternative to family. Nuns do not marry or bear children. Religious life is based on a principle of service to others and so the younger nuns took care of the elderly nuns in the same way a family is supposed to. However, with fewer young people entering religious orders, there are not enough young nuns to care for aging nuns (Mulligan 1993; Fitzgerald 2015). For Capuchin Priests, the financial cost of nursing-home care was unsustainable, so one friar went to nursing school to take on responsibility for his aging brethren (Associated Press 2003). Similarly, when the AIDS epidemic hit, many gay people had been abandoned by their families of origin and ACT UP, the political movement that developed to call for better treatment of gay men living with AIDS, also developed a service arm to provide care for the sick. Unfortunately, this reproduced the traditional gender roles by expecting lesbians to contribute care, but lesbians dealing with cancer did not have access to movement wide support (Winnow 1992). Ad hoc networks of friends have also become an important part of coping with serious illness, like cancer, and providing care for many. Another alternative form of family is the urban kibbutz.

Based on Israel's agricultural cooperatives that have been in decline as more young people move to the city, urban kibbutzim are cooperative living arrangements with shared apartments and living expenses and shared bank accounts (Ament 2008). More secular versions of cooperative housing with varying levels of integration also exist.

Unfortunately, most of these examples do not seem to address the issue of intergenerational transfers of care labor. The religious orders managed intergenerational care for hundreds of years, but with declining interest in religious life the system has broken down. Anyone choosing to enter an institution that promises intergenerational care transfers is going to wonder if the care is going to be there for them in the future. Young people are already asking this question about the American pay-as-you-go pension system. Cooperative housing arrangements, while often identifying as alternative families and sharing housework, do not emphasize any obligation of care. The example of ACT UP, while emphasizing care, does not even guarantee reciprocity of care between individuals at similar points in the life cycle. None of these examples incorporate care for children, but cooperative childcare arrangements tend to be built around a reciprocal principle that parents, who are responsible for care, can share that burden with other parents who are responsible for care (BBC News 2009). They do not instill a principle of responsibility that each of us as former children who received care and who will require care in the future have an obligation to care for others. Building intergenerational community and intergenerational trust will be a difficult challenge.

Post-families and the principle of universal obligation to care would ultimately require or effect transformations in other institutions. The housing stock in the United States is primarily built around nuclear families and neighborhoods have developed generationally, such that neighbors are often in the same age group. Managing care in intergenerational extended post-families would work better with a different mix of living arrangements. Universal obligation to care requires different work arrangements[5].

Another challenge facing post-families is one of the problems facing traditional families, the problem of migration. We need to consider how post-families will manage the care obligation when individuals are mobile. Presumably, religious orders managed this by having chapter houses in different locations. In this way an individual nun may have moved from one chapter house to another and still received care when her time came. Religious orders, however, are hierarchical organizations and post-families would be democratically run. Democratic decision-making is most efficient in smaller groups. Thus, there may be a trade-off between large post-families that can more easily share risk and manage mobility and smaller organizations that give greater voice to individual voices through a democratic process and resist becoming too impersonal.

Post-families represent an alternative that can be implemented on a small scale today and be developed and refined gradually over time. Initially, it could be difficult to get people to commit to enough care. Post-family projects would be most successful along other post-capitalist projects such as producer and consumer cooperatives, time banks, and alternative currencies where commitment to cooperative living precedes the institutions and, especially, where the organization of paid work can accommodate the obligation to care. Little by little the basic principle that care is both a universal right and a universal obligation can spread. Participants could observe the wisdom of a golden rule knowing that the norms they establish today will be those that they have to live under in their own old age. Hopefully, if we get it right, post-families can evolve into institutions that provide for people's needs without requiring growing population and growing environmental destruction.

Notes

1 Improvements in healthcare can both increase and decrease care needs. They may increase the probability of survival, such that an individual who otherwise would have perished quickly requires long-term care. It also likely raises the average age at which people need care or more extensive care. So, the change in the potential support ratio somewhat overstates the problem.
2 For an understanding of the relationship between capabilities and freedom, see Robeyns 2003.
3 Seventeen percent cited Medicaid and 25 percent cited Medicare as payment sources for in-home formal paid care (U.S. Department of Health and Human Services 2012).
4 See Folbre (2009, p.^pp.) for a discussion of self-interest and altruism in the history of economic thought.
5 See Hirsh et al. (2013) for a discussion of the ideal worker and the difficulty of balancing work with care obligations in the United States

References

Albert, M. and R. Hahnel (1992) 'Participatory Planning'. *Science and Society* 56 (1): 39–59.
Albert, M. and R. Hahnel (2002) 'In Defense of Participatory Economics'. *Science and Society* 66 (1): 7–21.
Ament, R. (2008) *The Israeli Urban Kibbutz Model, Now in Brooklyn*. The Jerusalem Post. August 28, 2008. Available at: http://www.jpost.com/Magazine/Features/The-Israeli-urban-kibbutz-model-now-in-Brooklyn. accessed on October 24, 2016.
Assisted Senior Living (2016) *The Cost of Assisted Living*. Available at: http://www.assistedseniorliving.net/ba/facility-costs.cfm/. accessed on October 20, 2016.
Associated Press (2003) *Caring for His Own: Priest Cares for Aging Brothers*. The Topeka Capital Journal. January 24, 2003. Available at: http://cjonline.com/stories/012403/ksp_priest.shtml#.WBzCXYWcGUl.
Barrett, M. and M. McIntosh (1982) *The Anti-Social Family* (London: Verso).
BBC News (2009) *Rethink on 'illegal' childcaring*. BBC News. September 28, 2009. Available at: http://news.bbc.co.uk/2/hi/uk_news/education/8279274.stm. accessed on Oct. 20, 2016.
Braunstein, E. and N. Folbre (2001) 'To Honour and Obey: Efficiency, Inequality, and Patriarchal Property Rights'. *Feminist Economics* 7 (1): 25–44.
Burczak, T.A. (2006) *Socialism after Hayek* (Ann Arbor: University of Michigan Press).

Burke, M., S.M. Hsiang and E. Miguel (2015) 'Global non-linear effect of temperature on economic production'. *Nature* 527 (7577): 235–239.

Coontz, S. (1988) *The Social Origins of Private Life: A History of American Families 1600–1900* (New York: Verso).

Coontz, S. (1992) *The Way We Never Were: American Families and the Nostalgia Trap* (New York, NY: BasicBooks).

Cooper, C., A. Selwood, M. Blanchard, et al. (2009) 'Abuse of people with dementia by family carers: representative cross sectional survey'. *BMJ* 338, http://www.bmj.com/content/bmj/338/bmj.b155.full.pdf.

Eaton, S.C. (2005) 'Eldercare in the United States: Inadequate, Inequitable, but Not a Lost Cause'. *Feminist Economics* 11 (2): 37–51.

Edelstone, S.F. (2002) 'Filial Responsibility: Can the Legal Duty to Support Our Parents Be Effectively Enforced?'. *Family Law Quarterly* 36 (3): 501–514.

Fischer, J. and J. Hayes (2013) 'The Importance of Social Security in the Incomes of Older Americans: Differences by Gender, Age, Race/Ethnicity, and Marital Status'. In: Research I.f.W.s.P. (ed) *Briefing Paper*. Washington, D.C.

Fitzgerald, J. (2015) *Aging Catholic Nuns Get Care at Jewish Nursing Home*. Salon. May 24, 2015. Available at: http://www.salon.com/2015/05/24/aging_catholic_nuns_get_care_at_jewish_nursing_home/. accessed on November 1, 2016.

Folbre, N. (1994) *Who Pays for the Kids? Gender and the Structures of Constraint* (London and New York: Routledge).

Folbre, N. (2009) *Greed, Lust and Gender: A History of Economic Ideas* (Oxford and New York: Oxford University Press).

Folbre, N. (2016) *Care Talk: Feminism and Political Economy*. Available at: https://blogs.umass.edu/folbre/2016/01/15/defining-alternative-systems/.

Folbre, N. and J. Nelson (2000) 'For Love or Money'. *Journal of Economic Perspectives* 14 (4): 123–140.

Gao, G. (2015) *Scientists more worried than public about world's growing population*. Available at: http://www.pewresearch.org/fact-tank/2015/06/08/scientists-more-worried-than-public-about-worlds-growing-population/. accessed on September 15, 2016.

Greene, K. (2012) *Are You on the Hook for Mom's Nursing-Home Bill?* Wall Street Journal. June 22, 2012. Available at: http://www.wsj.com/articles/SB10001424052702303506404577446410116857508.

Griscom, J.L. (2005) 'The Case of Sharon Kowalski and Karen Thompson: Ableism, Heterosexism, and Sexism'. In: Steele T.L. (ed), *Sex, Self, and Society: The Social Context of Sexuality* (Belmont, CA: Thomson, 162–169).

Hess, C. (2013) 'Women and the Care Crisis: Valuing In-Home Care in Policy and Practice'. *Institute for Women's Policy Research: Briefing Paper*. Washington.

Hess, C., J. Hayes and H. Hartmann (2011) 'Retirement on the Edge: Women, Men and Economic Insecurity After the Great Recession'. Washington, D.C.: Institute for Women's Policy Research.

Hirsh, E., H. Hollingdale and N. Stecy-Hildebrandt (2013) 'Gender inequality in the workplace'. In: Figart D.M. and Warnecke T.L. (eds) *Handbook of Research on Gender and Economic Life* (Cheltenham: Edward Elgar, 183–199).

Hodgson, G.M. (2002) 'Varieties of Capitalism and Varieties of Economic Theory'. In: Hodgson G.M. (ed) *A Modern Reader in Institutional and Evolutionary Economics* (Cheltenham, U.K. and Northampton, MA: Edward Elgar, 201–229).

Hodgson, G.M. (2006) *Economics in the Shadows of Darwin and Marx: Essays on Institutional and Evolutionary Themes* (Cheltenham, U.K.: Edward Elgar).

Hodgson, G.M. (2015) *Conceptualizing Capitalism: Institutions, Evolution, Future* (Chicago: University of Chicago Press).

Hyman, D.A. (2001) 'Health Care Fraud and Abuse: Market Change, Social Norms, and the Trust "Reposed in the Workmen"'. *Journal of Legal Studies* 30 (2): 531–567.

Kuné, J.B. (2001) 'The Controversy of Funding Versus Pay-As-You-Go: What Remains of the Debate?' *The Geneva Papers on Risk and Insurance* 26 (3): 418–434.

Lee, F.S. (2013) 'Heterodox economics and its critics'. In: Lee F.S. and Lavoie M. (eds) *In Defense of Post-Keynesian and Heterodox Economics: Responses to their critics* (London and New York: Routledge, 104–132).

Montgomery, R.J.V. (1999) 'The Family Role in the Context of Long-Term Care'. *Journal of Aging and Health* 11 (3): 383–416.

Mulligan, H.A. (1993) *Aging Nuns Transform Mobile Home Park*. Los Angeles Times. June 12, 1993. Available at: http://articles.latimes.com/1993-06-12/local/me-2351_1_mobile-home-park. accessed on November 1, 2016.

Muoio, D. (2015) *Japan is Running Out of People to Take Care of the Elderly, So It's Making Robots Instead*. Available at: http://www.techinsider.io/japan-developing-carebots-for-elderly-care-2015-11

Nelson, J.A. (2013) 'Gender and caring'. In: Figart D.M. and Warnecke T.L. (eds) *Handbook of Research on Gender and Economic Life* (Cheltenham: Edward Elgar, 62–76).

Newbold, T., L.N. Hudson, A.P. Arnell, et al. (2016) 'Has land use pushed terrestrial biodiversity beyond the planetary boundary? A global assessment'. *Science* 353 (6296): 288–291.

O'Donnell, L. (2016) 'The Crisis Facing America's Working Daughters'. *The Atlantic,* February 9, 2016.

O'Shaughnessy, C.V. (2014) 'National Spending for Long-Term Services and Supports'. National Health Policy Forum, George Washington University.

OECD (2014) *Society at a Glance 2014* (Paris: OECD Publishing).

OECD (2016) *Poverty Rate (indicator)*. 10.1787/0fe1315d-en accessed on November 3, 2016.

Power, M. (2004) 'Social Provisioning as a Starting Point for Feminist Economics'. *Feminist Economics* 10 (3): 3–19.

Robeyns, I. (2003) 'Sen's Capability Approach and Gender Inequality: Selecting Relevant Capabilities'. *Feminist Economics* 9 (2–3): 61–92.

Scheil-Adlung, X. (2015) 'Long-Term Care Protection for Older Persons: a Review of Coverage Deficits in 46 Countries '. In: Office I.L. (ed) *Extension of Social Security.* (Geneva: International Labour Office).

Shammas, C. (1994) 'Re-Assessing the Married Women's Property Acts'. *Journal of Women's History* 6 (1): 9–30.

Swagel, P. (2009) 'The Cost of the Financial Crisis: The Impact of the September 2008 Economic Collapse'. Briefing Paper #18, PEW Economic Policy Group.

Tedin, K.L., R.E. Matland and G.R. Weiher (2001) 'Age, Race, Self-Interest, and Financing Public Schools Through Referenda'. *The Journal of Politics* 63 (1): 270–294.

United Nations Department of Economic and Social Affairs Population Division (2015) *World Population Prospects: The 2015 Revision, Key Findings and Advance Tables* (New York: United Nations).

U.S. Department of Health and Human Services. (2012) 'Long Term Care Insurance'. *ASPE Research Brief*. Washington, D.C.: HHS Office of the Assistant Secretary for Planning and Evaluation Office of Disability, Aging and Long-Term Care Policy.

Willmore, L. (2004) 'Population Ageing and Pay-as-You-go Pensions'. *Ageing Horizons* (1): 1–11.

Winnow, J. (1992) 'Lesbians Evolving Heath Care: Cancer and AIDS'. *Feminist Review* (41): 68–76.

Worstall, T. (2016) *It's Not That Social Security Will Run Out of Cash – It's Whether Taxes Will Rise to Fund It*. Forbes. July 17, 2016. Available at: http://www.forbes.com/sites/timworstall/2016/07/17/its-not-that-social-security-will-run-out-of-cash-its-whether-taxes-will-rise-to-fund-it/#3c4c86b5664a. accessed on August 10, 2016.

7   World government is a necessity

Robert Albritton

"[T]he present generation of 'global problems' can truly be dealt with only by international management of an entirely new order." (Weiss 2012, xi)

Introduction

In this paper I shall advocate world government as the "international management of an entirely new order" that is required to deal with the array of global problems (both ecological and also social justice) that humanity faces. Such advocacy will seem utopian to many because the existing UN, NGOs, and other international organizations seem so far removed from a truly effective world government, and the kind of discussion that we need to move in this direction has hardly started. Indeed, many people probably think that an effective world government is not possible. As a result, my main focus will be on global problems that seem to require something like a world government for their resolution. I will not, however, give much attention to detailed institutional arrangements, for these will mainly need to be worked out by those directly involved.

If we knew the future, would we "act differently"? Some might think this is an empty question, because they may think that we cannot know the future. But this does not seem quite accurate. It is true that the further we go into the future, the less certain we can be about what will be the specific causes of particular outcomes. Yet the primary aim of science is not just to know more and more about the future, but also to have at least some knowledge of the likely causes of it evolving one way rather than another. No doubt the claims of some areas of research are less scientific than they claim (often economics?), but given the immense outpouring of funds aimed at denying climate science, as opposed to the immense body of well-grounded research that supports it, in this case it is important to realize the strength of most climate science. For climate science is an important basis of the radical thinking and action that is required if we want to extend our human lifespan on earth and make it more flourishing.

The purpose of these introductory philosophical paragraphs about science and acting differently is to set the stage for the main foci of this paper summarized here by two questions: Can a large majority of the world's people become citizens of the world? And can they act to bring about an effective world government? These two questions could become the center of dialogue, debate, and action over the future of the earth as that future unfolds. The problem is that there are many ways to act differently and given the enormous changes currently required, time is of the essence. Indeed, if we even come close to acting the same as we have been for much longer, the results will be a very rough and limited human lifespan on this planet.

There are many ways of acting differently in the current setting, but most informed people believe the primary one is to stop the annual increased out-pouring of greenhouse gases[1]. What we need to start seeing is a sharp reversal in our reliance on fossil fuels for our energy needs. Instead we see huge government subsidies to the fossil fuel industries that are increasing our annual reliance on fossil fuels, and as a result there are annual increases in global warming.

In a world in which nation-states are arming themselves more and more as they withdraw into themselves behind their respective borders, effective world government may strike one as a utopian dream. But I believe that such a vision could become a *practical* utopia in the sense that however long it takes to realize, it is a real possibility, and one worth struggling to achieve, however long that may take (Albritton 2012). Indeed, for some of the reasons that I hope will become clear in this essay, world government may not only be a possibility, but also a necessity if we want to avoid a descent into a hellish world.

Scientific research can make us more aware of the positive feedback between crises that are deepening each other, and, as a result, are increasing their destructive impact on the planet (e.g., if global warming thaws the frozen tundra of the arctic, the enormous release of methane gas will radically increase global warming, probably beyond our control). The warmer the world gets, the faster it will get yet warmer. And the global impact of these crises suggests the need for solutions that are, at least to an important degree, global solutions to global problems, solutions that are effective in the near future.

To the extent that the vast majority of people in the world come to see themselves as citizens of the world mobilized in an array of movements, it is conceivable that they might be able to construct a workable and democratic world government. But for this to happen we will need a vastly more egalitarian world: one in which people truly care for one another, and following from this, hold beliefs that no one deserves very much more wealth than anyone else. Our common humanness that leads us to feel spontaneous care for each other needs to be built upon and expanded in all areas of social life. This may take time because capitalism has so entrenched "possessive individualism" that it is not unusual for us to relate to other humans in very selfish ways (Macpherson 1962; Albritton 1991). As a result, many people would like to live in a castle made secure by guns, and surrounded with many moats to keep out those whose differences make them seem threatening. Sadly, this castle is most often made possible and even necessary by a violent world that could be much less violent.

Some problems that require global attention

Following are some typical problems that a world government would need to deal with. For example, should global warming increase to 4 degrees centigrade above average pre-industrial temperatures (a real possibility), eventually the world's ice would melt raising the oceans by approximately 60 meters[2]. Instead of the most powerful hurricanes being labelled as Category 5, there would now be Category 8 hurricanes (Griffin 2015, 63). Summer daytime highs in New York City (would there still be an NYC?) would reach as high or higher than 52 degrees centigrade, and there is a likelihood that 37 percent of plants and animals that inhabit global land would become extinct (Griffin 2015, 39, 63, 135; Kolbert 2014). According to Griffin (2015, 138), if global warming reaches 4 degrees centigrade, out of the 9 billion global population expected in 2050, the earth will eventually support only one-half billion (what will happen to the rest?).

The terrible consequences of such global warming make a very long list, and no doubt there are some consequences that are beyond our existing knowledge. However, we do know that without very high, very long, and very strong sea walls, backed up by very strong pumps, New York City as we know it would be largely underwater, with only taller buildings appearing as they stick their floors above water much as icebergs afloat in the oceans. We know this, and we know that to prevent this deluge, we have to act differently; that is, we have to act radically and with sufficient speed to stop global warming. But this does not seem to be happening, despite this particular piece of knowledge of the future, a knowledge that we have had for over 25 years[3]. The consumption of coal (a primary source of greenhouse gases) has increased globally from 4700 million tons in 2000 to 7900 million tons by 2013, and it continues to grow every year (State of the World 2015, 6). When will this truly be turned around? Since we have no world government, each nation-state will decide for itself, and the temptation within capitalist economies will always be profits and growth.

Unfortunately our social structures have usually limited us to thinking about the future in the short term. The main motivating force of capitalism is *short-term* profits, religions encourage thought about getting to heaven or at lease to purgatory at the end of a *lifetime*, and even family structures at their strongest seldom focus our attention beyond *three generations*. If we truly want a flourishing planet in the future, we have to act differently. Our current situation demands that humankind act in accord with likely happenings that may be several centuries off, a demand that is radically new and that requires us to totally alter our thought and action in relation to things as fundamental as space and time. In order to act differently, we need to think radically differently. Following are some examples that require global (spatial) and long-term (temporal) solutions.

Firstly, I will mention some problems generated primarily by global warming. One of our most basic needs is access to enough nutritious food to support a healthy life. Our achievements around this need are not very impressive, given other human achievements. Global malnutrition stemming from not enough food, food that is too expensive, or from unhealthy food is a growing problem (Albritton 2009; 2013). In the future food shortages are likely to become more severe due to the desertification of the land (the current annual loss of topsoil is 75 billion tons, and 44 percent of the world's food is grown on irrigated land) (Worldwatch Institute 2015, 67), while 11 percent of the world's irrigated land suffers from salination (Bardi 2014, 32, 35) and from extreme weather (droughts and floods), including daytime highs in some parts of the world eventually increasing to the 50- to 60-degree centigrade range. Since 2000, "land grabs" have absorbed over 36 million hectares (the size of Japan – and this is low compared to some estimations) of land and approximately one-third of this land will be used to grow bio-fuels, while in many cases peasants who have farmed the land for generations are pushed off the land (Worldwatch Institute 2015, 70). A strong indication of what is happening to global food availability is that in Egypt (not considered a particularly poor country), 38 percent of average household income goes to buy food (Worldwatch Institute 2015, 59).

What if, due to acidification, overfishing, and pollution of the oceans, saltwater fish and shellfish continue to become increasingly scarce? It is now estimated that over 3.5 billion people depend on the oceans as a primary source of food (Griffin 2015, 80, 88, 91, 105; Worldwatch Institute 2015, 15). As more and more populated areas face serious freshwater shortages due to drought, the loss of glaciers and snow pack, and the overuse of aquifers, what is to be done? Climate change itself will lead to severe droughts, flooding, and extreme weather. These problems will impact the availability of food on a global scale, and they are already leading to mass species extinction (Kolbert 2014; Griffin 2015, 135). We need to give a great deal of attention to finding long-term global solutions to these problems.

Does it make sense for the US to use over 40 percent of its corn crop (its largest crop) to make ethanol for the purpose of fueling automobiles? What does this do to the cost of food? It has been estimated that 2.8 billion people out of the current 7.4 billion who inhabit the earth (Power, 2016) make less than $2 a day. Is this enough income to afford a nutritious diet?

While many effective agricultural practices have been developed at a local level by peasant farmers over centuries, these need to be supplemented by an orientation that spreads the best agro-ecological practices both locally and globally, realizing that certain practices work best in particular soil, climate, availability of water, and so on, while other practices may have a broader reach, even global. Clearly, without radical changes now and in the near future, changes in climate, salination of land, desertification, lack of fresh water, and acidification of oceans will cause increasing food shortages.

As more and more places on earth become less inhabitable, the number of immigrants will necessarily increase. It has been estimated that there will be 250 million climate refugees by 2050 (probably a low estimate), and this will likely be supplemented by a much larger flow of refugees fleeing from violence, war, hunger, and repressive regimes. How will the world handle this? Already we see the traumatic impact of immigration on Europe, and this experience makes it clear that we will need a global policy that develops democratically agreed-upon criteria for immigrants to move globally in accord with the capacities of various countries and the needs of immigrants. Given all the media attention received by refugees fleeing to Europe, people may be unaware that Turkey, Pakistan, Lebanon, Iran, and Ethiopia host the most refugees. According to the latest report of the UN High Commission for Refugees (UNHCR), the global number of refugees has already reached 65.3 million (York 2016, A1).

China has large supplies of coal, making it by far the cheapest source of energy for its economy. Given China's energy needs and its predisposition to burn coal, it is contributing a great deal to global warming. This problem is severely exacerbated as a result of Australia's expanding coal industry, an expansion aimed precisely at profiting from exporting coal to help fill China's demand (Worldwatch Institute 2015, 51). So far the world has made little headway in limiting the consumption of fossil fuels, with the result that global warming increases every year and will continue to do so until we see some much more radical changes. Unfortunately, it is still the case that many nation-states spend billions annually to subsidize and thereby expand their biofuel or fossil-fuel industries. For example, "in Brazil almost a million acres a year of carbon-dioxide-absorbing tropical forest are being clear-cut and replaced by sugar cane for ethanol production or by open fields for grazing cattle. Authoritative studies show that the net effect is about 50 percent more carbon emissions than by fuelling automobiles with fossil fuels" (Morgan 2016, B2).

Let us consider another case that suggests the need for a global government that could come to the aid of particular countries, in this case Malawi. Malawi is one of the poorest countries in the world, and yet it is using a higher proportion of its land to grow tobacco than any other country. Deforestation is occurring at a rapid rate (from 1990 to 2010 Malawi lost 16.9 percent of its forest largely to either grow and cure tobacco or to make charcoal mainly for cooking or curing tobacco) (Vidal 2016; Onishi 2016), and this is likely to continue because this country depends on the tobacco industry for its survival. There is some international aid that may be helping the country cut back on the rate of deforestation, yet its dependence on tobacco is great and at the same time costly. Indeed, it takes 10 kg of wood to dry (cure) 1 kg of tobacco (Vidal 2016). The tobacco industry is the second largest employer in Malawi, with 350,000 farmers who grow tobacco, 70,000 hired laborers, and 10,000 in leaf-processing factories (Vidal 2016). And this is happening on a continent where hunger and malnutrition are widespread. Imagine the difference it would make if some of this land were to be used to grow nutritious crops. Clearly Malawi needs sufficient international aid to break the tobacco industry's control of its economy, a control fostered by giant tobacco multinationals that gather large short-term profits at Malawi's short-term and long-term expense.

Indonesia lets its rainforests burn to clear the land for agriculture, or it cuts them down for the lumber. As a result, large profits, more jobs, and an expanding GDP make the government look good, while air pollution diminishes the quality of life of millions, and deforestation contributes enormously to global warming now and in the future when rainforests, which are so important to the health of the world's ecosystems and climates supportive of life, may be permanently gone. I say this because it is unimaginable that the diversity of life to be found in a rainforest can be imitated by a human reforestation that is all too often a monoculture. It is not only the plant and animal diversity that is lost; rainforests play a key role in absorbing CO_2 and in generating rainfall, such that their loss can lead to eventual desertification. Clearly we need a global government that can step in and deal with this problem.

Secondly, the problems we face stem not only from global warming, but also from a growing scarcity of the earth's natural resources, starting with the great importance of fresh water and arable land that are such basic necessities of human life. Currently one-half of the people in the world have to cope with various degrees of water stress, and this situation is likely to worsen for numerous reasons (Griffin 2015, 80). One important reason stems from fracking for oil and natural gas. Fracking for oil uses on average 15 million liters of water per frack, and as a result the water becomes toxic. Fracking can also cause earthquakes (see the statistics for Oklahoma: Worldwatch Institute 2015, 29). As nature's economic inputs become more scarce, who will decide how they should be used? Markets are driven by short-term profits that ignore externalities (such as social and environmental costs) and not by considerations of long-term human and environmental flourishing. Hence markets by themselves will drive capitalists to maximize profits by maximizing fracking. And fracking is not the only questionable use of water spurred on by capitalist profits. Depending on how it is organized and under what conditions, irrigation can also waste water. Finally, water stress in the form of drought is up globally by 30 percent (Worldwatch Institute 2015, 61).

The continual loss of topsoil is a serious problem because it plays a crucial role in growing nutritious foods, and its loss means more reliance upon irrigation and chemicals. Some of the pesticides used widely are toxic and can cause health problems, and some of the mined fertilizers are already in low supply. For example, phosphorous is becoming less available, and 40 percent of the global arable land depends on this fertilizer for much of its productivity (Bardi 2014, 163).

It is not only the availability of arable land and fresh water that are in decline, but also many minerals. It takes more and more energy to mine minerals as they become increasingly scarce, and at some point the cost of the energy to mine and produce the mineral is greater that the value of the minerals themselves. Bardi (2014, 135) refers to this as a peak, and he claims that at least nickel, zinc, copper, tin, and silver will reach their peaks in 20 to 80 years, depending upon the rate they are mined.

A third problem area that requires the attention of world government is pollution and waste disposal. In 2012 it has been estimated that 7 million people died primarily from air pollution (Worldwatch Institute 2015, 5). At the same time, air pollution reduced the amount of the sun's energy reaching the earth, thus retarding global warming. In other words, if it weren't for massive air pollution, global warming would be worse. So we have a choice: let air pollution kill off 7 million people in the short run, or let global warming kill off most life on earth in the long term. Perhaps the better choice would be to sharply reduce both. And while we're at it, let us cut back sharply on both the pollution of salt water and fresh water. To deal effectively with all the above global problems, we will need a strong and democratic world government.

A world of peaceful nation-states?

Many academics focus on what they see as the positive advances of "multilateralism" and the degrees of "international governance," which already exist among some nation-states. While these two terms can be used positively to emphasize the need for greater international cooperation, they also are sometimes used to sink us into the status quo, or at most some conservative steps towards a little more cooperation. Few seriously discuss the future desirability of something as radical as world government. While there may be no immediate way of bringing it about, if we don't at least start some serious talk and action in this direction, there will never be a way of bringing it about even in the long run. Some may think that a slight strengthening of a combination of the United Nations, NGOs, treaties, regional common markets, various quasi-autonomous UN organizations, and more cooperative nation-states can achieve the enormous changes that are required, but this is doubtful, because these organizations are for the most part too embedded in existing economic and political institutions that are capitalist and therefore oriented to short-term profits. For obvious reasons, the UN is not very democratic, not only because of the veto powers of the permanent members of the Security Council, but also because of the general influence and power in the UN of rich countries and rich corporations both economically and politically. While some NGOs and UN semiautonomous organizations do display a degree of effectiveness in advancing global peace, health, caring, justice, and sustainability, still they are often faced with obstacles put in their way by the influence and power of capitalist corporations and what are often the narrow self-interests of powerful capitalist states.

Ever since the Treaty of Westphalia signed in 1648, the hegemonic countries of the capitalist world have for the most part tried to organize themselves into sovereign states whose rule within their boundaries is not to be interfered with by other states. Eventually the "sovereign" state was to become wherever possible a "nation-state." The "nation" was conceived to be a unified cultural entity loyal to the state, and nationalism became the primary ideology (like a religion in many ways) to mobilize the state's population for territorial expansion and war. In the twentieth century, the United States became the hegemonic world capitalist power. Typical nationalist phrases are to be found in the American Pledge of Allegiance and national anthem. For example, in the first we find the words "one nation under God, indivisible, with liberty and justice for all" and in the second the words "the bombs bursting in air, gave proof through the night that our flag was still there: Oh, say! Does that star-spangled banner yet wave O'er the land of the free and the home of the brave". In other words, the nation in this case is a sort of religious entity that is unified and directed by God.

Furthermore, it is a "home" with "liberty and justice for all" made up of "brave" individuals who will fight against rockets and bombs to keep the flag flying, and if necessary, sacrifice their lives for the good of the nation. In other words, if in the first instance the state was to be a totally autonomous legal person (i.e., sovereign within its boundaries), then the "nation" was to be a filled out and united national subjectivity, such that nationalism could call upon citizens to lay down their lives for the national interest. In short, the state increasingly became the legal subject and the nation the subjective content that was prepared to fight to its death when commanded by a state ultimately directed by God (as well as states, capitalist corporations are also legal subjects) (Albritton 1991). Indeed, God's guidance assured that the actions of the nation-state would be just, moral, and righteous.

Historically the nation-state's primary aims have been supplied by the growth of capitalism, which tends to develop deeply competitive relations among the richest and most powerful nation-states, all of whom would like to maximize their profits and become hegemonic. In other words, the most capitalist economies have found the nation-state to offer the most basic and congenial political forms for maximizing their wealth and to compete for world domination. The problem is that the competition is not always friendly. The result can be arms races and the sort of militarism that ends up being a military-industrial complex that plays a central role in political economic life even when a particular war is over. In other words, as militarism grows, arms production can become increasingly central to capitalist profits such that the international arms trade can support various degrees of warfare and armed violence as weapons are spread more thickly around the world (Pilisuk and Rountree 2015; Albritton 2015). It is sad that nationalism has been utilized so often in history to stir the citizens of a state into a frenzy of hatred against other nation-states or particular groups of people. Indeed, if there is one ideological element in the modern era that has been used most often to mobilize people for war, it is nationalism. And to this day the US and Russia, with 70,000 nuclear warheads between them (Bardi 2014, 54), have not only enough nuclear weapons to destroy the world many times over, but also the means to deliver these bombs anywhere on the globe at any time.

The Canadian political theorist C.B. Macpherson's (1962) widely read book on the British political theorists Hobbes and Locke is entitled *The Political Theory of Possessive Individualism*. Macpherson points out that Hobbes in particular starts his theory with the threat of "a war of all against all" that could occur without a strong state to make and enforce law and order. After all, Hobbes argues, if each individual competes with all other individuals to expand his private property (nearly all property was owned by males when Hobbes wrote), then without a strong state to make and enforce law and order, the result would be a tendency for competition to get out of hand and turn into generalized warfare. But if nation-states are simply very large legal persons or "possessive individuals" (individuals focused primarily on expanding their property in competition with other individuals), then can't they too easily tend towards warfare? Indeed, historically and up to the present we find it not unusual for nation-states to engage in conflicts over the smallest bits of territory, or over moving boundaries ever so slightly. Does it matter to the destiny of humanity in the long run whether a small island in the South China Sea belongs to China, the Philippines, Indonesia, or is an independent territory of some sort? One might think that the sword-rattling that can occur around small bits of territory is bizarre. Unfortunately, small sword-rattling or family feuds (World War I) can trigger wars of disastrous scope.

Even without a war-mongering state, citizens of capitalist nation-states often have strong feelings of loyalty and patriotism towards the state they identify with as their "home and native land." And sometimes particular nation-states deliver an array of desirable things and are seen as shining forth with greatness as citizens and the state are glorified. Although the capitalist focus on expanding profits and wealth in the short run may have had its attractions in parts of the nineteenth and twentieth centuries, humanity now faces a series of crises that make the capitalist nation-state increasingly outmoded when it comes to organizing the degree of transnational cooperation and orientation to the future that is now required. There are simply too many situations in which the short-term national interests of a particular capitalist state or the profit interests of a corporation can have immense long-term costs for humanity as a whole.

Nationalism is not always a bad thing, for it is also true that it has sometimes served to mobilize a people against imperialism or undemocratic practices. The problem is that such mobilizations may not benefit a nation very much in a capitalist world in the long run, since self-government may simply open a country to greater exploitation and corruption by capitalist political institutions, capitalist corporations, or authoritarianism. Sadly, this can easily produce a fully "failed" or semi "failed" state. Indeed, how many states in today's world can honestly be labeled "fully successful" states?

I don't mean to suggest that the nation-state is such an anachronism that it is on the verge of extinction; rather, I would argue that it has never been all that effective in maintaining peace domestically or internationally, and that whatever effectiveness it has had cannot for the most part deal effectively with the current unprecedented global problems. I strongly believe, therefore, that the future of humanity rests increasingly on the vast majority of the world's inhabitants supporting internationalist movements that can ultimately join together in order to build an effective world government.

Citizens of the world should support policies that they believe will most contribute to the flourishing of the global environment and of humans around the world in the long run, even if such policies go against the "national interest" of the nation-state that they have pledged to support with their lives. To some extent, the UN, NGOs, and semiautonomous organizations are already moving in this direction, though often their efforts are frustrated by undemocratic practices which are in turn fed by global capitalism. The central problem is that profits are the sine qua non of capitalism, but very often profit-making is largely blind to issues of democracy, justice, caring, equality, and sustainability.

In the past there have been movements for world government such as the "United World Federalists" whose primary aim was peace. While peace is still continually threatened, in order to deal with global warming, we need even much stronger movements whose aim is to remove a good deal of power from capital and nation-states and transfer it to a multilevel democratic world government. This is particularly necessary because global warming is the greatest crisis ever faced by humans, and the most difficult to deal with. It is truly a global problem that requires solutions at every level but particularly at a global level. How can we allow capitalist nation-states to do away with tropical rainforests that absorb so much CO_2, that are so rich in species, and have such a large impact on the weather?

High finance creates low life

A start in reforming the global financial system is to find ways (perhaps utilizing IT) to make it as transparent as possible and as a result to expose as illegal all forms of tax avoidance and all forms of corruption: shell corporations, transfer pricing, tax havens, manipulating the books, numbered accounts, payoffs, etc. If possible, all financial dealings of significance should be transparent. At the same time there should be far fewer financial dealings.

The purpose of capitalist financial systems is supposedly to mobilize all savings so that otherwise idle funds are used to maximize profits (including rent, interest, and pure commercial capital). Ideally, some of these idle funds would become credit given to consumers whose spending would stimulate the growth of capital, but the lion's share would presumably go to those capitalist corporations that can best use the funds to maximize the greatest profits by providing commodities and services that are wanted and can be paid for. Unfortunately, in today's financial capitalism more and more of total savings flow to making quick bucks from rent and interest and not from producing anything or offering useful services (Westra 2016). In other words, financial capital does little other than make the rich richer. The ownership of property and cash in itself is coupled with the pure manipulation of dollars by creditors to make more dollars. As a result there is a hollowing out of capitalism. It can no longer provide the jobs or provide the commodities and services that meet the needs of the vast majority (Lapavitsas 2013).

One solution to this problem is to tax away all profits and then redistribute them globally in accord with the requirements of long-term human (egalitarian) and environmental flourishing. In the first instance, this implies a very significant redistribution of wealth globally that would presumably be organized such that the countries with the highest per capita incomes and wealth would contribute accordingly to the global redistribution. The goal would be to move gradually towards a global redistribution that would make the difference between the richest and the poorest (in terms of wealth and income) some reasonable ratio such as 3:1, and would give everyone a basic income sufficient to lead a decent life well above the poverty line. And the redistribution would not simply be money but also services such as health, education, transportation, entertainment, and cultural expression.

Taxing away all profits as well as high incomes and high wealth would provide most of the resources, along with drastically cutting the manufacture of weapons of all sorts, the cutting of the international arms trade, and finally disarming the world.

While some companies would be shut down because of their negative impact on human and environmental flourishing, others would receive a portion of profits taxed away because they contribute to human flourishing. Suppose that a company can produce inexpensive housing with almost no long-term ecological foot print, and the demand for their product far exceeds the supply. In this instance the company (other things being equal) would receive a greater portion of the redistributed profit than they paid into it because it would be clear that they needed to expand production in order to meet a social need. Imagine a set of criteria that might serve to determine how the total profit would be distributed. For example, a switch to more sustainable ways of producing something (such as cement, which now contributes over 5 percent to global greenhouse gas emissions), more democracy in the workplace, more efficient and safer production, and less onerous work, these and other criteria would normally lead to a workplace receiving a larger share of the profit such that these changes would encourage the expansion of production and the spread of better workplace practices. The aim would not be to maximize profits but to maximize the quality of the product, the quality of the production process, the quality of life of workers, recycling waste, less pollution, more cooperation between units of production, increases to sustainability, and increases to research that would advance all these things. Not only would all profits be taxed away and then redistributed in order to advance global human and environmental flourishing, but so would high incomes and wealth be taxed away, ultimately resulting in a more egalitarian global society.

Basic incomes and property

A basic income relative to the cost of living could be provided for everyone globally at a level that would support a decent life whether one is employed or not. Housework, all kinds of caring work, and all kinds of productive work could be paid above a basic income. The aim might be that the income differential between the highest paid and lowest paid would be relatively small. Eventually all profits, all incomes more than three times higher (approximation) than the basic income, and all wealth based on private property would be taxed away and redistributed internationally with the ultimate aim of a high degree of equality. All debts would be cancelled or renegotiated. Banks and stock markets as they now exist would be done away with. People could take on only debts that would be relatively easy to repay, and even companies with losses instead of profits might be given the money to not only cover costs but also to expand assuming demand for the product or service and assuming that the company contributed to the flourishing of nature and people ("positive externalities").

Some oppose the Basic Income (BI) because they think it would simply result in people having to pay for social services out of their BI (such as education, health, and aspects of welfare) that are now paid for by the state in some countries. While one should be aware of this usage of BI by conservatives to drastically cut state spending and expand the commodification of things like education, we need to see that it can be used to enormously expand the quality of life of the vast majority by providing a lifetime of financial security and by getting rid of global poverty altogether. In other words, it is not simply a BI itself that I am advocating, but a BI in a very advanced and egalitarian welfare state.

Indeed, in most cases it would be desirable that the state provide far more services than it does now. Any general service where qualitative measures should strive towards an equalitarian approach such as health, education, transportation, housing, access to exercise, or access to culture could be provided free or at least largely subsidized by the state.

Others oppose a basic income because they think that people would have no incentive to work. But working people could be paid a wage on top of their basic income. Furthermore, for many people work is an important part of their lives, and with people having the option not to work, leaders in workplaces would be motivated to always improve the quality of life in the workplace, for otherwise they would lose their workers. Furthermore, to the extent that each workplace would become more democratic, the workers themselves would decide upon improvements to life in the workplace that would motivate them to continue to come to work. In a caring world, financial incentives would become much less important. Indeed, on the one hand, many people might opt for various kinds of volunteering, since their basic needs would be fulfilled by the basic income; on the other hand, it may be important that previous "volunteer" work of certain types be paid just as it may be important for other kinds of volunteer work not to be paid (e.g., some forms of work done as an expression of love or caring?).

One of the world's most serious problems today is unemployment, under-employment, and precarious employment. A BI would help deal with this problem, by always supporting a decent standard of living for all. A BI would enable otherwise unemployed people to get free training, become self-employed, or take some time to themselves. In other words, it would remove the terrible losses that can come with unemployment. Indeed, unemployment has become such a serious problem in our quasi-capitalist world that politicians are afraid to close down industries that contribute hugely to global warming, for fear of worsening unemployment. With a BI in place, however, unemployment would be less of a problem, since the unemployed would have sufficient income to lead a decent life, and society would have institutions designed to interconnect knowledge, labor, and needs or wants such that either employment or training could always be a possibility with a minimum of waiting. For example, someone with the idea to build a neighborhood park could present the idea to a local "bank," which in turn could help mobilize and finance the community, the expertise, tools, and labor-power to build the park in the most sustainable ways.

We need institutions that can make connections between people on a global scale with particular training or education, people who would like to get some specific training, and people with particular wants or needs. In a truly caring society there will always be caring needs that will improve people's lives and/ or the environment. "Banks" (think of a different name: e.g., "Urbanks") that are quite different from the ones we have now could mobilize social savings, social profits, and expertise to meet social needs and to enrich social life. Or they might decide upon particularly important areas of research and proceed to mobilize the expertise and funds required. The motivating factor would no longer be profits, but instead flourishing communities on a flourishing planet. It is important that this form of economic life would eventually spread around the planet, and "banks" would operate democratically at every level from global to local. Debt would be a small part of banking because consumers would be limited to small debts, and businesses would be supported by banks as needed without having to pay back a debt.

A shorter work week, say 30 hours to begin with, would not only require hiring more workers, but also would give full-time workers more time to do volunteer or caring work, whether to meet the needs of children, the disabled, the elderly, or do various sorts of community-oriented work. A good deal of caring work (for example, most day care) would likely be paid labor, but this issue could be decided by those concerned, given the free time and whether or not it makes sense to pay particular types of caring labor. For example, some parents are not only good at parenting, but also like it. At the same time they may want some time to themselves. Since children represent the next generation, care of children should be considered among the most important uses of time, including, among other things, nutritious diet, plenty of exercise, rich experiences and education, and most importantly lots of love, friendship, and support that they can pass on to others as they grow older. Adults would be able to decide how much time to spend in volunteer work, since they would receive a BI to meet their basic needs and wants. Indeed, they could spend all their working time doing volunteer work if they wanted to.

Where would the money come from? The money would come from social savings, taxing the profits of production and services, and taxing both income and wealth of the rich. Or, in other words, it would come from the social surplus that has been accumulated in the past or present. Consumers could assume debts, but only to a level that they could relatively easily pay off. Money for research would be given through competition based on criteria such as its potential importance in reducing long-term ecological costs, and it would be awarded by committees operating democratically. Banks would operate on various levels such as local, small regional, national, large regional, and global, and research money could be distributed democratically across levels according to criteria of social need, want, and sustainability.

Beyond what we could consider personal property, such as a shirt or a toothbrush, most property would be public with an array of use criteria. For example, farms may be public property used by a farmer as long as she/he meets certain use criteria, and, having met such criteria, they would be able to pass the farm on to family members when they retire. Farmers who cannot cover their costs for natural reasons (e.g., drought) would still receive a basic income plus a wage income. Finally farmers who make contributions to agro-ecology would receive a basic income, a wage, and a research reward.

In short, access and use of property will vary greatly given the type of property. Access to sports facilities might be free as long as one reserves their use in advance. In other words, property would become an issue of use, not of ownership: Who can use the property, for what purpose, for how long, under what conditions, and so on? Answers to these questions would vary with the type of property, though purely private property would mainly relate to products of personal consumption, particularly where personal choice is widely important, as with food or clothing.

Conclusions

I have said little about the sorts of institutions that might make up a world government, and though discussions about institutions need to occur primarily amongst those creating and experimenting with them, I want to conclude with a few very general reflections about a possible world government in the future.

First, I like the idea of calling it "United Peoples" rather than "United Nations." This is because I think in today's world nations are increasingly the hand-servants of giant corporations, and as such they are too pugnacious to do very much long-term uniting. Just as capitalists aim to maximize short-term profits, so nations want to pursue short-term national interests, particularly as they support and intertwine with capitalist profits. I would therefore suggest a global legislature that does not bury the voices of the marginalized, but instead makes it easy for their voices to be heard. The legislature may be unicameral, bicameral, or tricameral, but we need to find ways to really hear voices that have been marginalized in the past, including, for example, indigenous people, working-class people, small farmers, precarious workers, informal sector workers, unemployed, women, the poor, youth, domestic workers, immigrants, prisoners, war veterans, people who are discriminated against, and others. Hence, I like the name "United Peoples."

Second, if we have some kind of "House of Representatives," we might also consider a "House of Sustainability," in which people are selected into relatively autonomous groupings that focus on ecological concerns (e.g., land, salt water, fresh water, atmosphere, food, housing, energy, waste, toxicity). Each grouping might have a research branch and an implementation branch, and given overlaps they could consult with each other and make laws or policy that would advance sustainability in their area of concern and in related areas as well.

Third, there needs to be democratically controlled banking type institutions existing at more or less five levels (global, large regional, national, small regional, and local). They would direct savings and profits towards the most beneficial projects and policies by moving funds up and down through the levels as most needed.

Some people are more loving than others, some are more caring, some are gentler, some are more friendly. If anyone should be rewarded with wealth, shouldn't it be they? But does anybody's difference from others warrant gigantic monetary rewards? How about working at a job that is dangerous (road work) or that requires extraordinary energy? The merit of people who make important contributions to society can be rewarded by social recognition or by a one-time-only monetary reward (like many literary awards such as the British Booker Prize) that does not permanently place them in a class of extreme wealth, but rather is considered adequate recognition for their particular contribution. I am claiming here that the extremely rich never deserve their riches. No one is so much better than others that great wealth differences can be justified. Instead of awarding inventions or discoveries with long-term patents (e.g., 15 years) that often make them available only to the rich, they can also be treated like literary awards, with a single-time award distributed to those according to the role they played in the invention.

We desperately need a vast majority of people globally who identify themselves primarily as citizens of the world and who can sufficiently join together to build a world government, sometimes with small steps and sometimes with large.

Notes

1 According to an IMF study, global subsidies to fossil fuel industries add up to over $1.9 trillion per year (Roberts 2013).
2 Because of the number of variables involved, it is difficult to predict how long it would take global ice to melt at an average global increase of 4 degrees centigrade: maybe four centuries maybe less (Bardi 2014, 123).

3   "[T]he first major international gathering to set specific targets for emission reductions was the World Conference on the Changing Atmosphere, held in Toronto in 1988" (Klein 2014, p. 55).

References

Albritton, R. (1991) *A Japanese Approach to Stages of Capitalist Development*. London: Macmillan.

———(2009) *Let Them Eat Junk: How Capitalism Creates Hunger and Obesity*. Pluto.

——— (2012) "A Practical Utopia for the Twenty-First Century," in Vieira, P. and Marder, M. eds. *Existential Utopia: New Perspectives on Utopian Thought*. Continuum.

——— (2013) "Marxist Political Economy and Global Warming," *International Journal of Pluralism in Economic Education*, Vol. 4 No. 3, pp. 310–324.

——— (2015) "A Phase of Transition away from Capitalism," in Westra, R., Badeen, D., and Albritton, R. eds. *The Future of Capitalism after the Financial Crisis: The Varieties of Capitalism Debate in the Age of Austerity*. Routledge.

Bardi, U. (2014) *Extracted: How the Quest of Mineral Wealth Is Plundering the Planet*. Chelsea Green Publishing.

Griffin, D. R. (2015) *Unprecedented: Can Civilization Survive the CO_2 Crisis?* Clarity Press.

Klein, N. (2014) *This Changes Everything*. Alfred A. Knopf.

Kolbert, E. (2014) *The Sixth Extinction: An Unnatural History*. Henry Holt.

Lapavitsas, C. (2013) *Profiting without Producing: How Finance Exploits Us All*. Verso.

Macpherson, C.B. (1962) *The Political Theory of Possessive Individualism: Hobbes and Locke*. Clarendon Press.

Morgan, G. (2016) "Using 'Bio-Fuels' Is an Environmental Blunder," *Globe and Mail*, August 1, B2.

Onishi, N. (2016) "Charcoal Boom Devastating Africa's Environment," *New York Times International Weekly*, July 2–3.

Pilisuk, M. and Rountree, J. (2015) *The Hidden Structure of Violence: Who Benefits from Global Violence and War*. Monthly Review Press.

Power, S. (2016) "US Diplomacy: Realism and Reality," *New York Review of Books*, Vol. LXIII, No. 13, pp. 52–54, August 18.

Roberts, D. (2013) "The IMF Says that Global Subsidies to Fossil Fuels Amount to $1.9 billion per Year and that is Probably an Understatement," *Grist*, March 28.

Swift, R. (2014) *Alternatives to Capitalism*. Oxford: New Internationalist Press.

Vidal, J. (2016) *The Guardian*, "Malawi's Forests Going Up in Smoke as Tobacco Industry Takes Heavy Toll." August 31. https://www.theguardian.com/global-development/2015/jul/31/malawi-tobacco-industry-deforestation-chinkhoma

Weiss, T. (2012) *What's Wrong with the United Nations and How to Fix It*. Polity.

Westra, R. (2016) *Unleashing Usury: How Finance Opened the Door to Capitalism Then Swallowed It Whole*. Clarity Press.

State of the World (2015) *Confronting Hidden Threats to Sustainability*. Island Press.

York, G. (2016) "Poor Countries Bearing Brunt of Record Refugee Population." *Globe and Mail*, June 21, A1.

8 Alternative principles of labor

Liberation from labor and liberation through work[1]

Gui-yeon Jang

Introduction

The socialist bloc nations, including the Soviet Union, laid claim to having defeated capitalism, but they, in the end, returned to capitalism. Of course this does not mean that there is no alternative to capitalism. There is always the future. We can now analyze the many concrete factors leading to the failure of the socialist nations documented in history. But more fundamentally, there remains a question: Did this historically failed socialism realize an alternative to capitalism? In many ways, the societies of "real socialism" replicated the ills of capitalism.

Relating to this, one of the most significant aspects was the organization of labor. Even though ownership over the organization of production was not in the hands of private capital, there was no difference with capitalism in the actual organization of labor within production and the way production was carried out. The division of labor by criteria such as productivity and efficiency, as well as the technology and the managerial supervision structure for this, were adopted; thus, for workers, the labor process was little different from capitalism. Indeed, Lenin supported the introduction of Taylorism.

It would appear that the labor process was not thought to be an issue so long as the means of production were nationalized and production was used for the people of a workers' state. Though there were experiments aimed at "workers' self management" by involving workers in shop-floor organization and in management, in these cases as well, the labor process itself was hardly ever problematized. Workers' labor was organized to increase productivity and efficiency as much as possible, and workers were merely cogs in a wheel, adjuncts of the production organization. This was common to both societies under capitalism and under historically existing socialism.

As Marx once said, estranged labor is one of the root causes leading to the immiserization of workers' lives. Labor is a great part of our social lives, and if that labor is painful and even miserable, it cannot be easy to achieve happiness in our lives. This cannot be solved by simply abolishing exploitation of labor by capital, and is a different issue from participation in political and economic decisions.

Overcoming this form of labor is a vital piece of the larger endeavor of creating an alternative that removes the pains brought into our lives by capitalism. This chapter aims to propose the theoretical basis and elementary outline of alternative principles of labor.

First, I shall turn to Karl Marx as an important reference point. It is not only because Marx – among the modern theorists who focused on labor – delved so deeply into and theorized the concept of labor itself, but also because he tried to provide an alternative beyond capitalism. So I shall begin by tracing Marx's conceptualization of labor and estranged labor. Through this, I shall hearken back to and lay the underpinnings of the discussion on the necessity and direction for alternative principles of labor.

But Marx was not the only one who criticized the existing forms of labor. Because the pains of labor are real and practical, there have been varied efforts to find alternatives. So, next, I shall examine "post-work" and the "humanization of labor" as such attempts in theory and practice. Although these experiments each have their own limitations, they do provide practical help in thinking about alternative methods to organize labor.

Then I shall synthesize the discussion and return once again to Marx to conceptualize alternative principles of labor. In order to overcome the limitations and create alternative principles of labor, it is necessary to rethink the "abolition of the division of labor", which was core to Marx's ideas on communism, but which is considered utopian today. With this basis, I shall explore and propose some principles of labor in an alternative society.

Marx's labor and estranged labor

Marx saw labor as fundamental characteristic differentiating humankind from animals. Of course animals also carry out activities. However, the activities of animals are instinctive in nature, whereas human labor is activity directed by consciousness. In the *Economic and Philosophical Manuscripts* written in 1844, Marx defines labor as humankind's life activity: "The Animal is immediately one with its life activity. It does not distinguish itself from it. It is its life activity. Man makes his life activity itself the object of his will and of his consciousness. He has conscious life activity. Conscious life activity distinguishes man immediately from animal life activity" (MECW 3: 276)[2].

At first glance it may appear that consciousness is what differentiates human beings and animals; however, Marx is saying that it is when consciousness is materialized through labor[3] that human society and civilization can arise, and that consciousness alone can do nothing. Marx and Engels explain it in *The German Ideology*: "[Men] themselves begin to distinguish themselves from animals as soon as they begin to produce their means of subsistence, a step which is conditioned by their physical organization" (MECW 5, 31).

This also means that human labor – unlike the activity of animals – is fundamentally social. The process of producing the means of subsistence leads to social cooperation and the division of labor, with the overall results distributed among the members. If it were only that, however, ants, wolves, or herd animals could be said to display similar traits. But human labor goes beyond that. Based on social labor and the product thereof, human labor as conscious activity brings forth creative labor and new products by that labor once again. Even "when I am active scientifically, etc. – an activity which I can seldom perform in direct community with others – then my activity is social, because I perform it as a man. Not only is the material of my activity given to me as a social product (as is even the language in which the thinker is active): my own experience is social activity, is therefore that which I make of myself, I make of myself for society and with the consciousness of myself as a social being" (MECW 3, 298). To restate this, through labor, an individual contributes to the maintenance and development of society. So long as a human being is a part of society, his or her labor is an activity expressing his or herself as an individual from his or her position in society; that is, we can say it is the activity through which the individual attains self-actualization.

But human beings experience this labor – the trait differentiating human beings from other animals – as toil. Labor is something one has to do simply to make a living, and the purpose of labor comes to earning income for livelihood. Thus, paradoxically, "man (the worker) only feels himself freely active in his animal functions – eating, drinking, procreating, or at most in his dwelling and his dressing-up, etc.; and in his human functions he no longer feels himself to be anything but an animal" (MECW 3, 274–275).

Marx conceptualized this paradox as "estrangement (or *alienation*)," and discussed it in depth in the *Economic and Philosophical Manuscripts*. Alienation means the process by which the human activity of labor is estranging, and felt as an oppressive force externally imposed. Marx talked about two forms of estrangement: alienation from the product of one's labor, and alienation within the labor activity itself. That is, the product of my labor does not belong to me, and my work activity itself is not mine (MECW 3, 275).

How do workers actually experience this alienation? First, we cannot freely choose the type and amount of work. By inborn status in precapitalist society and through the commodification of our labor power in capitalism, the amount and type of work are usually decided externally, regardless of our intent. This resonates with what Marx said about the product of my labor not being mine. The product of my labor is received, not by me, but by another person, and the type and amount of work to make that product are decided, not by me, but by another person.

Furthermore, even during work there is no leeway to exert autonomy. This is strengthened in particular under the commodification of labor power in capitalism. Unlike the mode of production in precapitalist societies, where the product of labor was received by another, in capitalism, labor power itself is a commodity that can be bought. Because capital squeezes out the most in the hours it can use that labor power, the work intensity is accelerated and more direct control is exerted over workers' activities. Thus, commodification of labor power under capitalism means that not only do I have to sell my labor power in order to maintain livelihood, but additionally, having sold my labor power, my work activity itself is carried out according to the wishes of the buyer. As Marx said, the act of production within the labor process is not mine.

This estrangement from one's own work is exacerbated under the division of labor of the labor process. In order to get the most productivity and efficiency from the labor power that capital has purchased, the conception and execution are separated and each is further divided up into simple tasks in the labor process. Modern Taylorism can be said to be the most extreme form of this. It would be difficult for a worker, who has spent his or her working hours sitting at a conveyor belt repeating the task of inserting a chip into a component every 30 seconds, to see a fully assembled computer as the achievement of her or his labor; she or he may not know about the computer that is the product of her or his labor. That is, alienation from the labor process once again begets alienation from the product of one's labor.

Fundamentally, estranged labor is a consequence of class society in which the ruling class takes the product of workers' labor and controls the labor process. Marx and Engels saw the division of labor as the base of class society in *The German Ideology*. Class society started with social division of labor, in particular, the separation of intellectual and physical labor. And with the advent of modern capitalism, the alienation of labor deepened even further, as a division of labor throughout the labor process intensified beyond the social division of labor[4]. As a result, "as soon as no physical or other compulsion exists, labor is shunned like the plague" (MECW 3, 274).

In that case, if there were no class, would that mean that estranged labor would also cease? Perhaps that is how the socialist nations thought of it. They would have considered it the end of estranged labor, since private capital was eliminated and the means of production put in the hands of workers (or rather, the workers' state, to be precise). But the characteristics of labor in these socialist nations were little different from those in capitalist societies, and estranged labor remained, instead of labor being a way to actively fulfill oneself.

If the division of labor is the foundation of class society as Marx said, conversely, then one cannot say that class has been abolished in actuality so long as this way of dividing up labor that brought about alienation has persisted. This is a different issue from simply the issue of the ownership of the production organization, or of workers' income or material standard of living. Almost as if he presaged the mistakes of the socialist nations in the future, Marx wrote the following in his work treating the issue of labor and alienation, the *Economic and Philosophical Manuscripts*: "Indeed, even the equality of wages, as demanded by Proudhon, only transforms the relationship of the present-day worker to his labor into the relationship of all men to labor. Society is then conceived as an abstract capitalism" (MECW 3, 280). Even though private capital has ceased to exist, if labor remains merely a means to earn income rather than existing for the purpose of workers to fulfill themselves, then this society would be an abstract capitalist society without private capital. It is as though Marx had foretold that the states professing to be 20th-century socialism would eventually be called "state capitalism"[5].

Thus, in the face of this reality that places laying claim to socialism, as well as, of course, capitalist societies, have been unable to overcome the alienation of labor, we can think of two roads out. One is to minimize work itself, and the other is to make it such that work is not estranging. There have been contemporaneous discussions and experiments for these. We shall examine them in the next section.

Two alternatives

Post-work

The term "post-work" means just what it sounds like: to break from work. In particular, this line of thought became more compelling against the backdrop of high unemployment (Wheelock and Vail 1998). After the 1970s, the post-war "golden age" in the West drew to a close and unemployment began to grow rapidly. The Fordist production model had reached its limits, and there was a growing perception that the age of full employment based on Fordism was over. In actuality, from then until now, though there have been fluctuations in unemployment, it has been true that the age of full employment has not made a comeback.

The basic assumption underpinning post-work is that the reduction of employment is inevitable owing to technological development. With automation and informationization, not only the need for a clerical, production, and service workforce will have been declining rapidly, but also the quality of work itself will have been reduced to simple, tedious, and unskilled work. Those with a more optimistic view of the future predicted that, though the technology for automation and informationization would make unskilled work obsolete, work requiring intelligence and professional skills would flourish, or the jobs eliminated by automation would be replaced by the development of new industries absorbing the displaced workforce. But in reality, neither has happened. Now the advocates of post-work point to the reality that with technological development, companies have repeatedly downsized and reduced employment, and/or recruited precarious workers such as fixed-term contract workers, subcontracted workers, and temp-agency workers (Rifkin 1995; Gorz 1999).

Also, these advocates critiqued traditional leftists as having taken the wrong approach in this situation (Gorz 1982; 1999; Cleaver 2011). Traditional Marxists have a tendency to consider labor as humankind's species-essence and route to self-actualization, and the labor movement is demanding more jobs and full employment based on full-time, permanent employment. But this would just tighten a worker's own noose at the hands of capital (Lee 2006; Cleaver 2011).

But if we think outside the box, the age of joblessness could also give us an opportunity for "liberation from labor" (Rifkin 1995; Aronowitz and Cutler 1998). The development of technologies saving labor, such as automation and information technology, may currently be leading to workers' increasing poverty and precarious work; however, conversely it can contribute to making life fuller, with less labor and more leisure.

For this to happen, there needs to be a revolutionary change in the social paradigm. In today's work-centered society, individuals locate their identity through their job. Thus, being unable to work – being unemployed – brings not only economic hardship but also loss of identity and self-esteem. Those who do not work are those who have been unable to find their place in society. But in an age of joblessness, defining oneself mainly by the work one does would no longer be appropriate. If that paradigm persisted, then society would become a time bomb of rampant unrest and conflict by the social exclusion of so many jobless people (Rifkin 1995).

The advocates of post-work emphasize the shift away from this work-centered paradigm. Work is just one of the multiple activities of humankind. Most people neither derive joy from work nor actualize themselves through work. Rather, people can actualize their personalities and define their identities through other non-work activities. In particular, relational activities that strengthen a sense of fellowship and cultural activities that enable realization of one's creativity could be more important than labor in developing and expressing one's human potential. As such, we must make a shift such that an individual's self-definition and life revolve more heavily around social and cultural activities than around work (Gorz 1982; Kang 2014).

Of course this shift is not so much a problem of changing people's minds, but that of the underpinning social system and institutions. For this shift to post-work, some common-denominator preconditions have been proposed as follows (Rifkin 1995; Aronowitz and Cutler 1998; Gorz 1999; Kang 2014): The first and foremost prerequisite is, quite naturally, a drastic reduction of working hours. Along with a reduction of daily working hours or weekly working hours, there should be a reduction of working hours over one's lifetime. And people should be able to quit working or start working when they want to.

This reduction of work is coupled to an unconditional basic income system that universally guarantees people a certain income irrespective of whether they are working. The reason people today are trying so hard to get jobs and willing to work long hours is because they could not otherwise make their livelihood. Thus, to realize the post-work society, the guaranteed basic income must be sufficient for maintaining a livelihood. Then, work would be one option among a multitude of activities by the choice of an individual.

Finally, vitalization of the third sector or the culture and arts sector is important. If people simply idle their non-working hours, then the meaning of life would be lost. What post-work aspires to is for individuals' lives to no longer be centered around work, so that they can pursue far more diverse and enriching self-fulfillment activities. For this, it is necessary to revitalize activities for providing social solidarity in the civil society sector or opportunities to exercise creativity in the culture and arts sector.

It doesn't seem that all these policies – drastic reduction of working hours, guarantee of sufficient basic income, and vitalization of the civil society and of the culture and arts sector – are established in a society dominated by the might of capital. Because of this – although there are writers such as Rifkin (1995) who believe the post-work society can be born within a capitalist society by reform from within – post-work is considered a strategy within the anti-capitalist movement (Cleaver 2011)[6], and has also been presented as the picture of what an alternative society might look like after capitalism is overcome (Gorz 1982; 1999; Kang 2014). Thus, post-work aims for transformation of the entire society.

However, the definition of the concept of work in the post-work argument is too narrow. Work is either thought to be only capitalist wage labor, or, even when positing a post-capitalist society, work is still a foil to freedom and considered obligatory toil. Thus, "human activity is broadly differentiated into 'socially necessary work' and, separated out from this, 'free activity'" (Kang 2014, 359). Even when capitalism is overcome, the former is not only necessary and indispensable but also it has not lost its obligatory and toilsome character, though this type would be minimized and the latter activity maximized in the alternative society (Gorz 1982).

But we don't need to build a wall separating out socially necessary work and the free activity of individuals. An individual's free activity can contribute to social production and social needs. For example, today's free software and the creative commons are not so much carried out as occupational work but rather carried out for the pleasure of expressing personal creativity, yet they are becoming social production[7]. The most ideal situation would be that when an individual's free activity dovetails with socially necessary work and they are integrated. Of course that is the ideal situation, and in actuality it is not easy to integrate. But when a dichotomy of obligatory versus free is set up, this excludes the possibility of combining "individual free activity" and "socially necessary work" from the outset.

Since the advocates of post-work regard work as "toil" and thus focus on work as something to be minimized, they never think about how to transform the character of work itself. They talk of "liberation from labor" and take no account of "liberation through work". But even if social necessity makes work obligatory, by recomposing the labor process it can be made more enjoyable and include more possibility for autonomy. When that happens, the potential for individuals to find work fulfilling would increase as well as the potential for connections to be made between free activity and socially necessary work.

Humanization of work

On the contrary, of the post-work argument that preserves the character of labor as toil instead of aiming for overreaching social transformation, the "humanization of work" is an attempt to overcome the alienation within the labor process by focusing on the concrete labor process on the shop floor within the limitations of society today. Alienation in the labor process reached its peak in early 20th-century Taylorism. Under Taylorism – characterized by separation of conception and execution – work was subdivided into simple tasks, with the subordination of human beings to machines: workers were bereft of creativity, thought, and skill and were reduced to simple cogs in a machine. Eventually, with the growth of workers' grievances and the loss of voluntariness, the efficiency of work declined as well. Though of course Taylorism was designed to make production possible irrespective of workers' motivation, skill, or personality, efficiency improvements did reach their maximum limit, beyond which there could be no further increase.

So, the humanization of work also contained the goal of improving productivity, as desired by capital, in addition to the demands of the workers' side. In particular, "lean production" in Japan and the United States shared some characteristics with the humanization of work project – multitasking in the labor process, granting a certain level of authority and autonomy to workers, and discussion and participation – however, from its inception, it was initiated from the companies' interest in productivity improvements. Thus, here we shall focus more on the European cases where there was relatively more interest in breaking with the alienation of labor.

The "humanization of work project" began in the 1970s mainly in the Scandinavian countries and Germany, which differed from the cases in Japan and the United States in that the initiative began as a demand of labor. With the rapid economic growth and completion of welfare systems in the post-war golden age, the European working class had attained material abundance and turned their attention away from direct material compensation such as wages, and toward issues such as improving the quality of workers' lives. Because the trade unions in Germany and in Scandinavian states like Sweden and Norway were strong, they were in a position to proactively pursue these demands. Thus began two projects relating to work life at the shop floor: one was the participation of workers in management, beginning with codetermination, and the other was humanization of work to reorganize the labor process for the sublation of alienation.

Sociotechnical systems theory (STS theory) became the foundation to reorganize the labor process for the humanization of work (Kelly 1978; Susman and Chase 1986)[8]. STS theory sees the labor process as the result of the interaction of two systems, the technical system and the social system, with the social system here taken to mean the relational division of labor among workers. According to STS theory, there are many possible combinations of the technical and social systems, and searching for joint optimization was important. On the one hand, it pursues simultaneous transformation of the technical and social systems in critique of attempts such as human relations theory that left technical systems intact while trying to foster relationships between workers. On the other hand, while critiquing technological determinism, which views efficiency as set by technology, it posited that efficiency can be achieved from the optimized combination of technical and social systems in varied ways. For example, the existing combination of a conveyor-belt technology with a Taylorist division of labor cannot be the most optimal, and other technology and work organization combinations that achieve the humanization of work could deliver sufficient efficiency.

Based on this, the humanization of work project established the following organizational logic (Ketchun and Trist 1992): First and foremost, it is important to weaken the division of labor: the biggest contributor to alienation of labor is the division of labor that reduces workers to repeating a certain task without an understanding of the entire production process. Therefore, instead of just one function, workers were to have broader skills based on an understanding of the production process. This concept is different from the multitasking of lean production. Multitasking requires performing several tasks that have already been standardized and are already a product of the division of labor; whereas, this concept means that work is not predetermined by set orders, and workers can work in varied ways and autonomously. As such, autonomous working groups are emphasized here. These groups do not carry out an homogenized division of labor; rather, they are teams responsible for a broad range of work and are able to autonomously decide the labor process within the teams. Democratic participation and discussion are valued in this process. Unlike under the traditional hierarchical organization, the content and method of work are decided through participation, discussion, and consultation. Based on Habermas's communication theory, Sweden's Gustavsen saw this project as the process of extending democratic discourse into working life (Gustavsen 1985; Gustavsen and Enjgeldtad, 1986).

This humanization of work project is based on "flexible specialization" or "new production concepts". Use of computerized technology can integrate conception and execution of work and make artisan production possible; thus, alienation of labor could be overcome (Piore and Sable 1984; Kern and Schumann 1989). If automated computerized technology were combined with the work model pursued by the humanization of work project, then the basis for a "human-centered technical system" could be made possible (Badham 1991).

One of the most renowned cases was the Volvo Motor Uddevalla factory in Sweden. There, the trade union participated in everything, beginning with the design of the factory, eliminating the production line and introducing artisan production methods. Because auto plants in a large factory with a conveyor-belt system were notorious to Taylorism, there have been many humanization of work projects in this sector; however, the humanization of work project also has made attempts in the service sector and in clerical work as well. Ultimately, the goal of the humanization of work is to replace routine work with work that engages workers' knowledge and creative thinking (Purser and Pasmore 1992).

Because research into the humanization of work is applied theory rather than theoretical constructs, the accumulated studies can be concretely applied to an organization of labor process that overcomes the alienation of labor. In particular, these studies consider advanced technology as a method to realize humanization of the labor process, rather than seeing it negatively as the source of deskilling and loss of employment. This perspective can help us to design future alternative organizations of the production process practically, with advanced technology.

Actually, however, the humanization of work project can be considered as a failure in reality. Above all else, within capitalism the humanization of work is possible only within the limitations allowed by capital. The humanization of work project had to compromise with capital and could not ignore productivity and efficiency, even in cases where the trade unions proactively took part. In the end, the projects have been either given up, like the Uddevalla factory in Sweden, or subordinated to the efficiency standards set by the company.

With reference to this chapter, the more fundamental limitation is that it focuses only on the shop-floor labor process without consideration for the system of social distribution of labor. Of course the humanization of work project itself has an interest in the labor process, but the system of social distribution of labor – industrial structure, employment structure, working hours, etc. – also exerted significant influence on the organization of the labor process. Without addressing this, there could only be limitations to any attempt to humanize the labor process or overcome alienation. As such, one can say this is the limitation of pursuing change to only the labor process, irrespective of societal change on a larger scale. As a result, within capitalism this humanization of work project failed.

Alternative principles of labor

Abolition of the division of labor

As we saw, both the post-work and the humanization of work perspectives tried in their own ways to overcome the "suffering from labor" and to provide ideas for the application of alternative organizations of work. But before conceptualizing some alternative principles of labor, there is a basic question: Does overcoming the current form of labor – as expressed in the slogan "labor liberation" – mean "liberation from labor" or does it mean "liberation through labor"? Put another way, does the alternative society strive to minimize labor, or does it focus on making work become a means to self-actualization? We could say that post-work falls on the former trajectory, whereas humanization of work falls on the latter. And as we saw in the previous section, each had its own limitations.

Let us return to Marx. From his writings, there is some ambiguity as to which he had in mind. The *Economic and Philosophical Manuscripts* has been treated by many Marxists, including Althusser, as a work from Marx's early immature period, when he was still under the influence of Hegelianism. But references to labor as the proactive and conscious life activity differentiating man from animal, at the very least, consistently occur throughout his works: not only in the *Economic and Philosophical Manuscripts*, but also in *The German Ideology*, *A Contribution to the Critique of Political Economy*, *Capital*, and *Critique of the Gotha Program*. Further, he describes labor in the communist society that has overcome capitalism as self-realizing activity achieving "the all-around development of the individual". In *Critique of the Gotha Program*, written in his later years, Marx expresses this development of individuals: "In an higher phase of communist society, after the enslaving subordination of the individual to the division of labor, and thereby also the antithesis between mental and physical labor, has vanished; after labor has become not only a means of life but life's prime want; after the productive forces have also increased with the all-around development of the individual" (MECW 24, 87). From this it would appear as though Marx was thinking of "liberation through labor", as in his early years.

On the other hand, there are also passages conspicuous for showing Marx discussing labor with another meaning; sometimes we even see contradictory usage in the same work. In *The German Ideology*, Marx talks about individual development through labor in the society that has overcome capitalism: "Only at this stage [communism] does self-activity coincide with material life, which corresponds to the development of individuals into complete individuals and the casting-off of all natural limitations. The transformation of labor into self-activity" (MECW 5, 88). Yet in the same work, he proclaims that "the communist revolution ... does away with labor" (MECW 5, 52). In *A Contribution to the Critique of Political Economy* and *Capital*, he critiques Adam Smith's conception of labor as a curse, saying "[labor] is in itself a manifestation of freedom"(MECW 28, 530) and defining labor as "normal activity of living beings"(MECW 35, 57); however, in other passages he contrasts labor with freedom, saying that in the society beyond capitalism, "the true realm of freedom ... can blossom forth only with this realm of necessity as its basis. The shortening of working-day is its basic prerequisite" (MECW 37: 807), and as well, "wealth is no longer measured by labor time but by disposal time" (MECW 29, 94). In the latter passage, it would appear that he interprets it as "liberation from labor".

As such it would appear to give rise to the contradiction that "in his all stages of his work he [Marx] defines man as an *animal laborans* and then leads him into a society in which this greatest and most human power is no longer necessary" (Arendt 1958, 105). Because of this contradiction, "abolition of labor" could be seen as a core tenet of Marxist thought (Zilbersheid 2004)[9], but conversely, could also be seen as being captive to a capitalist view of labor (Lee 2006)[10]; that is, interpretations run the two extremes.

But sometimes the simplest interpretation is also the most accurate. Marx might think that estranged labor in class societies must be abolished, and individuals could reach all-around expression through labor in a future alternative society. The former "labor" and the latter "labor" hold different meaning, differentiating between labor in its current social form and that of a communist form. If we hypothesize that Marx thought this way, then his thoughts on labor liberation would not be contradictory but, rather, consistent from the start to the finish.

The point is the division of labor. As we saw earlier, the division of labor is not only a foundation for class society but also a source of alienation. "Individuals always proceed, and always proceed, from themselves. Their relations are the relations of their real life process. How does it happen that their relations assume an independent existence over against them? And that the forces of their own life become superior to them? In short: division of labor" (MECW 5, 93). As such, we can see in the many texts quoted that Marx was consistent in advocating the abolition of the division of labor as a condition for "the all-around development of the individual". Here the abolition of the division of labor includes not only the division in the labor process but also the social division of labor.

But this abolition of the division of labor is precisely what has been criticized as the most "utopian" element of Marxist thought. The idea that the division of labor is inevitable as human society developed and grew more complicated has been considered common sense since the beginning of modern sociology in the 19th century. It is impossible for one person to be a farmer, be a bureaucrat in government administration, and be a computer programmer at the same time. The same goes for division of labor in the labor process. The subdivision of the labor process has brought about extremely high productivity. It is felt that suggesting abolition would be the same as bringing everyone back to the preindustrial age. Thus even though this was one of the parts Marx strongly emphasized, abolition of the division of labor has been swept under the rug, something most Marxists don't see as worth discussing[11].

This is also where the separation of "liberation from labor" and "liberation through labor" arises. As we saw earlier, though the humanization of work project attempted to cautiously shed the division of labor within the limiting parameter of not reducing productivity, it did not consider the social division or redistribution of labor. Conversely, though the advocates of post-work make the assumption of reduced work and redistribution, they do not give much attention to transforming the character of labor as they hold fast to a concept of labor that is the opposite of freedom. This reflects just how unrealistic the abolition of the division of labor appears.

But if some people work in a factory and others manage the factory, if the people who design cars are separated from the people who assemble cars, if the person who wants to be a designer is reluctant to become a salesperson because he or she failed to gain a designer job, then, as Marx said, class and alienation have not been expunged even when such workers enjoy the same level of income and material life. And these situations will also make it difficult to enjoy happiness in the richness of individuals finding all-around development and expression. The very reason for trying to go beyond the class society of capitalism is for the happiness of every person; though, of course, the elimination or reduction of poverty and inequality would substantially alleviate suffering, that is not everything. As gleaned from the experience of socialist nations, where the division of labor and alienation persists, it is difficult to attain development of society based on the participation of individuals, and there remains a strong possibility for the resurgence of class distinctions and private property. Thus, even though it may seem difficult to realize immediately, the abolition of the division of labor needs to be set in the principles of the blueprint for the alternative society. The next sections will discuss the transformation of the character of labor and logic of social distribution for labor.

Changing the character of labor

The social activities of humankind can be divided into production and communication. As Marx said, the production of material life is not achieved by a solitary Robinson Crusoe but rather by social cooperation. Communication refers to a process where people gather to operate and lead diverse levels of social organization, which can be called political activity in a broader sense. This chapter will focus on the activity for production, namely, labor.

We designate production activity as labor, which itself can be divided into two types, with differing characteristics[12]. In English, there are two words: one is "labor", the other is "work". In actual usage, people barely distinguish the one word from the other. And, so far in this chapter, I also have used the two words interchangeably. The difference of the two words remains only as a trace in language. To provisionally distinguish between the two characteristics, let us set them off in quotations marks, as "labor" and "work".

"Labor" is something that must inescapably be carried out by necessity for living in itself. The products of "labor" are consumed soon for living. So "labor" is carried out endlessly and repetitiously. In contrast, "work" produces something added to the world. The products of "work" are durable, not just consumed.

Suffering from "labor" results from the fact that it is tedious and repetitious, not that it uses great physical and mental energy. There is no "end" to it. If you clean the house today, tomorrow you will need to clean again. Though you may feel a momentary sense of satisfaction looking at the tidy space, this 'achievement' is ephemeral and soon to be nothing. Furthermore, it makes little difference who does the labor; the result will not be significantly different. In other words, the process and product of labor are standardized, and there is little room for an individual to express originality. The division of labor utilizes this characteristic. Inserting the chip into the part on the conveyor belt is something anyone can do with the same homogeneity. In this job, ultimately, the individual is like a standardized part that can be easily replaced. Here, the important thing is that the division of labor process reduces all labor, even "work", into "labor". According to Arendt, the production of a car is "work" in itself, but in reality all workers who take part in the process of production do "labor".

On the other hand, the type of "work" activity that represents individuality is, as you have probably surmised, art. Artistic production results in a work of art, which is not only complete in itself but also unique, and another person cannot obtain the same result; indeed, the same artist may be unable to replicate his or her own artwork. "Work" activity doesn't involve the endlessly repeating production and consumption process. It produces something new that has been added to the world. Accordingly, it is not for the preservation of a person's life, but rather an enlargement or perhaps a development. Further, art is where individuals can best express their individuality. Zilbersheid, discussing Marx's thought regarding abolition of labor, writes "for Marx, the model for such new productive activity, which is not labor" (2004: 121). In this perspective, the abolition of the division of labor means that "labor" transforms into "work".

Of course all labor may not become artwork. But setting the direction is important. We should transform the character of labor into something exhibiting the properties of artistic activity as much as possible. Those properties, as discussed above, would be something expressing individuality and originality, and something new and changeable, not repetitious.

For this, technology and work organization are core issues. The experiences gained from the attempts at humanization of work can be valuable here. And the room for changing technology and work organization is considerably broader if production is not taking place under a capitalist society for the pursuit of profit. To make the labor process become "work" instead of just "labor," productivity and efficiency may be sacrificed to a certain extent. Simple labor can be replaced with automation; it would not be as in capitalism, where technology is neither developed nor used when labor force is cheaper.

But simple and repetitive labor cannot be completely eradicated. If automating technology is developed, there is a high possibility that the labor of running those machines would be even simpler, although the workforce and working hour for the jobs can dramatically decrease. At least, however, the division of labor can be reduced to change simple "labor" into something similar to "work" by integration to the extent possible.

Let us take the example of a factory. There needs to be R&D, design, production, managerial, and clerical activities. Currently, each area of activity and its corresponding workforce are separated, without mutual interchange among the areas. Further, even within each area, the labor process is fragmented and divided up. Let us consider what an alternative situation – having removed the division of labor as much as possible – might look like. Even if the market and profit were nonexistent, there would still be a need for managerial work, deciding things such as the production volume and type, and what kind of technology or how much workforce is needed. But there aren't separate managers as there are today. The people working in the factory could all participate in a producers' council that would hold the decision-making authority. Everyone could take turns doing all the different jobs by a job rotation system[13].

With regard to shop-floor work, social technical systems could be applied to the production process. The manufacturing process teams would have a certain level of autonomy. Simple tasks would be automated, and at the same time, diverse methods of assembly and experiments in the production process would be possible according to discussions and agreements between and within teams.

The autonomy of manufacturing process teams must be guaranteed as much as possible, yet the design by R&D could still be the foundation of the production. The research, development, and design work would be undertaken by each person rotating jobs, the same as with managerial, clerical, and manufacturing jobs. Perhaps all the workers may not be able to participate in the most specialized areas. But if the workers were provided with sufficient education in the workplace or in a social education system, then many of them would be able to participate even in these areas. The exchange of knowledge and experience between the shop floor and R&D processes would be achieved through this job rotation. When this happens, the producers can express their creativity in the process of production and feel that the resulting object produced is the product of their own work, though it may not be a work of art per se.

Social distribution of work

Above, we discussed the abolition of the division of labor in the labor process or in the production organization and the consequent change to the character of labor. For individuals to achieve their all-around development, along with this there must also be abolition of the division of labor on a larger social dimension. Of course, the abolition of the division of labor does not mean that one person must try to perform all the types of work existing on the planet. It means that all individuals must have unimpeded access to the opportunity to do the work they want in society. The provision of such an opportunity depends on the system for the distribution of work and the educational system. Here, the focus is on the system to distribute work.

The most basic preconditions are unconditional and sufficient basic income, and the sharp reduction of working hours, as the advocates of post-work have proposed. A sufficient basic income means at the level where an individual can choose not to work. The basic income does not necessarily need to be provided in currency. It could be defined as the right to use enough goods and services to guarantee a basic life.

The fewer the working hours, the better: As a very rough calculation in the case of Korea, if you divide the current total working hours of the employed by the numbers of the economically active population, the weekly working hours diminishes to about 25 hours per week. Even when the current industrial structure is maintained, if labor were equally divided among all, it would be enough to work only 25 hours a week. Though there would be differences by country depending on industrial structure, in modern society where labor-saving tech is rapidly developing, it would seem that the necessary working hours would not greatly exceed this. Of course there would be many variables. If not a society based on market capitalism, the necessary working hours for total industries could be reduced even further. For example, a significant amount of business services, personal services, as well as the advertising and entertainment industries would be greatly reduced if not vanish. Applied automation would decrease working hours even further. Conversely, if a certain amount of efficiency and productivity were sacrificed to change the character of labor, working hours could increase. But if there is no need to pursue profit anyway and social efforts were focused on the reduction of working hours, then the total amount of working hours is likely to decrease.

The total amount of necessary work can be calculated by the bottom-line labor needed to reproduce the society. There is no need for overproduction to pursue profits. Though human needs are developed and enlarged, those needs do not necessarily imply the enhancement of material products. Even the current level of material production is a burden on the ecological environment. Relentless consumer needs are a product of social relations in which one cannot express and realize one's individuality through other ways, and if such limitations were lifted, then ceaseless consumer needs would likely decrease. Anyway, we could determine the volume of social production and necessary labor, and then a social standard on working hours could be calculated accordingly. This could play a similar role to the statutory working hours we have today. But because the reduction of working hours would be a key aim, there would be a need to regulate overtime much more strictly than it is today. That is to say, with the exception of very unusual circumstances, most would not work in excess of the standard working hours.

As discussed above, with the abolition of the division of labor in the labor process, the types of jobs would be reduced, but the types of work needed to maintain society would still be diverse. The wants of individuals in society trying to fulfill themselves, and the types and volume of work socially necessary would not perfectly dovetail. Thus the numbers of socially necessary jobs and the numbers of jobs wanted by constituents of society will not be in an exact balance. In this situation, if the volume of socially necessary jobs is less than the number of people wanting to do that type of work, then those people would either select another type of work or receive the basic income while awaiting the next opportunity.

In comparison with this, the more difficult problem would arise when those applying for a certain type of work fall short of the volume of jobs socially needed. To resolve the problem of work most people avoid doing, there are two methods: provide incentives or make it obligatory. Shorter working hours than the statutory working hours – say, when the statutory weekly working hours are 25 hours, weekly working hours of 20 hours when working in commonly avoided jobs – could be given as a form of incentive. On the other hand, making it obligatory would entail fairly portioning out the volume of work each will be responsible for as a citizen's obligation. Taking the example of compulsory military service in Korea, there would not appear to be large administrative or technical obstacles to making the sharing of avoided work a citizen's obligation. Depending on the type of job that is commonly avoided and individual preference, one could choose to work in those jobs for a certain period in one's lifetime, as in the Korean compulsory military service, or work for a certain amount of time every year, as in the reserve forces or civil defense forces method in Korea.

The solution to job avoidance could be a mix of both: using incentives and making it obligatory. Making it obligatory would appear to have advantages. First, if we use incentives such as the further reduction of working hours for the avoided jobs, the jobs would need more workers. Second, it is likely that the avoided jobs are ones that involve simple "labor" activity and do not feel worthwhile doing, and if there are many people who must make it their principal social work thanks to the incentives, this would counteract the larger social goal of enabling people to seek self-actualization through work. Finally, if this avoided labor is meted out equally to all constituents as an obligation, then it would lead to greater efforts to transform that "labor" into a kind of "work" through technical developments or reorganization.

The final picture of these development processes would be a society where labor and freedom are no longer at odds. Individuals would fulfill themselves in society through their work. As they feel the joy of personal development and self-realization, it could become work. In truth, the boundaries between work, hobby, and art would slowly disappear. What is left would be the rich activity of humankind, and that in itself would make society.

Conclusion

The abolition of the division of labor and transformation of labor into activity for individual expression instead of for income, as discussed throughout this chapter, is not utopian but rather quite realistic. The ideas of the humanization of labor efforts and of post-work can be applied to many areas. Even the current level of productive capacity, science and technology, and administrative technique can also make these ideas a reality. The reason it sounds unrealistic is only because right now we have capitalism. The power of capital is just a set of social relations, but we feel it as a natural law. That's why alternative principles of labor seem to be a dream. So, the abolition of capitalism is the precondition for making this logic of labor possible.

But conversely, the abolition of capitalism is not a sufficient condition for the realization of alternative principles of labor. We know this even by looking at the experiences of the nations of real socialism. Of course it would be undesirable to draw a blueprint of the alternative society and force things to fit in, and such an approach would have a low probability of success.

But without some direction and principles of the alternative logic at all, the chances of failure would be high, too. Although it was thought that the removal of private capital alone would easily realize socialism that could develop into communism, ultimately the lesson of history has shown us the degeneration of socialist nations into collective capitalism. In this sense, it is vital to seek and establish some alternative logics, and this chapter aims to be a contribution to that crucial endeavor.

This chapter focused on labor: the organization of the labor process and the logic of socially distributing labor. But it is still at an abstract level. I was unable to draw out the more concrete contours of each individual's choice of work, the way avoided work could be handled – with incentives or obligation – and distribution of working hours, the structure of industry, and the types of jobs. Instead I am suggesting only the fundamental principles. Giving shape to these will be a challenge going forward, but to meet the challenge we would need to address at least three social institutions.

First is the method of decision-making. In capitalism, the distribution of labor and organization of the labor process are set by market principles and the profit motive, but in a society that is not market capitalism, these issues would be dealt with by constituents in the production organizations and communities at various levels. Thus, political institutions and processes in a broader sense exert decisive influence on the distribution and organization of labor. We should take not only production activities but also communication activities into consideration to picture how the principles of labor could work in an alternative society.

Second is the education system. The social distribution of labor is deeply related to the education system. Regarding this, there is no more explanation needed.

Third is the institution of the family. The family has been considered the place for reproduction of humankind and the private sphere in modern society. But in an alternative society, what form would the family take? Would activities for child-rearing and housework be undertaken as social labor, or would they be undertaken within the private family sphere? The distribution and organization of labor can vary depending on how such questions are answered.

As we expand to other institutions related to the distribution and organization of labor, the logic and direction of the alternative society will not only become clearer, it will also be possible to make the distribution and organizational logic of labor more concrete. We cannot cover so much ground in only one chapter. But this will be one part of a continuing research project.

Notes

1 This work is supported by the National Research Foundation of Korea Grant funded by the Korean Government (NRF-2013S1A5B8A01055117).
2 Also the following passage from *Capital* is often quoted in relation to this: "A spider conducts operations which resemble those of the weaver, and a bee would

put many a human architect to shame by the construction of its honeycomb cells.
But what distinguishes the worst architect from the best of bees is that the architect
builds the cell in his mind before he constructs it in wax. At the end of every labor
process, a result emerges which had already been conceived by the workers at the
beginning hence already existed ideally. Man not only effects a change of form in
the materials of nature: he also realizes his own purpose in those materials".

3 The *German Ideology* is the work in which the historical process of change
  concretely unfurls by the form of human division of labor and cooperation based
  on this definition.

4 The *German Ideology* has a concrete discussion with regard to the division of labor
  based in class society. *Capital* volume 1 also treats division of labor in the labor
  process.

5 In the same work Marx critiques this as "crude communism". In crude communism, "the category of the worker is not done away with, but extended to all
  men"(MECW 3: 294), and "the community is only a community of labor, and
  equality of wages by a communal capital = by the community as the universal
  capitalist" (MECW 3: 295).

6 In particular, in autonomist Marxism, labor is a category considered to be defined
  by capital, and thus "refusal of work" is posited as an anti-capitalist strategy.

7 There is also a discussion of peer production stemming from this free software
  methodology, as being able to realize Marx's concept of communist production
  (Rigi 2013).

8 Sociotechnical systems theory was originally conceptualized through workplace
  research conducted by the Tavistock Institute in the United Kingdom. The research
  had characteristics of a "movement" searching for the principles of social reform
  beyond humanization of the labor process and simply academic research.

9 Zilbersheid sees *Capital* as Marx's retreat from his early thoughts on labor abolition. He conceptualizes the overcoming of alienated labor appearing in the early
  works such as *Economic and Philosophical Manuscripts*, the *German Ideology*, as
  well as the *Critique of the Gotha Programme*, as "abolition of labor". But if we
  term self-realizing productive activity in the communist society also as labor, then
  Marx's thought could be both "abolition of (alienated) labor" at the same as "liberation through (self-fulfilling) labor" (I will call the latter type of labor as "work"
  in the following section). Zilbersheid or Arendt may have thought that Marx's
  concepts of labor and labor liberation were not consistent, because they did not
  differentiate between alienated labor in class society and self-realizing labor in a
  communist society in their use of the term.

10 Lee defines labor as the activity producing exchange value, with labor subjugated
   to capital in its very concept.

11 In the passage from the *German Ideology* following the description of the aftermath
   of the abolition of the division of labor – "in communist society, nobody has
   one exclusive sphere of activity but each can become accomplished in any branch
   he wishes, society regulates the general production and thus make it possible for
   me to do one thing today and another tomorrow, to hunt in the morning, fish in
   the afternoon, rear cattle in the evening, criticize after dinner, just as I have a mind,
   without ever becoming hunter, fisherman, shepherd or critic"(MECW 5: 47) –
   Marx has been critiqued for simply enumerating a preindustrial-era situation and
   failing to show how labor, which has been indispensably divided up in modern
   industrialized society, could be integrated through the abolition of the division
   of labor.

12 This distinctions are grounded in the discussion developed by Habermas (1984)
   and Arendt (1958).

13 See Albert's *Participatory Economics* (2003) for a related discussion.

References

MECW. 1975. – Marx and Engels Collected Works. New York: International Publishers.

Albert, M., 2003, *Parecon: Life after Capitalism*, Verso.

Arendt, H., 1958, *The Human Condition*, University of Chicago Press.

Aronowitz, S. and J. Cutler eds., 1998, *Post-Work: The Wages of Cybernation*, Routledge.

Badham, R., 1991, "The social dimension of computer-integrated manufacturing", *International Labour Review* 130.

Cleaver, H., 2011, "Work refusal and self-organisation", in Nelson and Timmerman eds. *Life without Money: Building Fair and Sustainable Economies*, Pluto Press.

Gorz, A., 1982, *Farewell to the Working Class*, Pluto Press.

Gorz, A., 1999, *Reclaiming Work: Beyond the Wage-Based Society*, Polity Press.

Gustavsen, B., 1985, "Workplace reform and democratic dialogue", *Economic and Industrial Democracy* 6(4).

Gustavsen, B. and P. H. Enjgeldtad, 1986, "The design of conference and the evolving role of democratic dialogue in changing working life", *Human Relations* 39(2).

Habermas, U., 1984, *The Theory of Communicative Action*, Beacon Press.

Kang, N., 2014, *Neo-liberalism and Cultural Political Economy*, Culture Science Press.

Kelly, J. E., 1978, "A reproposal of sociotechnical systems theory", *Human Relations* 31

Kern, H. and Schumann, 1989, "New concepts of production in West German plants", in P. J. Katazenstein ed. *Industry and Politics in West Germany*, Cornell University Press.

Ketchun, L. D. and E. L. Trist, 1992, *All Teams Are Not Created Equal: How Employee Empowerment Really Works*, Sage.

Lee, J., 2006, *Marxism in Future*, Greenbee Press.

Piore, M. and C. Sable, 1984, *The Second Industrial Divide*, Basic Books.

Purser, R. E. and W. A. Pasmore, 1992, *Organizing for Learning*, Loyola University Press.

Rifkin, J., 1995, *The End of Work*, G.P. Putnam's Sons.

Rigi, J., 2013, "Peer production and Marxian communism: Contours of a new emerging mode of production", *Capital and Class* 37(3).

Susman G. I. and R. B. Chase, 1986, "A sociotechnial analysis of the integrated factory", *Journal of Applied Behavioral Science* 22.

Wheelock, J. and J. Vail eds., 1998, *Work and Idleness*, Kluwer Academic Publishers.

Zilbersheid, U., 2004, "The vicissitudes of the idea of the abolition of labour in Marx's teachings – can the idea be revived?", *Critique* 35.

9 Building a (very) new road to socialism?

Cuba in the 21st century

Al Campbell

Both supporters and opponents of Cuba's 55-year effort to begin a process of constructing socialism are carefully watching the sweeping economic reforms[1] that have been introduced over the last 25 years. Ten years ago the pace of that process of change accelerated after Raúl Castro first temporarily assumed, and subsequently was elected to, the presidency. Five years ago the pace accelerated further following the publication of the *Lineamientos de la política económica y social del Partido y la Revolución* (hereafter referred to as the *Guidelines*) (PCC 2011). These were intended as a first contribution by the Communist Party of Cuba (PCC) and the government, following broad national popular input, to a comprehensive presentation of the nature of the new economic and social model that is being developed in Cuba. Based on both the practical experiences and the theoretical debates of the previous 20 years, they were intended, as their name implies, as broad guidelines for concrete laws and policies to be subsequently enacted. In April 2016 the PCC approved four additional documents intended as similar contributions to the continuously evolving discussion of the continuously evolving model. The two that will be referred to below are the *Conceptualización del modelo económico y social cubano de desarrollo socialista* (hereafter *Conceptualization*) and *Plan de desarrollo económico y social hasta 2030: Propuesta de visión de la nación, ejes y sectores estratégicos* (hereafter *LTP* for *Long-Term Plan*) (PCC 2016a, 2016b). The *LTP* is similar in nature to the *Guidelines*, intended to give broad directives for the specific content of the laws and policies to be subsequently enacted to create the new model, though over a longer time frame. The *Conceptualization*, on the other hand, is the first contribution by the PCC to the discussion that "presents the theoretical bases and essential characteristics of the Cuban Economic and Social Model of Development, which will result from the process of updating" (PCC 2016a, article 2).

All government documents discussing the nature of the updating stress that its goal is to build a new road to pursue the same goal as before, the construction of socialism. The opening sentence of the *Guidelines* from 2011 states their objective as "to guarantee the continuity and irreversibility of Socialism, the economic development of the country and the elevation of the standard of living of the population, together with the necessary creation of ethic and political values among our citizens" (PCC 2011, 5). The much-used phrase "prosperous and sustainable socialism" introduced by Raúl into the national discourse emphasizes this maintained goal, as well as tersely referring to the popularly perceived inadequacy of past material growth. From its full title onward throughout the document, the current *Conceptualization* stresses that the evolving new model of economic and social development in Cuba is a model of socialist development. Nevertheless, some supporters of Cuba's socialist project fear, and of course all its opponents hope, that the measures being taken will instead open a road back to capitalism.

This chapter will discuss three basic issues concerning Cuba's process of developing a new road intended for building socialism. First, it will review why the sweeping reforms were necessary. Second, it will indicate what have been, and will be, the most important fundamental changes in the way the economy operates, resulting from the profusion of reforms to date and those currently projected. Finally, against a background established by those two sections, the chapter will consider the fundamental question of the relation of the reforms to Cuba's declared goal of constructing socialism. It will look at this question from the perspectives of the two forms in which it is most discussed. First, it will examine the internationally much discussed issue of their potential contribution to a restoration of capitalism. Second, it will examine their potential contribution to improving the process of constructing socialism in Cuba today, their purpose according to the Cuban government which is implementing them.

Why the updating was necessary

The starting point for considering the nature of the updating of Cuba's economic model over the last 25 years and what that means for Cuba's socialist project has to be why the updating was necessary in the first place.

The primary reason that deep reforms to Cuba's pre-1990 economic model were necessary was the world-changing implosion of the non-capitalist economic and social systems in the USSR and its CMEA (Council for Mutual Economic Assistance, also abbreviated in English as COMECON) allies. Cuba's subsequent economic performance has been frequently and extensively documented, and there is neither space nor a reason to carefully review here yet again the severe detrimental effects of this implosion. Rather, what is necessary for the purpose of this chapter is to briefly indicate just enough of those effects on Cuba to show why the reforms had to sharply increase Cuba's ability to interact with the world capitalist economy.

The drop in Cuba's GDP from 1989 to 1993 was a bit over 35 percent, about the same fall over about the same length of time as the US Great Depression of the 1930s. But unlike the US, Cuba is a small and therefore a fairly open economy. To produce many goods (particularly manufactured goods) at any acceptable level of productivity requires that it produce at scales larger than its national market. As a small economy, it cannot do this for all steps in the productive chains for many products. This means that it needs to be able to import significant parts of the necessary inputs for production, and that it must have markets willing to buy what it produces above what it consumes internally. Cuba's production was integrated into CMEA such that both these conditions were guaranteed, and in addition it received technical assistance and credit needed for production.

Cuba's efforts to develop industry over the course of the Revolution had earned it the label of an industrializing country from the United Nations by 1989. But while GDP fell by "only" somewhat over a third, imports fell from 8.6 and 9.1 billion pesos in 1988 and 1989 before the crisis to 2.0 billion in 1993. Manufacturing capacity utilization in turn fell to only 10 to 15 percent in 1993 of what it had been in 1989. It was not only the size of the shock but also its nature that meant that this external shock by itself would have been enough to require sweeping economic reforms in Cuba, even if its economy had run perfectly before 1989. The possibility of regenerating the non-capitalist types of economic relations that the economy operated with before 1989 did not exist. The only way to reactivate the massive unemployed labor and productive capacity was to obtain the physically necessary inputs, and sell the outputs, in the world capitalist markets. From this it follows that the nature of the necessary updating of its economic mechanisms had to be such that it would make Cuba's economy able to function in this fundamentally different way. At the same time, the nature of the reforms was shaped by the intention to resist the pressure this change would generate to restore capitalism. Specifically, it was intended that the reforms that were necessary to enable Cuba to economically interact with the capitalist world would have a nature such that at the same time the Island could continue to try to build socialism.

There is an important set of secondary reasons for the necessity of deep reforms to Cuba's pre-1990 economic model. Even before it was hit by the massive external shock, Cuba had recognized that it had internal problems with its economy and its approach to building socialism. In narrow economic terms, its rate of growth had fallen precipitously in the second half of the 1980s[2]. More broadly, Cuba had already decided by the mid-1980s that its model for building socialism needed important changes. Just as today, the narrowly focused discussions on economic performance and the broader discussion on an appropriate model for constructing socialism were thoroughly intertwined in what became known as the Rectification Process[3]. An example of reforms that were central to this pre-1990 process is the issues of a reduction in the excessive over-centralization of the economy, and the related issue of a quantitative reduction and qualitative change in the nature of Cuba's bureaucracy. These additional considerations of why updating was necessary are important in that some key aspects of the current reforms have their roots more (not exclusively) in these internal factors, such as the important issues of decentralization and debureaucratization just referred to.

Central changes in how the Cuban economy operates as a result of the reforms

The multitude of reforms to the Cuban economy over the last 25 years has been frequently and extensively documented. For the concern of this chapter with their impact on Cuba's project of building socialism, what is important is what sorts of major changes this updating has made, and is projected to make in the future, to the nature of Cuba's economy. Here we will consider four aspects of the 1989 Cuban economy that were central to its performance then, have significantly changed in the current evolving new economic model, and are important issues in the discussions in Cuba today on what socialism is and how to build it. They are presented in the order they will be discussed in this and the next section, more or less from least to most in their importance to the determination of the socialist versus capitalist nature of what Cuba is building.

Cuban economy in 1989

In 1989 the Cuban economy

1 received external capital for productive investment, and hence both growth and development, beyond that available from domestic savings;
2 was extremely centralized;
3 was almost entirely state run and owned; and
4 produced according to a combination of long- and short-term plans.

This section will indicate how the Cuban economy has changed in regard to these four issues, while the next section will present some of the discussion and debates about what those changes could, or will, mean for Cuba's socialist project:

1 As a member of CMEA (particularly as a member considered less developed), Cuba received from it external capital for productive investment. This allowed more growth and development than would be possible from only domestic savings. This important contribution to Cuba's pre-1990 economy ended with the end of CMEA and the non-capitalist nature of the economies that composed it.

   While Cuba regularly publishes a large amount of data on its economic performance, data on the amounts of foreign investment since 1990 have been almost entirely unavailable to either foreign or Cuban researchers. The absence of this data is widely believed to be a response of the Cuban government to the permanent campaign of the US to disrupt whenever it can whatever foreign investment into Cuba it discovers.

   Notwithstanding this lack of data on investment, the well-documented overall performance of the Cuban economy makes it clear that two large inflows of private capitalist investment into the Island were important to both its survival in that first post-CMEA decade, and to the shape of its economy subsequent to that. The first was foreign investment into international tourism to Cuba. It needs to be underlined that Cuba also invested great amounts of its own resources, including both the conversion of much of its existing tourism facilities that were previously dedicated to domestic tourism, and much construction of new tourism facilities with Cuba's then very scarce investment resources. But the growth of this industry was far above what domestic resources could have funded. The short payback period on investment led to a tidal wave of foreign investment into this area. The result was a foreign tourist industry in Cuba that exploded from practically nonexistent in 1989 to being the engine of the Island's economic recovery from 1993 to the end of the decade.

The other major private foreign investment in the first decade of the reforms was into Cuba's nickel industry. This took longer to show the results. But by the second decade of the reforms this foreign investment (again, accompanied by major Cuban investment) raised the nickel industry's level of operation to where it rivaled tourism as the leading earner of foreign exchange[4].

In the first decade of the 21st century, Cuba received important capital inflows from sources other than private capitalists. Large credits from China (usually linked to purchasing Chinese goods) and from Brazil (for building the Mariel port) were important. Most important were numerous capital inflows from various arrangements and projects with Venezuela. Given the political situation there at the time this article is being written, it seems very possible that capital inflows from Venezuela will be dramatically reduced or completely suspended by 2018.

Given the lack of detailed data on what sort of capital inflows exist, it is hard for Cuban or foreign researchers to argue how much more is needed to obtain the rate of growth of 4 or 5 percent annually that is generally felt to be necessary to meet popular desires and create the intended "prosperous and sustainable socialism." Many economists in Cuba talk of the need to increase it massively, speculating on perhaps threefold or more.

Given this, Cuba is currently taking steps to attract more private foreign capitalist investment. The most fundamental reforms have been changes to its basic law on foreign investment, and subsequent enabling legislation and policies, with Law 77 in 1995 and Law 118 in 2014. Their central concern has been to make the investment process faster and less burdensome. In 2014 Cuba launched a new initiative, the preparation and dissemination of an official Portfolio of Opportunities for Foreign Investment. Presented at the Havana International Fair in November, they solicited 246 projects worth 8.7 billion dollars that year.

2 It is accepted by those working to build a new road to socialism, just as much as by those who would like to see a return to capitalism, that the Cuban economy was too centralized. The strong need for decentralization is the official position of the Cuban government, as reflected in the *Guidelines, Conceptualization* and *LTP*. In the pre-1990 model, while various economic decisions occurred at various locations in the economic and political structure, the more fundamental and strategic they were, the more they tended to be made in the various national ministries and by the national government, and at the national center of Communist Party. The further removed from the center they were, the more the decisions tended to concern implementation of an orientation determined more centrally. Three different processes of decentralization have been occurring over the course of the economic reforms, with a fourth process projected but not yet significantly advanced. Those who are trying to build a new road for constructing socialism and those who want a return to capitalism have very different things in mind when they argue for the need for decentralization.

One process of decentralization involves shifting economic activity out of the state sector and into the capitalist sector, which in Cuban statistics is the non-state noncooperative sector. In agriculture this has consisted of a shift from state farms to private individual farmers, Cooperatives of Credit and Services (CCSs), and especially recently to *usifructuarios*[5]. In the nonagricultural sector there is a shift to *cuentapropistas*, a category that, despite its name meaning "self-employed", includes petty commodity producers, small capitalists, and workers employed by the latter. As opposed to the other two processes of decentralization to be discussed below, we can get some measure of the quantitative dimension of this large expansion. In 1989 almost all the nonagricultural workforce worked in the state sector. By 2014, of the 4,030,700 workers in the nonagricultural sector of the economy, 483,400 were non-state noncooperative workers (*cuentapropistas*), 12.0 percent (ONEI 2015, Tables 7.2 and 7.3).

As of 2014 the cooperative sector was almost entirely agricultural. There were 226,000 members in the two types of agricultural cooperatives, *Cooperativas de Producción Agropecuario* (CPAs) and *Unidades Básicas de Producción Cooperativa* (UBPCs). There were only 5,500 members of the newly formed nonagricultural cooperatives (ONEI 2015, Table 7.2). It is nearly universally held in Cuba that from their inception mostly out of dissolved state farms in 1993, the UBPCs had minimal autonomy. The large majority of decisions on what to produce, where to sell it, prices to sell at, where to get inputs, etc., were made by the ministries and related central economic state institutions. Here it is asserted that while the CPAs had more autonomy, the state still made many (not all) of the fundamental decisions that determined their production, in particular concerning obtaining inputs and where to sell outputs, and on the prices to do so. As such, the shift from the centralized state economy to cooperative production should not yet be considered a form of decentralization. The government has stated that the newly forming nonagricultural cooperative sector, which is expected to grow dramatically, will have extensive autonomy, as likewise will the CPAs and even the UBPCs. It can be expected that the shift from the state sector to the cooperative sector will in the future be a fourth form of decentralization, but it cannot be considered to be so yet.

A second form of decentralization is the shift of the location of many economic decisions from the central state economic apparatus to the state productive enterprises. The importance attached to this decentralization by the government is indicated by its extensive discussion in the *Guidelines*, the *Conceptualization* and the *LTP*. No concrete quantitative data exists on how much this has changed to date from the previous model, though the government asserts the management model in state enterprises has already changed significantly in this regard, and will change further in the future as the new model continues to evolve. As all the guideline documents stress that the state sector is intended to remain the "fundamental" part of the Cuban economy, this has the potential to be a major part of the total decentralization of the economy.

The final form of decentralization is the shift of the location of many economic decisions from the central state economic apparatus to the regional and local state economic apparatuses. As for the decentralization of economic decisions to the state enterprises, no concrete quantitative data exists on how much this has changed to date from the previous model. As this is a form of the concept of "local development" which at present has significant support worldwide[6], this is one important dimension of several of the limited foreign aid projects Cuba receives. In particular the UNDP and the Swiss COSUDE have produced much material and held supporting seminars on local development in Cuba in recent years.

3 Employment data provide a useful metric for the shift in state ownership in the economy from 1989 to today. The agricultural sector comprised 20 percent of the Cuban workforce in 1989, and about the same in 2014. In 1989 20 percent of the workers in the agricultural sector were non-state workers. By 2014 the proportion of non-state workers had exploded to 94.7 percent, 889,600[7] out of the 939,100 agricultural workers. In 1989 in the nonagricultural 80 percent of the economy, almost the entire workforce was employed by the state. Of the 4,030,700 workers in that part of the economy in 2014, 488,900[8] worked in the non-state sector of the economy, 12.1 percent. At present Cuban government and academic figures speculate that this could continue expanding to 40 or even 50 percent.

4 It has been unequivocally indicated in the various guideline documents and in all government statements that Cuba intends that the economy will continue to be guided by conscious human planning. Already in

the first publication explaining the overall nature of the new evolving system, the first sentence of the first guideline reads: "The socialist planning system will continue to be the main way to direct the national economy" (PCC 2011, 8). The *Conceptualization* has dedicated the third of its four chapters, and 63 of its 330 articles, to a much fuller discussion of "The Planned Direction of the Economy".

For historical reasons, "socialist planning" came to be identified with the type of planning and economic structure developed in the USSR. There is nothing in the theories of the early socialists that indicates their desired planning and the related structure of the economy should take those particular forms. Of course, anything resembling the pre-1990 system of planning is not an option for Cuba in any case (this author would add "fortunately"). Hence, because it is committed to continuing to direct the economy via socialist planning, the nature of the planning will have to be radically different. Partly because the new economic structure for building socialism is still evolving, there is minimal writing on an appropriate new planning system even in Cuba. Just as one indication of how different the new planning system will be, it is worth noting that there is a broad consensus in Cuba that while the quantitative planning that was central in the old system will still have some role in particular sectors and at particular times, the new system will give a much greater role to planning and direction that use price and other indirect control mechanisms.

One aspect of the new planning system is particularly unclear. To be social planning, it must give direction to the full economy. The Cuban government has indicated it intends the new system to do this. "The system of planning includes all the actors in the economy and society, taking into account the definite policies and assuring their material backing" (PCC 2016a, article 217). It is not at all a priori clear how social planning, which sets goals to promote human development and well-being, will be able to plan for the performance of private capitalist operations, which pursue maximum return on their capital even when that is at the expense of social well-being.

Relation of Cuba's economic reforms to its process of building socialism

The major changes in the operation of the Cuban economy, which have resulted from its ongoing economic reforms, immediately pose the following question to both supporters and opponents of Cuba's goal of constructing socialism: Will the changes promote, as intended, or harm that project? This section will consider this question in relation to each of the four major changes in the operation of the Cuban economy discussed in the last section. It will consider the question from the perspectives of the two forms this question is discussed in most frequently. First, it will consider each change in relation to its potential contribution to a restoration of capitalism. Second, it will consider each change in relation to its potential contribution to what the Cuban government continually asserts is the goal of the updating, the improvement of the process of constructing socialism:

1 A first problem for Cuba with basing any of its growth and development on foreign capital inflows also holds for any developing country, the lack of sustainability. If the capital inflows stop or even slow for any reason, this will stop or slow the projected growth and development. This section will not elaborate on the potential problems for all developing economies from foreign investment based growth and development, since its specific concern is the impact of such an increased dependence on Cuba's project of building socialism. (For a clear exposition of the general problems with basing growth and development on international private capital flows, see Grabel 2003.)

Some supporters of Cuba's project to construct socialism fear that foreign capitalist investment could promote the Island's return to capitalism. Among the various channels through which it could do this, the following four are particularly important and frequently noted:

First, if a capitalist sector of foreign capital and joint ventures flourishes as desired, while the non-capitalist rest of the economy does less well or especially if it does poorly, the view that the project to construct socialism should be abandoned in favor of returning to capitalism could become socially widely accepted. Simply by providing higher individual wages, particularly in a country with low individual wages even if it has a high social wage, foreign private capital can promote the development of this social view.

Second, foreign capital can use its great wealth to directly intervene in Cuba's regulation of outside investment. In particular, foreign capital naturally wants to eliminate the barriers that restrict foreign investment to projects that benefit Cuba's growth and development (discussed next), and open up the economy to any investments it wants to make in pursuit of its own profits. In the first place, if this was allowed, it would make the obvious direct contribution to restoring capitalism from the resulting expansion of this capitalist sector. But beyond that, this would have the even more important indirect effect of supporting the ideology that whatever is privately profitable is socially beneficial – a view that if widely accepted would quickly generate a return to capitalism. Note that while some such "participation" by foreign capital in Cuba's determination of how to regulate it is legal (consultations, etc.), it is the potential illegal interventions, especially through corruption facilitated by its great wealth, that would generate the most powerful and dangerous support for a restoration of capitalism.

Third, given its desire to sharply increase foreign investment, the Cuban government could come to see the restriction of foreign investment to projects that contribute to national growth and development as a major disadvantage relative to its competitors for foreign investment. Then, as opposed to the elimination of such restrictions resulting from the efforts by foreign capital just discussed, their elimination could result from the aspirations of the Cuban government itself. The resulting increased dangers of a return to capitalism from the same elimination of the restrictions on foreign investment would, of course, be the same.

Finally, in a setting where a domestic capitalist sector is also developing, a foreign capitalist sector can promote the growth of the domestic sector either consciously or simply through the way capitalist enterprises operate. To begin with, this enhancement of the development of a domestic capitalist sector could promote a return to capitalism in the same way discussed above for the expansion of the foreign capitalist sector itself, through its effects on popular consciousness if the private domestic sector does better and offers better earnings than the non-capitalist sector. But beyond that, and a more immediate danger from foreign capital's enhancement of the development of a domestic capitalist sector, is that this would increase the number and the scale of operation of domestic capitalists. A restoration of capitalism can be effected only by a domestic capitalist class, even if it is dependent and comprador; it cannot be effected directly by foreign capital.

While there clearly is nothing in foreign capitalist investment that could deepen the socialist nature of Island's economy (unlike subsequent changes to be discussed), it has the potential to contribute to the Cuba's project of building socialism by contributing to its overall economic growth and development. The various documents that give the guidelines for the new model of socialist development and the general laws governing foreign investment are not only very specific on what contributions Cuba is looking for from foreign investment, but they also require that proposed foreign investment make some such contribution to be accepted. Foreign investment must satisfy various objectives, such as access to advanced technologies and methods of management, diversification and expansion of export markets, import substitution, the supply of medium- and long-term financing for realizing a productive goal and the provision of working capital for its operation, and the generation of new employment (PCC 2011, article 97).

The expansion of foreign capitalist investment has already made important contributions to Cuba's growth and development, and in that way to its socialist project, over the last 25 years. At the same time, foreign capitalist investments have the potential to contribute to a return to capitalism through various channels. The Cuban government is aware of these potential dangers to its socialist project. Its continued commitment to building socialism indicates that it believes it is capable of neutralizing these threats, not only at the current level of foreign investment, but also at a level two or three times greater that it hopes to achieve.

2 The debates on the dangers and advantages to Cuba's project of building socialism from decentralization are confused by two issues. The first is the failure to distinguish between decentralization and capitalist desta-tization. The second is the failure to distinguish between the idea that not only the Cuban model that existed in 1989 but also what exists today strongly need decentralization, and the idea that more decentralization is a priori always better for constructing socialism.

When people who desire a restoration of capitalism on the Island speak of the economic need for decentralization in Cuba, they have in mind the first form of decentralization discussed above, the change from production governed by centralized economic decisions by the state to capitalist production. As indicated in the discussions on the expansion of the capitalist sector in the preceding and following parts of this sec-tion, that expansion does involve dangers of contributing to a restoration of capitalism. Likewise negative, it does not contribute to the deepening of the socialist nature of Cuba's economy, though it can contribute to Cuba's socialist project, as discussed. But these results come from the capitalist destatization involved in this form of decentralization, not from decentralization itself. The processes of decentralization through coop-erative destatization and state decentralization discussed above do not involve these contributions to the danger of the restoration of capitalism, nor do they have the absence of contributions to the deepening of the socialist nature of Cuba's economy.

Those who want to see a restoration of capitalism in Cuba of course favor as much decentralization as possible, where for them, as noted, decentralization means transforming centralized state production to capi-talist production. For those who support the construction of socialism, the starting point for a consideration of centralization must be the neces-sity under socialism for people to collectively control all the institutions that they are part of. The appropriate group for a person to collectively make decisions with is all others "significantly affected" by such a decision, where of course the appropriate group to make a given decision will be an issue that must be repeatedly socially decided. Since people have local, regional, and national interests, decision-making by all "significantly affected" people needs to mirror these various scales. The theoretical cri-terion for the appropriate level of centralization to make a decision at is straightforward, though of course putting it into practice always involves a political debate: each economic decision should be made at the most appropriate level of centralization/decentralization. Local communities should not be deciding by themselves if there will be a cement factory in their community, given the small number needed for the country, and central authorities should have next to nothing to say about how many tomatoes are grown in a given neighborhood. A correct centralization/decentralization balance is necessary. Either too much centraliza-tion or too much decentralization impedes the socialist goal of people democratically controlling all the institutions they are part of. While the various guideline documents make clear that extensively increased decentralization is a key characteristic of the projected new model, they also make clear that some centralized aspects remain essential.

Increased decentralization that does not increase the size of the capitalist sector will not increase the danger of a capitalist restoration. To the contrary, this key reform, when carried out in the frame of achieving the appropriate centralized/decentralized balance for socialism, will deepen the socialist nature of Cuba's project, in that it will increase the power of people to collectively control all the institutions that they are part of.

3 If the reduction in state property involved only the expansion of real self-employment, it would pose little significant support for a capitalist restoration. Real self-employment involves not living off the labor of others, not capturing the surplus value created by others, no exploitation. It is petty commodity production and not capitalism. But a significant part of the nearly half-million *cuentapropistas* in Cuba today are actually hired labor. Two important issues indicate Cuba's awareness of some of the dangers from an actual domestic capitalist sector, and its reactions to them. First, in the East Bloc a significant part of the restoration of capitalism resulted from the privatizing (generally at very low prices) of state enterprises. This generated major capitals quickly. Cuba has indicated it will not sell off any functioning state enterprises. Second, even large numbers of small capitalists cannot restore capitalism. Restoring capitalism requires the political leadership and coordination of large capital. In regard to this, Cuba has stated that while private capital will be part of its updated economic model, it will not be allowed to become large. At the very beginning of the *Guidelines* it states: "In the forms of non-State management, the concentration of property in the hands of any natural or legal person shall not be allowed" (PCC 2011, guideline 3). The repeated changes in the restrictions on the allowed number of tables and employees over the last decade in the *paladares* (small private restaurants) are the best-known example of Cuba's actual efforts to limit the concentration of capital. Though less discussed, the prohibition of chains of *paladares* is actually a more important restriction on the concentration of capital; individuals cannot own more than one *paladar*[9].

The starting point for looking at the possible effects of Cuba's expansion of non-state property in the means of production on its project of building socialism has to be a consideration of the goals of socialism. It will suffice for the examination here to use the widely accepted goal among socialists of collective self-governance of all institutions of society by their members[10]. Under capitalism, ownership of some aliquot of society's means of production gives the owner both the legal right to determine how they will (or will not) be used, and claim to the output produced with them by the hired labor. Marx, Engels and many early socialists therefore advocated the following procedure: First, "win the battle of democracy" (Marx and Engels [1848], 504), replacing the dominant political power of the minority capitalists with that of the majority laboring classes. Second, "wrest, by degree, all capital from the bourgeoisie, to centralize all instruments of production in the hands of the State, i.e., of the proletariat organized as the ruling class" (ibid.). Then, with the state popularly controlled by the proletariat, the desired collective self-governance of the economy is achieved.

The history of the 20th century demonstrated that control of the economy by the state did not guarantee control of the economy by society, the socialist goal of collective self-governance of the economic sphere. In an attempt to reassert the original socialist goal, by the end of the 20th and beginning of the 21st century a number of socialists began to call for "socialized property" as directly counterpoised to "state property".

The essence of socialized property is that it is collectively governed by the people affected by it. One position is that it is necessary but not sufficient for the state to own something for it to be social property. The main concern here is that if the workers own the enterprise, they could choose to pursue profits for themselves, in effect becoming "group capitalists". Hence some ownership by society on a social scale above the collective must have ultimate power to assure this does not happen. The alternative current view is that what is important is control of the operation of an enterprise by those strongly affected by it (usually the workers and members of the adjacent communities). To understand the issue involved, consider if there is an important difference in this regard between a cooperative that owns its means of production, a cooperative that owns its means of production but is not allowed to sell them, a cooperative that rents its means of production from the state (as some do in Cuba), and Marx's minimally specified idea of Associated Producers, where they worked in enterprises in which the state owns the means of production.

This chapter cannot enter into the many facets of this discussion of whether, in the construction of socialism, all the means of production must be the property of the socially controlled state. Rather, it will here indicate only two points about Cuba's position today on the role of state property in the means of production in the construction of socialism.

a The position that ownership of the means of production is of secondary importance to the issue of their collective self-governance by the people who use them is particularly strong among advocates of cooperatives in Cuba.

> What characterizes a cooperative is not the legal ownership of the means of production (facilities, land, machinery) by the collective or group of people who make up the cooperative, but the fact that the decisions about their utilization are made collectively by all

members, either directly or through elected representatives, under the conditions and with the powers that the members decide

(Piñeiro Harnecker 2013, 6).

b In government documents, cooperatives are considered "part of the socialist property system" (PCC 2016a, article 159). Their nature as part of the socialist property system does not depend on if they own their means of production, but rather that they "apply collective principles of production and distribution of their product" (ibid.). If who owns the means of production is not determinant of what is a cooperative, as here and in point (a), then the inclusion of cooperatives as part of the socialist property system implies that state ownership of the means of production is not needed to build socialism.

c However, at the same time that the Cuban government defines cooperative property as part of the socialist property system, it repeatedly stresses that it intends that

> In the Model, socialist property of all the people (meaning state-owned property) over the means of production is fundamental and determines the relations of production, distribution, exchange, and consumption, including the appropriation of wealth, which constitutes a principle characteristic of our socialism
>
> (PCC 2016a, articles 118).

Hence one sees the two points on Cuba's position on the role of state property in constructing socialism. First, the logic of their position on the socialist nature of cooperatives regardless of ownership of the means of production implies they hold that socialism does not require state ownership of the means of production. Second, Cuba has nevertheless clearly indicated that it intends for the core of its socialist economy to be state property.

4 Maintaining conscious and comprehensive social planning and direction of the economy cannot be argued to support a return to capitalism. Because such planning is incompatible with capitalism, the opposite proposition actually holds. Conscious and comprehensive direction of the economy would need to be eliminated for a restoration of capitalism.

Comprehensive social planning promotes the deepening of Cuba's socialist project in two ways. First, as just indicated, in the absence of the determination of production by capital's drive for self-expansion, conscious planning is necessary simply to make an economy operate. But, much more profound for the goal of constructing socialism, social planning deepens Cuba's socialist project in that it represents the form of collective self-governance, applied to the economy, which is a goal of socialism.

> Centralized planning is the way of being of a socialist society, its defining category and the point where man's consciousness eventually manages to synthesize and channel the economy toward

its goal: the full liberation of human beings in the frame of a communist society

(Ché, translated into English in Álvarez 2013, 114).

Conclusion

For the last 25 years, Cuba has been engaged in carrying out the most sweeping reforms to its economy since it declared its goal of building socialism in 1961. Recalling the reform processes of many non-capitalist economies at the end of the 20th century, many supporters of Cuba's socialist goal fear its reforms will similarly restore capitalism to the Island. The Cuban government, to the contrary, has consistently maintained the updating not only will not return Cuba to capitalism, it will to the contrary significantly improve its process of constructing socialism. This review of its reforms reaches two conclusions in regard to this issue. First, it concludes that the reforms indeed bring with them a significant possibility of opening the door to a return to capitalism. Second, it agrees with the position of the Cuban government that if the updating process is carried out correctly economically, politically, and socially/ideologically, the reforms do have the potential not only to avoid promoting capitalism, but also to significantly improve Cuba's socialist project. The outcome of which way Cuba ends up going will be determined by the course of the class struggle between capitalism and socialism that is going on today, both inside Cuba and around the world.

Notes

1　The Cuban government refers to them as an "updating" of its previous economic model to stress the continuity of the goal of the new models with previous ones, to build a socialist economy. Furthermore, the word "reforms" was used by other non-capitalist economies to describe the very different process of their intentional return to capitalism. As the plethora of new procedures involves major changes as well as this central continuity and hence is reform, this chapter will use the terms "updating" and "reforms" interchangeably.

2　Beyond the usual ideological reasons for arguments about Cuban data, there is legitimate debate about the rate of growth of the Island's GDP over the first several decades of the Revolution, because Cuba then kept its economic data in the Soviet accounting system. This author holds that the most careful and ideologically neutral treatment of the conversion of that data into standard National Accounts data was done by Zimbalist and Brundenius (1989, 165). They found that in Latin America over the period of 1960 to 1985, only Brazil grew faster than Cuba's average 3.1 percent. This dropped to around 1 percent at the end of the 1980s, even before the effects of the external shock were to cause the subsequent much greater declines.

3　See Castro (1989) for an indication of both the issues involved in the Rectification Process, and how the Cuban government saw those issues.

4　Low commodity prices after the Great Recession and a renewed expansion of tourism growth and earnings after December 17, 2014, mean that foreign exchange earnings by tourism are again well above those of nickel, but nickel remains among the most important sectors of the economy.

5 "Cooperatives" is used in Cuban data only to refer to workers' cooperatives. The CCSs are producers' cooperatives, small capitalist farmers that coordinate their use of equipment, credit, and so forth. The *usifructuarios* are people given the right to farm specified state-owned land. For a detailed discussion of the expansion of these groups beyond what is useful for the topic of this chapter, see Campbell (2016).
6 The difference between Cuba's interpretation of local development and its usual capitalist interpretation is returned to in the next section.
7 In 1989 non-state agricultural workers consisted of private individual farmers and CCS members, plus CPA cooperativists. In 2014 the total of 889,600 non-state agricultural workers consisted of 351,300 private farmers and CCS members, 312,300 farmers in the new private category of *usufructuarios*, and 226,000 cooperativists in CPAs and the new UBPCs (ONEI 2015; Tables 7.2, 7.3l and 9.4) in 2014.
8 That is, 483,400 *cuentapropistas* and 5,500 nonagricultural cooperativists (ONEI 2015, Tables 7.2 and 7.3).
9 Naturally, some people work around this restriction by having family members and relatives as the official owners of additional units. So while the prohibition is not impervious, it does serve its purpose, to prevent the large concentrations of capital of big restaurant chains.
10 For a brief but much fuller treatment of the goals of socialism that presents this as a sub-goal of the central goal of human development, see Campbell (2006, 113).

References

Álvarez, Elena (2013) Medium- and Long-Range Planning in Cuba. In Al Campbell (ed.), *Cuban Economists on the Cuban Economy*. Gainesville, FL: University of Florida Press.
Campbell, Al (2016) Updating Cuba's Economic Model: Socialism, Human Development, Markets and Capitalism. *Socialism and Democracy*, 30(1), 1–29.
Campbell, Al (2006) Competition, Conscious Collective Cooperation and Capabilities: The Political Economy of Socialism and the Transition. *Critique*, 34(2), 105–126.
Castro, Fidel (1989) *Por el camino correcto*. Tercera Edición. Havana: Editora Política.
Grabel, Ilene (2003) International Private Capital Flows and Developing Countries. In Ha-Joon Chang (ed.), *Rethinking Development Economics*, London: Anthem Press, 325–345.
Marx, Karl and Frederick Engels (1984[1848]) Manifesto of the Communist Party. In *Karl Marx Frederick Engle's Collected Works*. Moscow: Progress Publishers, 477–519.
ONEI (Oficina Nacional de Estadística e Información (2015) *Anuario Estadístico de Cuba*. Havana: ONEI.
PCC (Partido Comunista de Cuba) (2016a) *Conceptualización del Modelo Económico y Social Cubano de Desarrollo Socialista*. Available at www.granma.cu/file/pdf/gaceta/Copia para el Sitio Web.pdf (Accessed September 30, 2011.)
PCC (Partido Comunista de Cuba) (2016b) *Plan Nacional de Desarrollo Económico y Social hasta 2030: Propuesta de Visión de la Nación, Ejes y Sectores Estratégicos*. Available at www.granma.cu/file/pdf/gaceta/Copia para el Sitio Web.pdf (Accessed September 30, 2011.)
PCC (Partido Comunista de Cuba) (2011) *Lineamientos de la Política Económica y Social del Partido y la Revolución*. Available at www.cubadebate.cu/wp-content/uploads/2011/05/folleto-lineamientos-vi-cong.pdf (Accessed September 30, 2011).
Piñeiro Harnecker, Camila (2013) Introduction. In Camila Piñeiro Harnecker (ed.), *Cooperatives and Socialism*. Houndsmill. UK: Palgrave Macmillan.
Zimbalist, Andrew and Claes Brundenius (1989) *The Cuban Economy*. Baltimore, MD: Johns Hopkins University Press.

10 South African *commoning* of medicines and water beyond human rights rhetoric

Patrick Bond

Introduction

Can an alternative, proto-socialist economic system be built up from within the ashes of a dying system, in which the very poorest members of a society have fought back and retained access to shrinking state services on grounds not of liberal reform, but of radical non-reformist reforms? The pages below answer in the affirmative based on social struggles within the world's most unequal society, in campaigning areas including medicines and water which are vital for the survival of HIV+ people and low-income urban residents. The argument is that the South African activists involved inexorably worked through socio-economic "Rights Talk" and discovered its limits in what is otherwise a celebrated liberal constitution. Those limits took many of the activists forward to a different strategy, moving *through* human rights narratives and identifying commons instead. The *commoning* strategy presents one of the most interesting current efforts at establishing an alternative economic system, based on principles and concrete victories won, from below, in pitched battles with those who would commodify even the most basic needs.

The traditions involved in this kind of strategy date back centuries. UN-Habitat (2012:118), the United Nations' Nairobi-based housing advocacy agency, issued a 2012 *State of the World's Cities* report with language that requires thorough deliberation:

> The "Right to the Commons" is an ancient concept in legal jurisprudence originating in feudal England, where it referred to the extension of user rights for all on a manor's grazing land. Lately, the notion has resurfaced in urban settings (including public goods, societal institutional arrangements, public culture, and heritage sites), where it is perceived as an effective way of countering not just rampant enclosures and appropriations, but also the rise of duality under the form of inequity and segregation.

Yet along with other UN institutions and the multilateral development banks, UN-Habitat (2012:117) remains committed to a society grounded in private property rights, and accordingly, commoning can be repurposed to fit the broader neoliberal agenda by contributing to 'balancing' the urban capital accumulation process:

> The "Commons" reinforce the social function of property and that of the city as a whole, while recognizing the dynamism of private assets. Laws, regulations and institutions as factors of restraint, opportunity and action, act as the levers that can optimize the social function of property and balance it out with private rights and assets. It must be stressed here that this social function is not about ownership rights or their transactional implications.

In South Africa and internationally, there is an emerging debate about how and *whether* to invoke "rights talk" – the appeal to a higher juristic source of power than standard state social policy – so that the dispossessed may gain access to greater levels of state services and subsidized goods. As a framing device, *commoning* is posed as the alternative approach and the distinctions are worth exploring (in spite of conceptual confusion introduced by the UN-Habitat authors).

Many strategists of social justice have become more familiar with the Commons idea in recent years, following the 2009 Nobel Prize in Economics awarded to the late Elinor Ostrom based on her 1990 book *Governing the Commons*. On the left, there is awareness of the problem of Ostrom's contradictions and ambivalences – because, after all, she labored as an academic within the conservative discipline of political science in one of the world's most backward sites of intellectual and social solidarity, the United States, where she played a heroic role in contesting neoliberal *homo economicus* dogma, in which rational actors are merely individually self-interested. Ostrom thus was compelled to ask rather limited questions based largely on efficiency criteria, and so her legacy requires us to go "Beyond Ostrom" (i.e., not "against" but "through"). Scale is of great importance here. The limitation of around 15,000 people served by a Commons (Ostrom's highest level of collaboration) is obviously inadequate for the societal-scale changes that will be required for the next mode of production, after capitalism is fully exhausted. David Harvey (2012:69) sets out the problem:

> As we "jump scales" (as geographers like to put it), so the whole nature of the commons problem and the prospects of finding a solution change dramatically. What looks like a good way to resolve problems at one scale does not hold at another scale. Even worse, patently good solutions at one scale (the 'local,' say) do not necessarily aggregate up (or cascade down) to make for good solutions at another scale (the global, for example).

The single most portentous site for societal reconstruction, with scale politics as a central challenge, is the giant metropolis that characterizes late capitalism. There are increasing struggles for social and economic justice, as well as ecological rebalancing, going on in cities across the world. To some extent these reflect the campaigns by political forces to influence what happens in a national capital city, but in a great many sites, the catalyzing force that generates unrest is specific to the urban character of the site of struggle.

As a result, the idea of a "right to the city" as a rallying cry has gained popularity, for good reasons. It potentially offers a profound critique of neoliberal urban exclusion. The Brazilian urban left pushed hard for the idea to be officially recognized in the government's 2001 *City Statute*. In one field especially, water and sanitation services, the right is increasingly adjudicated in courts, and South Africa has had the most advanced case to date, one that lasted from 2003 to 2009. However, because of intrinsic liberal limitations, applying the rights talk here ended in defeat, reminding of the warning by Karen Bakker (2007:447) that a narrow juristic approach to rights can be "individualistic, anthropocentric, state-centric, and compatible with private sector provision". Attempts to expand liberal socio-economic rights through incremental strategies may offer victories at the margins, but some of the lessons of the 2009 defeat bear close examination in order that social movements do not make the mistake of considering rights as a foundational philosophical stance.

Still, most urban radical activists have at some stage embraced rights talk, perhaps because there is propaganda value and mobilizing potential in accusing opponents of violating rights, and also as a result of the waning respectability of more explicitly socialist narratives. In 2004–05, the World Charter for the Right to the City (2005) was developed in Quito, Barcelona, and Porto Alegre by networks associated with the World Social Forum. To illustrate using the case of water, its twelfth article made the following points:

Right to water and to access and supply of domestic and urban public services

1 Cities should guarantee for all their citizens permanent access to public services of potable water, sanitation, waste removal, energy and telecommunications services, and facilities for health care, education, basic-goods supply, and recreation, in co-responsibility with other public or private bodies, in accordance with the legal framework established in international rights and by each country.
2 In regard to public services, cities should guarantee accessible social fees and adequate service for all persons, including vulnerable persons or groups and the unemployed – even in the case of privatization of public services predating adoption of this charter.
3 Cities should commit to guarantee that public services depend on the administrative level closest to the population, with citizen participation

in their management and fiscal oversight. These services should remain under a legal regimen as public goods, impeding their privatization.
4 Cities should establish systems of social control over the quality of the services provided by public or private entities, in particular relative to quality control, cost determination, and attention to the public.

Although one might argue that far too many concessions are made to water commercialization (i.e., supply by "private entities"), this is a reflection of the reality too many activists confront, *using weak liberal tools to pry concessions from neoliberal municipalities*. The arguments above require reforms that pay close attention to both technical and socially just (if not necessarily ecological) considerations about water services, as well as subsidiarity and community control principles. But as part of a broader right to the city, can the right to water be recast in more radical terms set out by urban revolutionaries such as Henri Lefebvre and David Harvey?

The "right to the city", in Lefebvre's (1996:154) class-conscious understanding of community, meant that

[o]nly groups, social classes and class fractions capable of revolutionary initiative can take over and realize to fruition solutions to urban problems. It is from these social and political forces that the renewed city will become the oeuvre. The first thing to do is to defeat currently dominant strategies and ideologies ... In itself reformist, the strategy of urban renewal becomes 'inevitably' revolutionary, not by force of circumstance, but against the established order. Urban strategy resting on the science of the city needs a social support and political forces to be effective. It cannot act on its own. It cannot but depend on the presence and action of the working class, the only one able to put an end to a segregation directed essentially against it. Only this class, as a class, can decisively contribute to the reconstruction of centrality destroyed by a strategy of segregation found again in the menacing form of centres of decision-making.

There is today no one "class" that can destroy class segregation. Still, at a time in South Africa (and everywhere) when debate is intensifying about the alliances required to overthrow urban neoliberalism, as discussed below, we should heed Lefebvre's suggestion about the centrality of the working class to these struggles. The broadest definition of that class is now appropriate, as contradictions within capital accumulation play out in cities, in the process generating a potentially unifying class struggle, as Harvey (2008) argues:

A process of displacement and what I call "accumulation by dispossession" lie at the core of urbanization under capitalism. It is the mirror-image of capital absorption through urban redevelopment, and is giving rise to numerous conflicts over the capture of valuable land from low-income populations that may have lived there for many years ... Since the urban process is a major channel of surplus use, establishing democratic management over its urban deployment constitutes the right to the city. Throughout capitalist history, some of the surplus value has been taxed, and in social-democratic phases the proportion at the state's disposal rose significantly. The neoliberal project over the last thirty years has been oriented towards privatizing that control.

The right to the city should therefore be deployed not foremost to backstop liberal constitutionalism, but as a vehicle for political empowerment, Harvey (2008) continues:

> One step towards unifying these struggles is to adopt the right to the city as both working slogan and political ideal, precisely because it focuses on the question of who commands the necessary connection between urbanization and surplus production and use. The democratization of that right, and the construction of a broad social movement to enforce its will is imperative if the dispossessed are to take back the control which they have for so long been denied, and if they are to institute new modes of urbanization.

Rights with neoliberal and liberal framings

Contrast such radical analysis with a near-simultaneous technicist statement – in a 2010 booklet, *Systems of Cities: Integrating National and Local Policies, Connecting Institutions and Infrastructure* – from what many consider to be the brain of urban neoliberalism, the World Bank. There is, to be sure, a confession that the neoliberal project was not successful in what the Bank had advertised since at least its 1986 New Urban Management policy (Bond 2000). The Bank (2010:24) brags that "many developing country governments and donors adopted an 'enabling markets' approach to housing, based on policies encouraged by the World Bank".

The core urban neoliberal policy strategy introduced more decisive property rights to land, cost recovery for water, electricity and municipal services, fewer subsidies within state housing institutions, and expanded mortgage credit. On the last component, private housing finance, the Bank's earlier "hope has been that pushing this and other aspects of the formal sector housing systems down market would eventually reach lower income households". But it didn't work, the Bank (2010:25) finally admitted:

> Despite some successes, affordability problems persist, and informality in the housing and land sectors abounds. By the mid-2000s, it became clear that the enabling markets approach was far too sanguine about the difficulties in creating well-functioning housing markets where everyone is adequately housed for a reasonable share of income on residential land at a reasonable price. The general principles of enabling markets are still valid, but must be combined with sensible policies and pragmatic approaches to urban planning and targeted subsidies for the

urban poor … Experience suggests that only a few regulations are critical: minimum plot sizes and minimum apartment sizes, limitations on floor area ratios, zoning plans that limit the type of use and the intensity of use of urban land, and land subdivision ratios of developable and saleable land in new greenfield developments.

Unlike Harvey, the Bank has virtually nothing at all to say about "human rights" (except property rights and "rights of way" for new roads and rail), and nothing at all to say about urban social movements. The closest is the document's reference to 'community-based organizations' which operate in "partnerships" in Jamaica and Brazil to "combine microfinance, land tenure, crime and violence prevention, investments in social infrastructure for day care, youth training, and health care with local community action and physical upgrading of slums". Civil society in its most civilized form hence lubricates markets (even though it is evident that microfinance is replete with literally fatal flaws, such as the 250,000 debt-related farmer suicides in India between 2005 and 2010 (Bond 2011) and acts as a social safety net for when municipal states fail.

Yet notwithstanding the confession, the Bank's (2010:24) discursive strategy leaves states with more scope to support markets, because rapid Third World urbanization generates market failures: "The general principles of enabling markets are still valid, but must be combined with sensible policies and pragmatic approaches to urban planning and targeted subsidies for the urban poor". Recall that from the late 1980s, the World Bank had conclusively turned away from public housing and public services as central objectives of its lending and policy advice. Instead, the Bank drove its municipal partners to enhance the productivity of urban capital as it flowed through urban land markets (now enhanced by titles and registration); housing finance systems (featuring solely private sector delivery and an end to state subsidies); the much-celebrated (but extremely exploitative) informal economy, urban services (often newly privatized) such as transport, sewage, water and even primary health care services (via intensified cost-recovery); and the like. Recall, too, the rising barriers to access associated with the 1990s' turn to commercialized (sometimes privatized) urban water, electricity and transport services, and with the 2000s' real-estate bubble. As a result, no matter the rhetoric now favoring "targeted subsidies", there are few cases where state financing has been sufficient to overcome the market-based *barriers* to the "right to the city", a point we will conclude with.

As Erik Swyngedouw (2008:3) pointed out, the context included a general realization about the limits to commodification in the private sector, if not the World Bank:

> This seems to be the world topsy-turvy. International and national governmental agencies insist on the market and the private sector as the main conduit to cure the world water's woes, while key private sector

representatives retort that, despite great willingness to invest if the profit prospects are right, they cannot and will not take charge; the profits are just not forthcoming, the risks too high to manage, civil societies too demanding, contractual obligations too stringent, and subsidies have often been outlawed (the latter often exactly in order to produce a level playing field that permits open and fair competition).

These contradictions were especially important where social and natural processes overlapped. During the 1990s, the "Integrated Water Resource Management" perspective began to focus on the nexus of bulk supply and retail water provision – in which water becomes an economic good first and foremost – but only to a very limited extent did it link consumption processes (especially overconsumption by firms and wealthy households) to ecosystem sustainability. Hence the rights of those affected by water extraction, especially those displaced by mega-dams that supplied cities like Johannesburg, have typically been ignored.

This is where liberal rights talk appears so attractive. Since the United Nations (UN) Declaration of Human Rights, the idea that all individuals have certain basic human rights, or entitlements to political, social, or economic goods (food, water, etc.) has become a key framework for politics and political discourse. In appealing to human rights, groups and individuals attempt to legitimize their cause and to accuse their opponents of "denial of rights". As water is essential to human life, social conflict surrounding water is now framed in terms of the 'human right' to water. In this "culture of rights", social groups use "rights talk" as a blanket justification for the provision of water; in some cases, however, even popularly elected governments dispute their exact responsibilities for water provision and management.

During apartheid, water was a relatively low-cost luxury for white South Africans, with per capita enjoyment of home swimming pools at amongst the world's highest levels. In contrast, black South Africans largely suffered vulnerability in urban townships and in the segregated "Bantustan" system of rural homelands, which supplied male migrant workers to the white-owned mines, factories, and plantations. These rural homelands had weak or nonexistent water and irrigation infrastructures, as the apartheid government directed investment to the white-dominated cities and suburbs, and also, in much more limited volumes, to black urban townships.

After 1994, racial apartheid ended, but South Africa immediately confronted international trends endorsing municipal cost-recovery, commercialization (in which state agencies converted water into a commodity that must be purchased at the cost of production), and even the prospect of long-term municipal water management contracts roughly equivalent to privatization. At the same time, across the world, commercialization of water was being introduced so as to address classic problems associated with state control: inefficiencies, excessive administrative centralization, lack of competition, unaccounted-for consumption, weak billing, and political interference.

Across a broad spectrum, the commercialization options have included private outsourcing and the management or partial/full ownership of the service. At least seven institutional steps can be taken towards privatization: short-term service contracts, short/medium-term management contracts, medium/long-term leases, long-term concessions, long-term Build (Own) Operate Transfer contracts, full permanent divestiture, and an additional category of community provision which also exists in some settings. Aside from French and British water corporations, the most aggressive promoters of these strategies are a few giant aid agencies, especially USAID, the British Department for International Development, and the World Bank. As a result of pressure to commercialize, water was soon priced beyond the reach of many poor South African households, by 2003 resulting in an estimated 1.5 million people disconnected each year due to inability to pay (Muller 2004).

The South African Constitution, however, included socio-economic clauses meant to do away with the injustices of apartheid, including 'Everyone has the right to have access to sufficient food and water' and 'Everyone has the right to an environment that is not harmful to their health or well-being' (Republic of South Africa 1996:s27(1)(b)). The Water Services Act 108 of 1997 put these sentiments into law as "the main object": "the right of access to basic water supply and the right to basic sanitation necessary to secure sufficient water and an environment not harmful to human health or well-being" (Republic of South Africa 1997:s2(a)). Grassroots water activists seized on these guarantees to clean water, and their discourses soon invoked rights talk. They insisted upon a social entitlement to an acceptable supply of clean water, amounting to at least 50 liters supplied per person per day, delivered via a metering system based on credit, not "pre-payment".

The surge in confidence felt by radicals when invoking the liberal rights narrative left their neoliberal critics bemoaning a new 'culture of entitlement' in which the government was expected to solve all social ills. As Lungile Madywabe (2005) of the (pro-market) Helen Suzman Foundation put it:

> Cynics fear that a culture of entitlement is growing. But the left finds such statements insulting and dehumanizing, and argues that it is crass to suggest that people are unwilling to pay for services when unemployment exceeds 40 per cent ... A turning point in the African National Congress government's thinking came in 1995, when Nelson Mandela returned from Europe and spoke in favor of privatization.

The commercialization of water was viewed with great enthusiasm by the new South African government. In South Africa, the shift to a market-based system of water access has been protested in various ways, including informal/illegal reconnections to official water supplies, destruction of prepayment meters, and even a constitutional challenge over water services in Soweto. While such protests confront powerful commercial interests, they attempt to shift policy from market-based approaches to those more conducive to "social justice". Nevertheless, this article draws on the 2008 to 2009 courtroom dramas to argue that a rights discourse has significant limitations so long as it remains primarily focused on the social domain.

The objective of those promoting water rights should be to make water primarily an eco-social rather than a commercial good. Including eco-systemic processes in discussions of water rights potentially links consumption processes (including overconsumption by firms, farms and wealthy households) to environmental sustainability. However, the lawyers developing strategy in the seminal *Mazibuko v. Johannesburg Water* case (discussed below) decided to maintain only the narrowest perspective of household water usage, since to link with other issues would have complicated the simple requests for relief. Hence, given the lawyers' defeat, the most fruitful strategic approach may be to move beyond the "rights" of consumption to reinstate a notion of the Commons which includes the broader hydropolitical systems in which water extraction, production, distribution, financing, consumption, and disposal occur.

The judges' wariness of supporting social movements requesting even basic civil and political rights was on display on Human Rights Day, 21 March 2004. Just before the grand opening of the Constitutional Court's new building in central Johannesburg, at the site of the old Fort Prison where Nelson Mandela had been incarcerated, community activists in the Anti-Privatization Forum (APF) called a march to demand their rights to water. They were specifically protesting against the installation of prepaid water meters in Soweto by the French company Suez, which was running the city's outsourced water company. City officials banned the peaceful protest on grounds of potential traffic disturbances – on a Sunday. The police arrested 52 activists and bystanders, some simply because they were wearing red shirts, and blocked travel of APF buses into Johannesburg. Neither the judges nor Mbeki – who attended the opening ceremony – uttered a word in the protesters' defense, revealing the true extent of their underlying regard for civil and political rights.

The country's highest court had by then heard several major cases on socioeconomic rights. The first, in 1997, led to the death of a man, 41-year-old Thiagraj Subramoney, who was denied renal kidney dialysis treatment because the judges deemed it too expensive. Inspired by the Constitution, Subramoney and his lawyers had insisted, "No one may be refused emergency medical treatment" and "Everyone has the right to life". Chief Justice Arthur Chaskalson replied, "The obligations imposed on the state by sections 26 and 27 in regard to access to housing, health care, food, water and social security are dependent upon the resources available for such purposes, and that the corresponding rights themselves are limited by reason of the lack of resources" (*Soobramoney v. Minister of Health* (Kwazulu-Natal), 1997). The South African state was in the process of repaying illegitimate apartheid debt ($25 billion) and cutting the corporate tax rate from 48 to 28 per cent, which escaped Chaskalson's notice. The day after the ruling, Subramoney's plug was pulled and he died.

The next high-profile Constitutional Court case on socio-economic rights was over emergency municipal services, in a lawsuit brought by plaintiff Irene Grootboom in her Cape Town ghetto of Wallacedene. Although she won, the outcome was not positive, for the Court decided simply that the 1994 *Water Supply and Sanitation White Paper* that was Housing Minister Joe Slovo's last major initiative before he died of cancer in 1994 was unconstitutional for not considering the needs of poor people. That document had as its main priority the 'normalization of the market' for housing in townships. By 2000, when the Grootboom case went to the Constitutional Court, the Slovo policy had left national, provincial, and municipal housing authorities without a mandate and plan to supply emergency housing and associated services.

The Court's decision was, however, merely 'negative', for it slapped down existing policy for failing to meet constitutional standards. But the Court did not have the courage and self-mandate to prescribe the policies and practices that *would* be considered of minimal acceptability. As a result, Grootboom and her community remained as destitute as ever, and by 2008, it was tragic yet also logical to read the headline, "Grootboom dies homeless and penniless", according to Pearlie Joubert (2008) in the *Mail & Guardian*:

Judge Richard Goldstone, a Constitutional Court judge at the time of the hearing, described the Grootboom judgement as unique, saying it will be remembered as "the first building block in creating a jurisprudence of socio-economic rights". Grootboom's victory gave legal muscle to the poorest of the poor and has been studied around the world. Her legal representative at the time, Ismail Jamie, said the Grootboom decision was "undoubtedly one of the two or three most important judgements the Constitutional Court has made since its inception." This week Jamie said that Grootboom's death "and the fact that she died homeless shows how the legal system and civil society failed her. I am sorry that we didn't do enough following-up after judgment was given in her favour. We should've done more. I feel a deep regret today", he said.

The third high-profile case was more encouraging. In 2001 the Treatment Action Campaign (TAC) insisted that the drug nevirapine be offered to HIV-positive women who were pregnant in order to prevent transmission of the virus to their children. Recall that a year earlier, Mbeki spokesperson Parks Mankahlana had explained the state's reluctance in an interview with *Science* magazine in cost-benefit terms, essentially arguing that refusing to supply nevirapine was logical in terms of saving state resources. The callous nature of his cost-benefit analysis was confirmed by state AIDS policies, often termed by critics as being basically "denialist". The result, according to Harvard School of Public Health researchers: "More than 330,000 people died prematurely from HIV/AIDS between 2000 and 2005 due to the Mbeki government's obstruction of life-saving treatment, and at least 35,000 babies were born with HIV infections that could have been prevented" (Roeder 2009). The word for this scale of death, *genocide*, was used to describe Mbeki's policies by the then-president of the Medical Research Council Malegapuru Makgoba, by leader of the SA Medical Association Kgosi Letlape, by Pan Africanist Congress health desk secretary Costa Gazi, by leading public intellectual Sipho Seepe, by Young Communist League of SA leader Buti Manamela, and by others.

In its mid-2002 judgment, the Constitutional Court criticized the state: "The policy of confining nevirapine to research and training sites fails to address the needs of mothers and their newborn children who do not have access to these sites. It fails to distinguish between the evaluation of programs for reducing mother-to-child transmission and the need to provide access to health care services required by those who do not have access to the sites". One of the lawyers on the successful case, Geoff Budlender (2002), observed that this victory "was simply the conclusion of a battle that TAC had already won outside the courts, but with the skilful use of the courts as part of a broader struggle". As argued below, the lessons learned from the TAC struggle are vital to further political development in South Africa, with or without constitutional components.

However, the limits of rights talk became evident in the fourth of the highest profile socio-economic rights cases, over the right to water. Activists in the Phiri neighbourhood of Soweto insisted upon a social entitlement to an acceptable supply of clean water, amounting to at least 50 liters per person per day and delivered via a metering system based on credit and not prepayment meters. In October 2009, the Constitutional Court overturned a seminal finding in lower courts that human rights activists had hoped would substantially expand water access to poor people: *Mazibuko et al. v. Johannesburg Water*. In the first ruling, Johannesburg High Court Judge Moroa Tsoka had found that prepayment meters were "unconstitutional and unlawful", and ordered the city to provide each applicant and other residents with a "free basic water supply of 50 liters per person per day and the option of a metered supply installed at the cost of the City of Johannesburg". Tsoka accused city officials of racism for imposing credit control via prepayment "in the historically poor black areas and not the historically rich white areas". He noted that meter installation apparently occurred "in terms of color or geographical area". It was the first South African case to adjudicate the constitutional right of access to sufficient water (Bond and Dugard 2008).

Johannesburg's appeal was also joined by the national water ministry, and was based on the decision by Johannesburg officials, just a few weeks prior to Judge Tsoka's decision, to retract the ANC promise of universal free basic water service. In the 2000 municipal election campaign, the ANC's statement had been clear: "The ANC-led local government will provide all residents with a free basic amount of water, electricity and other municipal services so as to help the poor. Those who use more than the basic amounts will pay for the extra they use." Initially, Johannesburg Water officials reinterpreted the "right to water" mandate regressively by adopting a relatively steep-rising tariff curve. In this fee structure, all households received 6,000 liters per month for free, but were then faced with a much higher second block (i.e., the curve was convex-up), in contrast to a concave-up curve starting with a larger lifeline block, which would have better served the interests of lower-income residents. The dramatic increase in their per-unit charges in the second block meant that for many poor people there was no meaningful difference to their average monthly bills even after the first free 6kl. Moreover, the marginal tariff for industrial/commercial users of water, while higher than residential, actually declined after large-volume consumption was reached.

What is the impact of these kinds of water price increases on consumption? The "price elasticity" – the negative impact of a price increase on consumption – for Durban was measured during the doubling of the real (after-inflation) water price from 1997 to 2004. For rich people, the price hike resulted in less than a 10 per cent reduction in use. In contrast, the impact of higher prices was mainly felt by low-income people (the bottom one-third of Durban's bill-paying residents, in one study), who recorded a very high 0.55 price elasticity, compared to just 0.10 for the highest-income third of the population (Bailey and Buckley 2005). Johannesburg and other cities' data are not available, but there is no reason to suspect the figures would be much different, and international evidence also bears out the excessive impact of high prices on poor people's consumption. Hence, ironically, as the "right to water" was fulfilled through Free Basic Water, the result of price changes at higher blocks in Durban and Johannesburg was further water deprivation for the poor alongside increasing consumption in the wealthier suburbs – with this in turn creating demand for more bulk water supply projects (including another Lesotho Highlands Water Project dam) which would then have to be paid for by all groups, and which would have major environmental impacts.

Resistance strategies and tactics developed over time. Activists attempted to evolve what was already a popular township survival tactic on diverse fronts – illicitly reconnecting power once it was disconnected by state officials due to nonpayment, for example (in 2001, 13 per cent of Gauteng's connections were illegal) – to a more general strategy. Thus socialist, but bottom-up, ideological statements of self-empowerment were regularly made by the APF and member organizations such as the Soweto Electricity Crisis Committee. Indeed, within a few months of Johannesburg Water's official commercialization in 2000, the APF had united nearly two dozen community groups across Gauteng, sponsoring periodic mass marches of workers and residents. And the APF was also the core activist group in the Coalition Against Water Privatization, which supported the Phiri complainants in a court process that lasted from 2003 through 2009.

The Constitutional Court's October 2009 ruling, however, vindicated Johannesburg Water, affirming that the original amount of 25 liters per person per day plus prepayment meters were "reasonable and lawful" because self-disconnections were only a "discontinuation", not a denial of water services: "The water supply does not cease to exist when a prepaid meter temporarily stops the supply of water. It is suspended until either the customer purchases further credit or the new month commences with a new monthly basic water supply whereupon the water supply recommences. It is better understood as a temporary suspension in supply, not a discontinuation" (*Mazibuko et al. v. Johannesburg Water*, 2009).

The Coalition Against Water Privatization (2009:1) was disgusted with the Court's logic, however: "We have the highest court in the land saying that those poor people with pre-paid water meters must not think that their water supply has discontinued when their taps run dry ... Such 'logic,' and even worse that it is wrapped up in legal dressing and has such crucial practical consequences, is nothing less than mind boggling and an insult both to the poor and to the constitutional imperatives of justice and equality."

The case was useful nonetheless in revealing the broader limits to the merely constitutional framing of socio-economic rights (Danchin 2010, Dugard 2010a, 2010b). One such limitation is the concomitant 'domestication' of the politics of need, as Tshepo Madlingozi (2007) put it. By taking militants off the street and putting them into courts where their arguments had to be panel-beat – removing any progressive and quasi-socialist intent, for example – the vain hope was to acquire judges' approval. Another critical legal scholar, Marius Pieterse (2007:797), complained that "the transformative potential of rights is significantly thwarted by the fact that they are typically formulated, interpreted, and enforced by institutions that are embedded in the political, social, and economic status quo". Added Daniel Brand (2005:18–19), "The law, including adjudication, works in a variety of ways to destroy the societal structures necessary for politics, to close down space for political contestation". Brand specifically accuses courts of depolitizing poverty by casting cases "as private or familial issues rather than public or political".

Commoning medicines during the AIDS pandemic

One solution, both proposed and acted upon, has been the moving of rights talk to that of *commoning*, articulating more clearly and politically the collective claim for public goods: For this, in turn, can represent a more consistent form of sustained resistance to neoliberalism, one potentially ranging from mass protest to micro-level mutual aid. The AIDS victory in the Constitutional Court could not have been achieved without the broader political sensibility won in 1999–2002 by activists who converted AIDS from a personal health stigma into a social cause that required a commoning of medicines that had earlier been privately consumed, at great cost, by only those with class and race privileges.

Because so many lives were lost in the early 2000s, and because the struggle to save subsequent lives of millions of HIV+ South Africans was ultimately victorious, it is worth understanding in detail how a small, beleaguered group of activists with compromised immune systems had such an extraordinary impact on public policy while also challenging the whole notion of commodified health care. The South African government's 1997 Medicines Act had actually made provision for compulsory licensing of patented drugs, and this in turn helped to catalyse the formation in 1998 of a

Treatment Action Campaign (TAC) that lobbied for AIDS drugs. In the late 1990s, such antiretroviral medicines (ARVs) were prohibitively expensive for nearly all the five million people who would need them once their blood counts ("CD4") fell below 250.

That campaign was immediately confronted by the US State Department's "full court press" against the Medicines Act (the formal description provided to the US Congress), in large part to protect intellectual property rights generally, and specifically to prevent the emergence of a parallel inexpensive supply of AIDS medicines that would undermine lucrative Western markets. The campaign included US Vice President Al Gore's direct intervention with SA government leaders in 1998–99 to revoke the law (significantly, in July 1999, Gore launched his 2000 presidential election bid, a campaign generously funded by big pharmaceutical corporations). As an explicit counterweight, TAC's allies in the AIDS Coalition to Unleash Power (ACT UP) began to protest at Gore's campaign events in the United States. The protests ultimately threatened to cost Gore far more in adverse publicity than he was raising in Big Pharma contributions, so he changed sides and withdrew his opposition to the Medicines Act – as did Bill Clinton a few weeks later at the World Trade Organization's Seattle Summit.

Big Pharma did not give up, of course. The main South African affiliates of the companies that held patents filed a 1999 lawsuit against the constitutionality of the Medicines Act, counterproductively entitled *Pharmaceutical Manufacturers Association of SA and Another: In re ex parte President of the Republic of South Africa and Others* (a case which even *Wall Street Journal* editorialists found offensive). It went to court in early 2001, but by April there were also additional TAC solidarity protests worldwide against pharmaceutical corporations in several cities by Medicins sans Frontieres, Oxfam, and other TAC solidarity groups. Such public pressure compelled the pharmaceutical manufacturers to withdraw the suit and by late 2001, the Doha Agenda of the World Trade Organization adopted explicit language permitting violation of the Agreement on Trade-Related Aspects of Intellectual Property Rights for the sake of medical emergencies.

It is also true that Big Pharma's reluctance to surrender property rights so as to meet needs in the large but far from lucrative African market coincided with the rise of philanthropic and aid initiatives to provide branded medicines. The Bill and Melinda Gates Foundation's parallel health services in sites like Botswana undermined state health services; it was no coincidence that Gates himself stood more to lose than anyone on the planet in the event intellectual property was threatened. Given such prevailing power relationships, the South African government did not invoke any compulsory licensing of medicines even after the 2001 lawsuit was withdrawn. Local generics manufacturers Aspen and Adcock Ingram did, however, lower costs substantially through voluntary licensing of the major AIDS drugs. It is in this sense that not only decommodification, but also deglobalization of capital, was considered vital to expanding access to the ARVs. Similar local licensing arrangements were soon arranged for firms in Kampala, Harare, and other sites.

This struggle was one of the most inspiring in the context of Mbeki's neoliberal-nationalist years. Elsewhere in South Africa, independent left movements struggled to turn basic needs into human rights, making far-reaching demands (and even occasionally winning important partial victories): the provision of improved health services (which led to endorsement of a National Health Insurance in 2010); an increase in free electricity from the tokenistic 50 kilowatt hours per household per month, especially given the vast Eskom price increases starting in 2008; thoroughgoing land reform; a prohibition on evictions and the disconnection of services; free education; lifeline (free) access to cellphone calls and SMS texts; and even a 'Basic Income Grant', as advocated by churches and trade unions. The idea in most such campaigns was that services should be provided to all as a human right by a genuinely democratic state, and to the degree that it was feasible, financed through cross-subsidization by imposition of much higher prices for luxury consumption.

Because the "commodification of everything" was still under way across Africa, however, *de*commodification could actually form the basis of a unifying agenda for a broad social reform movement, if linked to the demand to "rescale" many political-economic responsibilities that were handled by embryonic world-state institutions. The decommodification principle was already an enormous threat to the West's imperial interests, as in, for example, the denial of private corporate monopolies based on "intellectual property"; resistance to biopiracy and the exclusion of genetically modified seeds from African agricultural systems; the renationalization of industries and utilities (particularly when privatization strategies systematically failed, as happened across Africa); the recapture of indigenous people's territory via land grabs; and the empowerment of African labor forces against multinational and local corporate exploitation.

To make further progress along these lines, delinking from the most destructive circuits of global capital will also be necessary, combining local decommodification strategies with traditional social movements' calls to close the World Bank, IMF, and WTO, and with rejection of the United Nations' neoliberal functions and lubrication of US imperialism. Beyond that, the challenge for Africa's and South Africa's progressive forces, as ever, is to establish the difference between "reformist reforms" and reforms that advanced a 'non-reformist' agenda (in the terminology of Andre Gorz, 1967).

The latter attempts were to win gains that did not strengthen the internal logic of the system, but that instead empowered the system's opponents. Hence, unlike reformist reforms, non-reformist reforms would not have a co-optive character. Neither would they lessen the momentum of reformers (as did many successful reformist reforms). Rather, they heightened the level of meaningful confrontation by opening up new terrains of struggle. The non-reformist reform strategy would include generous social policies stressing decommodification, exchange controls, and more inward-oriented industrial strategies allowing democratic control of finance and ultimately of production itself. These sorts of reforms can strengthen democratic movements, directly empower producers (especially women) and, over time, open the door to the contestation of capitalism itself.

We have briefly considered how these struggles play out in the realm of AIDS medicines and how they link to broader decommodification agendas. Then how might we return to debates about the right to the city, especially given the understanding of rights limitations when it comes to water?

The right to the city *and* to the water commons in South Africa

Making hydro-socio-ecological connections within South Africa's cities will be one of the crucial challenges for those invoking the right to water. As Lefebvre (1996:72) put it:

> Carried by the urban fabric, urban society and life penetrate the countryside. Such a way of living entails systems of objects and of values. The best known elements of the urban system of objects include water, electricity, gas (butane in the countryside), not to mention the car, the television, plastic utensils, 'modern' furniture, which entail new demands with regard to services.

Indeed, the ecological challenge of mobilizing water has, traditionally, been an important process of more general social and spatial organization (Strang 2004). As Lefebvre (1996:106) explained:

> One knows that there was and there still is the oriental city, expression and projection on the ground, effect and cause, of the Asiatic mode of production; in this mode of production State power, resting on the city, organizes economically a more or less extensive agrarian zone, regulates and controls water, irrigation and drainage, the use of land, in brief, agricultural production.

Each different struggle for the right to the city is located within a specific political-economic context in which urbanization has been shaped by access to water. The early "oriental despotism" that Karl Wittfogel (1957) discovered would follow as this Asiatic mode of production's emphasis on a strong central state's control of the water works gave way, in successive eras of city-building, to the central square role of water fountains in medieval market cities, and to huge infrastructural investments in capitalist cities. Within the latter, the neoliberal capitalist city has adopted a variety of techniques that individualize and commodify water consumption, delinking it from sourcing and disposal even though both these tasks are more difficult to accomplish through public–private partnerships. Given the emphasis on decentralization, as Bakker (2007:436) suggests, "The biophysical properties of resources, together with local governance frameworks, strongly influence the types of neoliberal reforms which are likely to be introduced".

The next logical step on a civilizational ladder of water consumption would not, however, be simply a *Mazibuko*-style expansion of poor people's access (and technology) within the confines of the existing system. Acquiring a genuine right to water will require its *commoning*, both horizontally across the populace, and vertically from the raindrop above or borehole below, all the way to the sewage outfall and the sea. But to get to the next mode of financing, extraction, production, distribution, consumption, and disposal of water requires a formidable social force to take us through and beyond rights, to the water commons.

Tactically, anger about violations of the right to water has taken forms ranging from direct protests, to informal/illegal reconnections and destruction of prepayment meters, to a constitutional challenge over water services in Soweto. Rights advocates argue that they have the potential to shift policy from market-based approaches to a narrative more conducive to "social justice", even in the face of powerful commercial interests and imperatives. Yet the limits of a rights discourse are increasingly evident, as South Africa's 2008–09 courtroom dramas indicated. If the objective of those promoting the right to the city includes making water primarily an eco-social rather than a commercial good, these limits will have to be transcended. The need to encompass eco-systemic issues in rights discourses is illustrated by the enormous health impacts of unpurified water use (Global Health Watch 2005:207–224).

Thus once we interrogate the limits to rights in the South African context, the most fruitful strategic approach may be to move from and beyond 'consumption-rights' to reinstate a notion of the commons, which includes broader hydro-political systems. To do so, however, the South African struggle for water shows that social protests will need to intensify, to force concessions that help remake the urban built environment. As expressed by David Harvey (2009), "My argument is that if this crisis is basically a crisis of urbanization then the solution should be urbanization of a different sort and this is where the struggle for the right to the city becomes crucial because we have the opportunity to do something different".

One of the first strategies, however, is defense. The struggle for the right to water entails staying in place in the face of water disconnections and even evictions. Apartheid-era resistance to evictions is one precedent, but another is the moment in which the prior downturn in South Africa's "Kuznets Cycle" (of roughly 15-year ups and downs in real-estate prices) occurred, the early 1990s. The resulting "negative equity" generated housing "bonds boycotts" in South Africa's black townships. The few years of prior financial liberalization after 1985 combined with a class differentiation strategy by apartheid's rulers was manifest in the granting of 200,000 mortgages ("bonds") to first-time black borrowers over the subsequent four years. But the long 1989–93 recession left 500,000 freshly unemployed workers and their families unable to pay for housing. This in turn helped generate a collective refusal to repay housing bonds until certain conditions were met. The tactic moved from the site of the Uitenhage Volkswagen auto strike in the Eastern Cape to the Johannesburg area in 1990, as a consequence of two factors: shoddy housing construction (for which the homebuyers had no other means of recourse than boycotting the housing bond) and the rise in interest rates from 12.5 per cent (−6 per cent in real terms) in 1988 to 21 per cent (+7 per cent in real terms) in late 1989, which in most cases doubled monthly bond repayments (Bond 2000).

As a result of the resistance, township housing foreclosures which could not be consummated due to refusal of the defaulting borrowers (supported by the community) to vacate their houses, and the leading financier's US$700 million black housing bond exposure in September 1992 was the reason that its holding company (Nedcor) lost 20 per cent of its Johannesburg Stock Exchange share value (in excess of US$150 million lost) in a single week, following a threat of a national bond boycott from the national civic organization. Locally, if a bank did bring in a sheriff to foreclose and evict defaulters, it was not uncommon for a street committee of activists to burn the house down before the new owners completed the purchase and moved in. Such power, in turn, allowed both the national and local civic associations to negotiate concessions from the banks (Mayekiso 1996).

However, there are few links between the early 1990s civics which used these micro-Polanyian tactics successfully, and the 2000s generation of "new social movements" which shifted to decommodification of water and electricity through illegal reconnections (Desai 2002). The differences partly reflect how few of the late 2000s' mobilizing opportunities came from formal sector housing, and instead related to higher utility bills or forced removals of shack settlements. Still, there are profound lessons from the recent upsurge of social activism for resistance, not only to the implications of world capitalist crisis in South Africa, but also elsewhere.

The lessons come from deglobalization and decommodification strategies used to acquire basic needs goods, as exemplified in South Africa by the national Treatment Action Campaign (TAC) and Johannesburg Anti-Privatization Forum, which have won, respectively, antiretroviral medicines needed to fight AIDS and publicly provided water (Bond 2006). The drugs are now made locally in Africa – in Johannesburg, Kampala, Harare, and so on – and on a generic, not a branded, basis and generally provided free of charge, a great advance upon the US$15,000/patient/year cost of branded AIDS medicines a decade earlier (in South Africa, nearly a million people now receive them for free). The right to health care in the South African city, hence, requires the *commoning* of intellectual property rights, which were successfully achieved by the TAC by mid-decade in the 2000s after a period of extreme resistance to the United States and South African governments, the World Trade Organization's Trade-Related Intellectual Property Rights regime, and global pharmaceutical capital.

The ability of social movements such as in the health, water, and housing sectors to win major concessions from the capitalist state's courts under conditions of crisis is hotly contested, and will have further implications for movement strategies in the future (see Huchzermeyer 2009 for the standard view that the South African Constitution mandates "an equal right to the city"). Leftist critics of rights talk point to the ceilings imposed by the Constitutional Court in the water case, and they consider a move *through and beyond* human rights rhetoric necessary on grounds not only that – following the Critical Legal Scholarship tradition – rights talk is only conjuncturally and contingently useful (Roithmayr 2011). In addition, in political terms, Ashwin Desai (2010) summarises the South African urban social movements:

> If one surveys the jurisprudence of how socio-economic rights have been approached by our courts there is, despite all the chatter, one central and striking feature. Cases where the decision would have caused government substantial outlay of money or a major change in how they make their gross budgetary allocations, have all been lost.

In addition, the limits of neoliberal capitalist democracy sometimes stand exposed when battles between grassroots-based social movements and the state must be decided in a manner cognizant of the costs of labor power's reproduction. At that point, if a demand upon the state to provide much greater subsidies to working-class people in turn impinges upon capital's (and rich people's) prerogatives, we can expect rejection, in much the same way Rod Burgess (1978) criticized an earlier version of relatively unambitious Urban Reform (John Turner's self-help housing), on grounds that it fit into the process by which capital lowered its labor reproduction costs. It may be too early to tell whether court victories won by social movements for AIDS medicines and housing access represent a more durable pattern, one that justifies such rights talk, or whether the defeat of the Soweto water-rights movement is more typical. Sceptics of rights talk suggest, instead, a 'commons' strategy, by way of resource sharing and illegal commandeering of water pipes and electricity lines during times of crisis (Desai 2002, Bond 2002, Naidoo 2009, Ngwane 2009). This is a very different commons, of course, than the more decentralized – and thus potentially neoliberal – strategy proposed for public service provision and smaller, autonomous units by Ostrom (see Harvey 2012:70 for a critique).

The challenge for South Africans committed to a different society, economy, and city is combining requisite humility based upon the limited gains social movements have won so far (in many cases matched by regular defeats on economic terrain) with the soaring ambitions required to match the scale of the systemic crisis and the extent of social protest. Looking retrospectively, it is easy to see that the independent left – radical urban social movements, the landless movement, serious environmentalists and the left intelligentsia – peaked too early, in the impressive marches against Durban's World Conference Against Racism in 2001 and Johannesburg's World Summit on Sustainable Development in 2002. The 2003 protests against the US and UK for the Iraq war were impressive, too. But in retrospect, although in each case they out-organized the Alliance (i.e., the ruling nationalists, the trade unionists, and the SA Communist Party), the harsh reality of weak local organization outside the three largest cities – plus interminable splits within the community, labor, and environmental left – allowed for a steady decline in subsequent years.

The irony is that the upsurge of recent protest of a "popcorn' character" – i.e., rising quickly in all directions but then immediately subsiding – screams out for the kind of organization that once worked so well in parts of Johannesburg, Durban, and Cape Town. The radical urban movements have not jumped in to effectively marshal or even join the thousands of 'service delivery protests' and trade union strikes and student revolts and environmental critiques of the past years. The independent left's organizers and intelligentsia have so far been unable to inject a structural analysis into the protest narratives, or to help network this discontent.

Moreover, there are ideological, strategic, and material problems that South Africa's independent left has failed to overcome, including the division between autonomist and socialist currents, and the lack of mutual respect for various left traditions, including Trotskyism, anarchism, Black Consciousness, and feminism. A synthetic approach still appears impossible. For example, one strategic problem – capable of dividing major urban social movements – is whether to field candidates at elections. Another problem is the independent left's reliance upon a few radical funding sources instead of following trade union traditions by raising funds from members (the willingness of German voters to vote Die Linke may have more than a little influence on the South African left).

By all accounts, the crucial leap forward comes when leftist trade unions and the more serious South African Communist Party members ally with the independent left. The left within the Congress of South African Trade Unions (Cosatu), especially in the 350,000-member National Union of Metalworkers of South Africa (Numsa), reached the limits of their project within the Alliance in late 2013. By 2014, the more conservative federation leadership had fired its leftist secretary general, Zwelinzima Vavi (on the pretext of a sex scandal), and a legalistic reinstatement in 2015 proved temporary. By 2016, Vavi was working hard to start a new federation so as to draw in many more members than are available in the traditional metal sectors. Numsa is agitating that a workers' party be formed to contest the 2019 national elections. Meantime, the African National Congress Youth League's leader Julius Malema was expelled in 2012 and by 2014 had won 6 per cent of the national vote for his fearless Economic Freedom Fighters (EFF), as the first serious parliamentary opponents of the ANC. In the 2016 municipal elections he raised this to 8.4 per cent, which allowed the EFF to vote the ANC out of power in the vital cities of Johannesburg and the capital of Pretoria (leading to a period of centre-right urban management with far less corruption than during the ANC's rule). Add to the mix the dubious legitimacy of President Jacob Zuma and the economic crisis associated with the rapid fall in mining commodities (e.g., coal and platinum by more than half in the five years after mid-2011) and in approval of ANC neoliberalism by the main credit rating agencies. This is a fluid situation – one in which the distinction between Rights Talk and *commoning* is less vital in macro-politics.

Yet it is in South Africa's intense confrontations during capitalist crisis that we may soon see, as we did in the mid-1980s and early 2000s, a resurgence of perhaps the world's most impressive urban social movements along with metalworkers and other radical trade unionists, Economic Freedom Fighters, university students, feminists, environmentalists, and others (Bond 2014, 2016). They will have less and less satisfaction with constitutionalism, as the courts protect property in times of stress, and give credence to the police push-back on protest (from 2005 to 2015, the number of "violent protests" had risen from 600 per year to more than 2,200, according to the main source of that violence, the police themselves). En route, the society is girding for degeneration into far worse conditions than even now prevail, in a post-apartheid South Africa more economically unequal, more environmentally unsustainable, and more justified in fostering anger-ridden grassroots expectations than during apartheid itself. One of the central questions, once dust settles following battle after battle and activists compare notes, is whether the cadres persist with rights talk, or move *through rights to the Commons*, and then travel *beyond Ostrom* to a *commoning* that is ecosocialist in character.

References

Bailey, R. and C. Buckley (2005), 'Modeling Domestic Water Tariffs', Presentation to the University of KwaZulu-Natal Centre for Civil Society, Durban, 7 November.

Bakker, K. (2007), 'The "Commons" versus the "Commodity": Alter-globalization, Anti-privatization and the Human Right to Water in the Global South', *Antipode*, vol 39, no 3, pp 430–455.

Bond, P. (2000), *Cities of Gold, Townships of Coal*, Africa World Press, Trenton.

Bond, P. (2002), *Unsustainable South Africa*, Merlin Press, London.

Bond, P. (2006), *Talk Left Walk Right*, University of KwaZulu-Natal Press, Pietermaritzburg.

Bond, P. (2011), 'A Run on Grameen Bank's Integrity', *Counterpunch*, 27 April. http://www.counterpunch.org/2011/04/27/a-run-on-grameen-bank-s-integrity/.

Bond, P. (2014), *Elite Transition*, Pluto Press, London.

Bond, P. (2016), 'South Africa's Next Revolt: Eco-Socialist Opportunities', in L. Panitch and G. Albo (eds), *Socialist Register 2017*, Merlin Press, London.

Bond, P. and J. Dugard (2008), 'The Case of Johannesburg Water: What Really Happened at the Pre-paid "Parish Pump"', *Law, Democracy and Development*, vol 12, no 1, pp 1–28.

Brand, D. (2005), 'The Politics of Need Interpretation and the Adjudication of Socio-Economic Rights Claims in South Africa', in A.J. van der Walt (ed), *Theories of Social and Economic Justice*, Stellenbosch University Press, Stellenbosch.

Budlender, G. (2002), 'A Paper Dog with Real Teeth', *Mail & Guardian*, 12 July.

Burgess, R. (1978), 'Petty Ccommodity Housing or Dweller Control?' *World Development*, vol 6, no 9/10, pp 1105–1133.

Coalition Against Water Privatization (2009), 'Press Statement: "Phiri Water case: Constitutional Court Fails the Poor and the Constitution"', Johannesburg, 2 October.

Danchin, P. (2010), 'A Human Right to Water? The South African Constitutional Court's Decision in the Mazibuko Case', *EJIL Talk, European Journal of International Law*, 13 January, www.ejiltalk.org/a-human-right-to-water-the-south-african-constitutional-court's-decision-in-the-mazibuko-case.

Desai, A. (2002), *We are the Poors*, Monthly Review Press, New York.

Desai, A. (2010), 'The State of the Social Movements', Presented to the CCS/Wolpe Lecture Panel 'Social justice ideas in civil society politics, global and local: A colloquium of scholar-activists', Centre for Civil Society, Durban, 29 July.

Dugard, J. (2010a), 'Civic Action and Legal Mobilisation: The Phiri Water Meters Case', in J. Handmaker and R. Berkhout (eds), *Mobilising Social Justice in South Africa Perspectives from Researchers and Practitioners*, Pretoria University Law Press, Pretoria.

Dugard, J. (2010b), 'Reply', *EJIL Talk, European Journal of International Law*, 17 April, www.ejiltalk.org/a-human-right-to-water-the-south-african-constitutional-court's-decision-in-the-mazibuko-case.

Global Health Watch (2005), *Global Health Watch*, Zed Books, London.

Gorz, A. (1967), *Strategy for Labor*, Beacon Press, Boston.

Harvey, D. (2008), 'The Right to the City', *New Left Review*, no 53, https://newleftreview.org/II/53/david-harvey-the-right-to-the-city.

Harvey, D. (2009), Opening speech at the Urban Reform Tent. World Social Forum, Belem, 29 January.

Harvey, D. (2012), *Rebel Cities*, Verso Press, London.

Huchzermeyer, M. (2009), 'Does Recent Litigation Bring Us Any Closer to a Right to the City?', Paper presented at the University of Johannesburg workshop on Intellectuals, Ideology, Protests and Civil Society, 30 October.

Joubert, P. (2008), 'Grootboom Dies Homeless and Penniless', *Mail & Guardian*, 8 August.

Lefebvre, H. (1996), *Writings on Cities*, Basil Blackwell, Oxford.

Madlingozi, T. (2007), 'Good Victim, Bad Victim: Apartheid's Beneficiaries, Victims and the Struggle for Social Justice', in W. le Roux and K. van Marle (eds), *Law, Memory and the Legacy of Apartheid: Ten Years after AZAPO v. President of South Africa*, University of Pretoria Press, Pretoria.

Madywabe, L. (2005), "A compelling need for African innovation", The Helen Suzman Foundation, Johannesburg, 2 March. http://70.84.171.10/~etools/newsbrief/2005/news0303.txt.

Mayekiso, M. (1996), *Townships Politics*. Monthly Review Press, New York.

Mazibuko et al. v. the Johannesburg Water (2008), Unreported case no 06/13865 in the Johannesburg High Court.

Muller, M. (2004), 'Keeping the Taps Open,' *Mail & Guardian*, 30 June, http://mg.co.za/article/2004-06-30-keeping-the-taps-open.

Naidoo, P. (2009), 'The Making of "The Poor" in Post-apartheid South Africa', Masters research thesis, University of KwaZulu-Natal School of Development Studies, Durban.

Ngwane, T. (2009), 'Ideology and Agency in Protest Politics', Masters research thesis proposal, University of KwaZulu-Natal School of Development Studies, Durban.

Ostrom, E. (1990), *Governing the Commons: The Evolution of Institutions for Collective Action*, Cambridge University Press, Cambridge.

Pharmaceutical Manufacturers Association of SA and Another: In re ex parte President of the Republic of South Africa and Others (2000), (2) SA 674 (CC); 2000 (3) BCLR 241 (CC).

Pieterse, M. (2007), 'Eating Socioeconomic Rights: The Usefulness of Rights Talk in Alleviating Social Hardship Revisited', *Human Rights Quarterly*, 29, pp.796–822.

Republic of South Africa (1994), *Water Supply and Sanitation White Paper*, Cape Town.

Republic of South Africa (1996), *Constitution of the Republic of South Africa Act 108 of 1996*, Cape Town.

Republic of South Africa (1997), *Water Services Act 108 of 1997*, Cape Town.

Roeder, A. (2009), 'The Human Cost of South Africa's Misguided AIDS Policies', *Harvard Public Health*, Spring, http://www.hsph.harvard.edu/news/magazine/spring-2009/spr09aids.html.

Roithmayr, D. (2011), 'Lessons from *Mazibuko*: Persistent Inequality and the Commons', *Constitutional Court Review*, 1.

Strang, V. (2004), *The Meaning of Water*, Berg Publishers, Oxford.

Soobramoney v. Minister of Health (Kwazulu-Natal) (1997), 'Soobramoney Decision,' http://www.escr-net.org/usr_doc/Soobramoney_Decision.pdf.

Swyngedouw, E. (2008), 'Retooling the Washington Consensus: The Contradictions of H2O under Neo-liberalism and the Tyranny of Participatory Governance', Paper presented to the Centre for Civil Society, Durban, 3 July.

United Nations Habitat (2012), *State of the World's Cities*, Nairobi.

Wittvogel, K. (1957), *Oriental Despotism: A Comparative Study of Total Power*, Yale University Press, New Haven.

World Bank (2010), *Systems of Cities: Integrating National and Local Policies, Connecting Institutions and Infrastructure*, Washington, DC.

World Charter for the Right to the City (2005), Porto Alegre, http://www.urbanreinventors.net/3/wsf.pdf.

Part III

New thinking towards a new future

11 Foundations and pathways to a progressive, socialist, eco-sustainable future

Richard Westra

Virtually since its dawn, capitalism has been subject to variegated critique over the inability of capitalist societies to deliver on the human liberationist promises of modernity. Of this critique Marxism, the body of thought tracing its lineage to the writings of Karl Marx, has proved the most enduring and powerful with its vision of socialism as a society which ultimately consummates the historical march of human beings toward freedom. In summarizing Marx's vision of socialism, Friedrich Engels put the supersession of capitalism by socialism in terms of "humanity's leap from the kingdom of necessity to the kingdom of freedom" (Engels 1954, 391–3). What Engels is referring to here is Marx's concurring with bourgeois claims for capitalism "freeing" human beings from the interpersonal bonds of domination and subordination along with the extra-economic coercions in which their material lives were ensnared in precapitalist societies. Marx further lauded the bourgeois cultivation of a "public sphere" of civil and political society as a cornerstone of human freedom. Marx, however, was crisply clear: in capitalist society, one glaring un-freedom remains. This is the fact of human subjugation to the blind economic forces of the capitalist market which yokes human beings to its economic compulsions. Marx discerned how economic compulsion in capitalist economies confronts human beings as a natural force to which they must conform and argued that the leap to the kingdom of freedom necessitated a superstructure of free associations of free human beings managing the economic substructure of society for their concrete human purposes and needs.

Where Marx was not as clear, however, was on the specifics of the organizational or institutional forms of socialist superstructure management of the economic substructure of society or how the economic substructure itself will be configured to deliver the socialist vision of the new society as the kingdom of freedom. Though Marx left no sustained, systematic discussion of socialism, excavation of his writings show numerous shifting conceptions of its elements (Hudis 2013). These culminate in Marx's article *Critique of the Gotha Programme*, where he treated the two related questions of the conditions within capitalist society marking initial socialist transformation and how socialist development should proceed to realize socialist goals (Marx 1875 [2016]).

But the sketchiness of Marx's remarks on socialism, even in the *Critique*, enabled their overriding by forceful yet highly misleading revolutionary statements Marx made in the first volume of *Capital* that have dominated socialist thinking, certainly for leaders of 20th-century revolutions, although persisting in many Marxist quarters, to this day.

In chapter 32 of the first volume of *Capital*, the only volume Marx himself saw to the printer, Marx declares: "Centralization of the means of production and socialization of labour at last reach a point where they become incompatible with their capitalist integument. This integument is burst asunder ... The expropriators are expropriated" (Marx 1867 [2016]). Marx's reference to the "socialization" of labor here ties in to related comments in the concluding sections of the first volume of *Capital* on the "socializing" tendencies of capital as purportedly manifested in business monopolization culminating in the spread of joint stock corporations. *Capital*, of course, when all three volumes of it are explored as a coherent whole, is most definitely not about the historical trajectory of capitalism. As per its title, *Capital* is an economic treatise exposing the deep causal mechanisms or "inner logical" structure of capital as the economic operating system of each historical society which qualifies for the name "capitalist". In the second and third volumes of *Capital* Marx explains his remarks on socialization as referring to *capitalist* socialization where capital perpetually struggles to overcome the anarchy of private production. Marx's misleading statement in the first volume of *Capital* rather follows from his pithy theory of history sketched in a few paragraph *Preface* to an earlier work (Marx 1859 [2016]).

In that famous *Preface*, Marx suggested that human history progressed through successive modes of production, each characterized by discrete sets of forces and relations of production or "fixes" between the level of technological development and social class structure of society. Processes of historical change within modes of production ultimately placed new production and technological possibilities on the horizon, yet to unleash their potentialities necessitated transformation of the existing social class structure along with the political and ideological superstructure. To realize that transformation punctuates intervening historical periods between modes of production with significant social tumult and dislocation. The "dark age" transition from antiquity to feudalism along with wars and human displacement in the transition from feudalism to capitalism in Western Europe illustrated the point. While Marx's theory of history is extremely perceptive and offers in broad sweep an unrivalled historical framework for thinking about social change, it was never posed by him in terms of supposed historical "laws" carrying with them a determinate automaticity. Nor was Marx's approach to human history, in toto codified as the doctrine of historical materialism, even the centerpiece of his research agenda; a point we will return to below.

Nevertheless, as argued elsewhere, under the influence of Second International Marxist doyen Karl Kaustky, a generation of Marxist scholars and revolutionary activists were inculcated with precisely such views (Westra 2015). Effectively, this rendered Marx's *Capital* but a subtheory of historical materialism as an overarching theory of historical directionality, wherein *Capital* simply demonstrates the working out of opaque historical forces in a given historical context – that being capitalism. The alleged historical force driving towards socialism in capitalism was the "contradiction" between development of the productive forces as large-scale industry drawing legions of workers into cooperative production endeavors *and* social class relations, which saw the fruits of collective labor privately appropriated by capitalist-class-owned businesses. The only remaining questions, according to this schema, were (1) when the mounting "incompatibility" between development of the centralized, large-scale production edifice and capitalist class rule reached the "point" where revolutionary upheaval remained the sole resolution to the "contradiction", and (2) what the spark would be which would animate the working class to assume their historic role as revolutionary agent. Indeed, critique of the Second International among theorists of "imperialism", with imperialism viewed as a new "stage" in the transformation of capitalism, swirled precisely around the latter of the two questions. With capitalism deemed ripe for revolution, the changes it underwent during the imperialist era, tending to divide the working class and dampening its revolutionary aspirations in the most advanced capitalist economies, led the leader of the Russian revolution to formulate his claim for working-class revolution occurring at the weakest "link" in the "imperialist chain" (Westra 2015).

With the question of revolutionary agency thus resolved, and the "expropriators expropriated", the "building" of socialism was seen as simply extrapolating from the socializing tendencies exhibited by capitalism in its advanced heartland. Eric Hobsbawm explains it thus (Hobsbawm 2011, 86):

> The shape of the future and tasks of action could be discerned only by discovering the process of social development which would lead them, and this discovery itself became possible only at a certain stage of development. If this limited the vision of the future to a few rough structural principles ... it gave to socialist hopes the certainty of historical inevitability.

So sanguine was Lenin about the "inevitability" of socialism and the building of the new society with socialized capitalism as its antechamber that he unabashedly declared (Lenin 1920 [2016]),

> Communism is Soviet power plus the electrification of the whole country ... Communism implies Soviet power as a political organ, enabling the mass of the oppressed to run all state affairs ... Economic success, however, can be assured only when the Russian proletarian state effectively controls a huge industrial machine built on up-to-day technology; that means electrification.

In fact, Lenin speaks here to one of the great ironies of the whole socialist or communist enterprise conceived in terms of historical materialism: that no socialist revolution ever occurs in a state where the productive forces were developed or "socialized" to the point of their "incompatibility" with the relations of production. Even these relations themselves, under the impetus of development of the forces of production, nowhere in the societies where socialist revolution occurred produced the mass cooperative, collective proletarian revolutionary "subject", thus spawning the agonizing "soviet style" authoritarian experience of the "vanguard" communist party responsible for inculcating proletarian values throughout society simultaneously with guiding the socializing of capitalist productive forces for socialism.

Rethinking Marxism and socialism for the 21st century

As touched upon above, in his crowning economic work *Capital*, Marx theorized *capital* as the deep inner logical operating system of all capitalist societies. In this fashion Marx produced a "synthetic" definition of capital across the three volumes of *Capital* as a "totality" of logically interconnected commodity economic categories. The epistemological warrant for Marx's theorizing and "defining" of capital as such, capturing capital in its most fundamental incarnation, arises from its peculiar ontological properties as an object of study in the social world (Albritton 1999). Economic historian Karl Polanyi sought to grasp these in terms of the way capitalist market activities tend to "disembed" human economic life from other social practices (Polanyi 1971). However, Polanyi's metaphor of the economic "levitating" from politics, religion, ideology, culture, and so forth with which it was always enmeshed is, from the perspective of Marx's writings a century prior, an imprecise rendering of what Marx understood as reification. That is, the economic appears "transparently" for theory to explore for the first time in human history in the age of capital, because, while capital is socially and historically constituted, its market operations tend to objectify the very subjects whose individual self seeking purposive actions set it in motion. Its tendencies toward reification, in other words, distill human actions into outcomes that no one intended but which (if capital has its way) satisfy the capitalist chrematistic of value augmentation or profit-making.

Why we even need economic *science* or theory is because it is *not* possible to study human economic life *directly*, as it *only* appears "transparently" in its reified form in the capitalist era. Hence the task of economic theory as initially set out in Marx's unfinished *Capital* is threefold: to unfold all the categories of the capitalist commodity economy to show how it is possible for capital to wield economic life of a human society as a byproduct of value augmentation or profit-making in the first place; to shed light on the basic constituents or "general norms" of economic life, disentangled from their capitalist integument, to understand organization of material life in past historical societies as well how it may be organized in socialist societies of the future; and to offer a critique of existing bourgeois political economy and economic theory.

In Marx's *Capital*, the fundamental "contradiction" at the root of the inner logical structure of capital is that between *value* and *use value*. Use value is the substantive foundation of human material existence. No human society could survive without the metabolic interchange between human beings and nature through which the labor and production process furnishes the useful goods necessary for human material reproduction. Value, on the other hand, is the historically specific abstract, homogenizing, quantitative principle of capital. Use value poses a contradiction or "opposition" for value in the way value is forced to abstract from the sensuous, qualitative heterogeneity of use value as it brings diverse goods into the homogenizing quantitative pricing relations of the capitalist market. Theory construction in Marx's economics is thus "reality assisted" and generates the categories of capital by studying the way capital surmounts the contradictions or oppositions posed by use-value obstacles. It is in following the real (read "material") processes of abstraction in the capitalist economy that disciplined thought (why the term "transparently" is placed in quotation marks) is able to unfold a complete set of basic economic categories of capital shorn of this or that ideological prejudice.

What is most important to grasp from this is that, because the very condition of possibility for the study of economic phenomena is the historical existence of capitalism, the *cognitive sequence* in Marxism necessarily runs from Marx's analysis of capital to historical materialism. Only in the context of the analysis of capital could Marx, for example, have discerned how value striving to manage the use-value obstacles posed by human labor power rendered as a commodity would manifest itself in the contradiction or "fix" between the forces of production as the technology complex wielded by capital and the capital labor relation. Indeed, the very conceptualizing of an economic *substructure* as separate from a political and ideological superstructure is dependent upon the tendency of value toward self-movement or reification. It is so often overlooked that Marx's writing of the *Preface* and formulation of his pithy theory of history followed over two decades intensive study of the capitalist economy, as attested to in his work book for *Capital* subsequently published as the *Grundrisse*. And, no sooner did Marx write the iconic *Preface*, he turned to that project which ultimately consumed his life – *Capital*. Hence the study of both precapitalist economies and postcapitalist society begins in the comparative light of study of the capitalist economy.

Flowing from this perspective on Marxist theory, the conceptualizing of socialism commences not as a function of a purported law of history operating through capitalism such that socialization of capitalism is taken as the antechamber of socialism. Rather, at the most abstract level, if capitalism in its most fundamental incarnation constitutes a reified society where human material life is reproduced as a byproduct of value augmentation or profit-making, then socialism at its root must be conceived as the opposite of capitalism. Put differently, socialism is not built by capitalism but by human beings seeking to undo capitalist subsumption of human economic life. On the foundation of the cognitive sequence in Marx's writing, creative thinking about socialism marshals all areas of the Marxist research agenda to elucidate varying possibilities for configuring human material life to realize socialist goals. If the study of capital holds out any certainty for socialists, it is this: in conclusively demonstrating how capital manages to satisfy the general norms of economic life to reproduce material existence of an entire society as a byproduct of abstract value augmentation, the economic theory of capital simultaneously confirms the possibility of those same general norms being met through decision-making by free associations of human beings organizing their economic world for concrete human purposes and needs (see Figure 11.1).

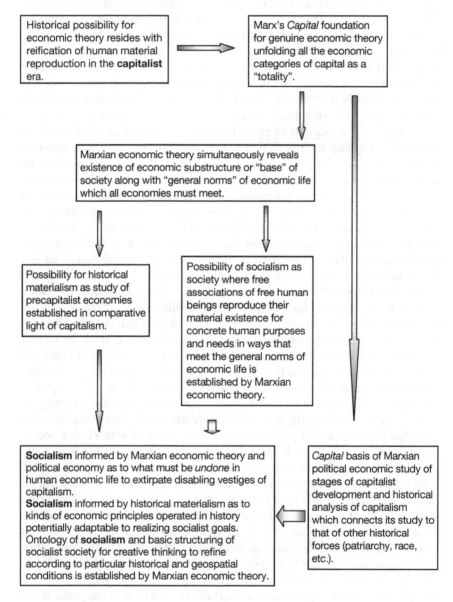

Figure 11.1 Socialism and the cognitive sequence in Marxism

Ontology of socialism and economic principles for socialist material reproduction

Setting out ontological principles of socialism, I have argued, follows from thinking about a society that is the antithesis of capitalism in several key respects (Westra 2002; 2014, 76–9). First, if capital tends to reify human economic life, reproducing it as a byproduct of augmenting abstract mercantile wealth, then socialism must be conceived in its basic incarnation as a non-reified society where responsibility for organizing human material reproduction is vested in the hands of free associations of free human beings and managed for their concrete, freely chosen, human purposes. Second, given the fact of commodification of labor power as the sine qua non of capitalism, socialism requires decommodification of labor power. However, what may be derived from historical materialist study of precapitalist economies as well as Marx's grasp of the role capitalism plays on the road to human freedom, with its "freeing" of work from interpersonal relations of domination and subordination, decommodification of labor power must proceed without reinstating extra-economic compulsion. The latter was one element of what made soviet-style societies unappealing in parts of the world where people had experienced advanced capitalist economic life, notwithstanding the fact of significant contributions to social welfare made in soviet-style societies, beyond that characteristic of societies under similar conditions of relatively limited development which were not seeking to build socialism. That is, capitalism in its developed economies paradigmatically entails economic compulsion for work, which constitutes an advance over interpersonal, extra-economic bonds of precapitalist economies and the reinstatement of extra-economic coercion in a new guise by soviet-style societies. Work, in genuine socialist transitions, must become self-motivated or, as Marx himself puts it in *Critique of the Gotha Programme*, "life's prime want" (Marx 1875 [2016]). Without institutional enabling of self-motivation for work in all its forms, workers and the ordinary mass public will continue to "choose" abstract, economic compulsion of capitalism.

Third, but crucially, in wielding human material life as a byproduct of value augmentation through the abstract, quantitative operating calculus of its market activities, capital necessarily manifests a studied indifference to use value except as a vehicle subsumable by value in its chrematistic of value augmentation. In the broadest sense, of course, use value embodies not only the useful goods human beings refashion nature to produce, but nature itself, in all its concrete, sensuous, qualitative terrestrial, geospatial and biospheric heterogeneity. The indifference to use value at the heart of capital is what sees capitalism regularly produce toxic goods (for nature and human beings) as vehicles of value augmentation. As capitalist production-centered societies spread their tentacles across the globe over the past two centuries, the technologies, production systems and energy sources which power these societies in service of abstract value augmentation have wreaked such murderous providence upon nature and the biosphere as to threaten human existence itself. Thus a genuine socialism must ensure the reinstatement and primacy of qualitative use-value considerations in the reproduction of human economic life and the suppression, to the greatest extent possible, of abstract quantitative considerations.

Yet, for socialist practice in building the sort of practical utopias this volume makes the case for, the foregoing ontological principles still remain, at best, vague foundational signposts. To concretize these, I have argued elsewhere, it is necessary to think more precisely about the specific principles of economy through which the ontological principles will be given life in the institutional configuring of actual socialist societies (Westra 2014, 138–48). To foreground the discussion, it is important to remind ourselves that the challenges for building a socialist future today are far greater than envisioned by Marx, even in his major single writing on socialism, the aforementioned *Critique of the Gotha Programme*.

First, bracketing debate over whether Marx ultimately recognized the innate anti-environmental thrust of capitalism, eco-sustainability is probably the most pressing human concern when it comes to creative thinking about a socialist future. It is a concern with dimensions that are both "local", pertaining to the very organizing of social and material reproductive community life, as well as "global", in that not only are environmental decisions impossible to "contain" geospatially, but also the planet and biosphere are in desperate need of a cleanup that will require concerted international effort.

Second, without entering at this point in our discussion into the pathway that building socialism will assume, the world economic forces euphemized as "globalization" have disarticulated much of the once integrated productive apparatuses of society. Whether socialists came to power in Marx's era through working-class revolutionary upsurges or the electoral route, as advocated during the famous "Revisionist Controversy" (Westra 2015), on taking power socialists expected to have at their disposal the accouterment of a "national" economy upon which to "build" the new socialist society. To be sure, capitalist economies have always been intertwined in international trading networks, but as late as the 1960s most basic goods and foodstuffs populations were reliant on were produced within the nation-state geospatial unit. Today, that this is no longer the case saddles prospective socialist transitions with a daunting task of remaking economic life at local and regional levels from the bottom up.

Absence of the foregoing constraints had lent support and credibility to the initial socialist scheme of building socialism upon the foundation of full-scale industrialized capitalist economies, where socialism largely entailed eliminating the anarchy of private ownership of production by imposing public ownership over commanding heights of the economy. Following upon planned economic management, a deepened democracy, egalitarian social outcomes, equitable resource redistributions, empowering of the direct producers, mass systems of social wage support and free public and social services were all expected to be emplaced. When mounting evidence of the miscarrying of soviet-style societies regarding much of the above became far too glaring for international socialists to ignore, the major remedies proposed held to two overarching visions of single society-wide models (Westra 2009, 202–6).

First, economic inadequacies of soviet-style systems were to be addressed by the reinstating of markets in what are dubbed models of "market socialism". However, the major argument against this is that in imbibing the dogmas of neoclassical economics, proponents simply cannot grasp the fact of the impossibility of decoupling the *capitalist* market, the productivity and efficiency gains of which they hope to harness, from capitalism with its "extra-human" reified outcomes. We will return below to the issue of differentiating between market activities of a "small *m*" type, as had existed in precapitalist societies, and the operation of the specifically capitalist market, with its metric of quantitative calculus. But, as alluded to above in this chapter, the society-wide calculus of capitalist market operations is attuned to value augmentation and is indifferent to the qualitative use-value considerations in human material reproduction. Yet, to treat issues of environmental sustainability and the disarticulation of national economies, it is precisely use-value considerations in human material existence which must be placed at the forefront of creative future-directed thinking.

Second, the democratic deficit of soviet-style societies, combined with the insensitivity of centralized authoritarian state planning to consumption desires of socialist mass publics, were viewed as the main culprits in sowing disfavor with socialism among both those living in soviet-style societies and supporters of socialism around the world. To resolve the twin socialist discontents, models of "participatory planning" were proposed which, with few exceptions, advocated democratic aggregating of various levels of "deliberatory" public committee inputs into plan formulation while operating the plan through computer programs or economic calculus procedures which simulated equilibrium outcomes purportedly arrived at by market activities as captured in neoclassical economics. Yet, as with so-called market socialism, society-wide participatory planning models remained too much a prisoner of capitalism and never genuinely grappled with Marx's concern with the use-value dimension of human material life, which capitalism, or simulation of its quantitative market pricing mechanism, necessarily manifests indifference towards.

In fact, the very narrowing of the socialist menu to two choices, that between market and state, mimics debates within advanced capitalist societies between neoliberals and social democratic proponents of the welfare state. Marx, however, had maintained in his schema of historical materialism that capitalism, like other historical societies, was destined to be outpaced by history. The core indicator for Marx of the historical exhaustion of capitalism was the emergence on the horizon of a use-value complex and available technologies that would satisfy new human material wants but which were impossible for capital to manage the production of as a byproduct of value augmentation, given the innate recalcitrance to value of these use values. Indeed, words of Nobel

Laureate Joseph Stiglitz capture the issue here with supreme irony: "Heavy industry was particularly well suited for the control mechanisms employed by the socialist system … [T]here may have been a short window of time, the period of … steel, autos … and so on, in which some variant of socialism may have been able to work" (Stiglitz 1994, 204–5).

Actually, steel and ultimately automobile production demanded capitalist states themselves employ a wide array of "control mechanisms" to manage their production. Steel companies of the early 20th century were already deemed too big to fail, and states marshaled protectionist and imperialist policies on their behalf. Mid-20th-century automobile and other consumer-durable-producing corporations were supported by a gamut of state policies, from macroeconomic countercyclical programming to extensive social wage entitlements, to ensure ongoing mass consumption, which was the necessary corollary to their profit model of high-throughput mass production. But neither society-wide centralized soviet-style state planning nor capitalist market operations cocooned by welfare state programming are up to the task of moving beyond the highly urbanized automobile and petroleum economy toward the necessary future eco-sustainable world of alternative energies, once-and-for-all public transportation systems, reconfigured living spaces and agroecology beckoning humanity today. That is, given the sweep of human history, the "short window of time" for capitalism to "have been able to work" is that taken up by capitalist mass industrial production of paradigmatic use values, from textiles through automobiles, which lent themselves to suppression of qualitative considerations in human economic life in favor of quantitative ones. In short, in its advanced, latest stage of automobile society, capitalism was only "able to work" to augment value supported by abundant extra-capitalist, state and other social practices. Soviet-style state central planning was "able to work" in the age of steel, but faltered in its "competition" with capitalism in the post-WWII consumer durable/mass consumption era.

Thus, the argument, quite simply, is that, considering both major issues of eco-sustainability and the disarticulation of global production systems (the latter, incidentally, involving the consumer durable complex which powered advanced economy growth and employment to the 1970s, though is composed of products and processes that are most unsustainable environmentally today), and adding into the mix ills of the current social morass such as democratic deficits, perverse wealth asymmetries, "financialization" of economies which accompanied the disintegrating of their material production edifices, a new nimbleness in terms of economic organization is indispensible (Westra 2014, 138ff). Following up on writings by ecosocialists (Foster et al. 2010; Williams 2010), and informed by economic history and economic anthropology (Polanyi 1971; Graeber 2011), and further integrating work on political organization by anarchist Murray Bookchin (1990), I argue that whatever the pathway taken to reach the socialist future, economy, polity and society must be reconfigured and rescaled in reduced and layered interconnected geospatial units with layered components operated by the appropriate economic principle.

To rejuvenate "local" community economic life and build eco-sustainable agriculture that services consumption at local and regional levels to the fullest extent climatically and topographically possible, as well as to ensure deepening of democratic participation and decision-making, politico-economic units large enough to contain diversity of population to engage in farming, light goods and forms of craft production, and basic services are to become the foundations of material reproduction in new societies. The socialist village of Marinaleda in Andalusia, Spain, is one example of how property ownership may be reconfigured, with land held in common by the "cooperative", though families live in private homes and their "property" may also be used for cafes, restaurants, vegetable gardens, craft centers and so forth. While its population is approximately 3000, it sports a cultural center with Internet café, athletic facilities, swimming pool, basic medical facilities, schools, a park and so forth (Hancox 2013). Such cooperatives will form part of larger *community-scale economies* of 150,000 to 200,000 that manage the basics of material reproduction of society. The central economic principle through which economic life is managed here is *reciprocity*, which potentially includes varieties of small-*m* market operations such as local exchange/employment and trading systems (LETS), community currency systems (CCs), barter, "need exchanges", "gift giving" and so forth. Essential services, including care, are socialized and provision of basic goods democratically planned, but beyond this, ample space is guaranteed for multifarious "private" initiatives based upon individual/family interests and capabilities. Utilization of LETS and CCs which incorporate community monies serves the function of money as means of exchange and unit of account but forestalls the function of money as store of value upon which capital accumulation and stark inequality in society may resurface.

In the proposed design, the bedrock *community-scale economies* which, following Sekine (1990), I have also referred to as "qualitative goods sectors" in reference to their extirpating of commodity economic, quantitative value relations in material life (Westra 2014) are linked to *state production* and *state administrative* sectors. Precisely, how many *community-scale economies* will be serviced by a *state production* and *state administrative* sector depends upon the total population size of the socialist "state"/region (whether the building of the new society adheres to current nation-state containers or is constructed along other geospatial contours will be determined in practice), along with economic and political governance considerations. At the outset of the transformatory process, assuming it proceeds under impetus of democratic movements within current societies rather than under conditions of duress following from crises and/or war, the whole edifice proposed here will largely be superimposed upon existing cities and surrounding areas with divisions among *community-scale economies*, *state production* and *state administrative* sector communities, essentially made according to existing boroughs, districts, counties, wards and so forth according to economic and political criteria.

Summarily stated, the key economic question is how to ensure the eco-sustainable material economic reproducibility of the society, while achieving the redistributive egalitarian outcomes that socialists have long called for, under robust institutional conditions that protect self-motivation for work and social contribution and forestall reemergence of a new social class-like stratum of more wealthy and privileged elements of the society, as occurred in soviet-style systems. The answer is to ensure that flow of control and ownership of "heavy" complex production assets of the *state production sector* are in hands of the members of the bedrock communities these service in terms of both management and staffing decisions. Most of the producer and transportation goods and infrastructure, along with electronic technologies and their products, plus heavy construction materials and energy infrastructure, require economies of scale beyond 200,000-member communities. Yet, analysis of the Soviet Union, for example, revealed that it was precisely through their superintendence of commanding heights industries that high-level managerial personnel, associated bureaucrats and ultimately industry representative Ministers assumed ruling-class-like powers over the direct producers as they utilized their positions to appropriate greater material benefits than did workers (Resnick and Wolf 1993; 1994).

To prevent such an outcome, a separate unit of account or "currency" needs to be deployed for transactions among *state production sector* units and between these and *community-scale economies* and a firewall emplaced, ensuring that "currency" of the former has no direct purchase in the internal economic intercourse of the latter. That way, while the initial transition period to the new economy will certainly entail reliance upon existing stock of human expertise and administrative capacities in society, given that the consumption and lifestyle possibilities of these cohorts will be embedded in *community-scale economic* life within the ambit of community LETS and CCs, there is scant potential for a new soviet-style elite to spawn. This is also the case for the *state administrative* sector, which is charged with managing the integrated production systems of *state production sector* units. Yet, both state sectors, whether these are geospatially separated or separated as policy communities, are "owned" (potentially through shareholding mechanisms) and managed/staffed under auspices of *community-scale economies*.

Reemphasis is warranted here on the point that such a design is not far off the mark in terms of practicality, from existing proposals for current urban agglomerations as set out in a recent *Guardian* article (Engelen et al. 2014). In the piece it is stated: "The idea of a heterogeneous economy means only that the economy has different spheres or zones which run on different principles … [each "sphere" with] different internal logics and variable salience for material welfare". The sphere within today's cities that has received the least attention and mismanagement, according to the authors, is what they dub the "foundational economy", responsible for the basic goods and services that support the welfare of the bulk of urban inhabitants. My contribution to this debate is to achieve clarity and specification over divisions of "zones" and "spheres", and on what precise economic principles will best operate in these, to achieve the desired outcomes that socialists and other Left progressives have called for in terms of redistribution, economic empowerment and participation, environmental sustainability and so forth.

The "foundational economy" is the *community-scale economy*. As historian of cities Lewis Mumford shows, cities battened upon surrounding environs which furnished them with basic goods, until transportation and development enabled attaining of such goods from great distances and urban encroachment upon lands that fed cities proceeded apace. Modern suburbanization for parks and greenery usurping surrounding arable farmland was the final step in this unsustainable dynamic (Mumford 1961). Today, even the production of many basic material goods the factories for which initially compelled movement from within cities to suburbs, are now produced continents away, only exacerbating environmental ills along with a raft of social malignancies related to work, income and wealth distribution in urban society. Apprehending the fundamental place and "logic" of a "foundational" *community-scale economy* speaks to this. In the design envisaged here, self-motivation for work is institutionally fostered by the cooperative ownership structure and "foundational" nature for human material reproduction of the gamut of goods this sector produces, whether it is carved out of existing "greater" city areas or not. Environmental sanctity is engendered initially by attention to power and waste management that emerges with local provisioning and the rescaling of social and economic spaces.

Economically, management of the *state production sector* requires a form of redistributive participatory democratic planning as its core economic principle. Its labor force will come from the bedrock *community-scale economies*. This poses some problems for motivation and remuneration. Regarding the former, the production of state-sector goods entails multiple "roundabout" processes which distance work activities from final consumption to a far greater degree than occurs in community economies, meaning that alienation akin to that existing in work in capitalist social democracies in like production and technology conditions will persist. Regarding the latter, remuneration cannot be in the state currency that is used for intrastate-sector transaction, as that has no purchase in communities where individual consumption and much production for direct consumption takes place. To remedy both problems simultaneously, a process of democratic rotation of labor forces, from *community-scale economies* to the state sector, will be required, and remuneration in the LETS and CCs of communities will need to be calculated. Given that ultimately the decisions over the democratically planned economy are vested in the hands of communities it services, production and distribution modalities, along with transportation networks connecting the whole edifice, will be promoted in a fashion ensuring eco-sustainable outcomes. And participatory planning is not society-wide but limited to producer and infrastructure goods, leaving foundational community economies operating according to principles more sensitive to direct community needs.

Finally, the *state administrative* sector is essentially the structure of government and ministries which exists in current democratic societies. The differences, of course, are, firstly, like the state sector, while decisions are made by administrative workers that allocate state currency, neither this function nor the fact that such a cohort actually "handles" large sums of units of account offers administrators opportunities to accumulate personal wealth or enjoy elite-class consumption habits compared to other categories of worker, as their remuneration is in the LETS and CCs of their residence. Secondly, the flow of power in the system as a whole follows that proposed by anarchists such as Murray Bookchin. Power germinates in a direct democratic milieu at the micro level of the cooperatives and neighborhood districts of the *community-scale economies*. It is there that immediately recallable representatives are chosen for more meso-level administrative functions within the community as a whole. Meso-level representatives, in turn, will be nominated or elected to staff the macro management functions of the *state production sector* and political functions of the *state administrative* sector. Macro functionaries are also directly and immediately recallable (see Figure 11.2). While this process of decision-making might, to some, appear cumbersome, it mirrors in many ways the hierarchy of decision-making operating today in modern societies with one major caveat. The proposed model is democratic at each level and creates no opportunities for excessive economic benefits to accrue to those who will staff the positions, helping to guarantee that the best qualified and committed citizens will seek public life. To be sure, the regularization and habituation of the new order until the state "withers away" will take a generation, as the hegemony of new practices takes hold.

Debating pathways to practical socialist utopia

In the early 20th century, as the first mass experiments for socialist change were put into play, the signal area of debate over the procedure and pathway for change was that springing from the aforementioned Revisionist Controversy. Quite simply, the "orthodox" viewpoint attributed to Marx was that socialism will follow the revolutionary overthrow of the ruling class and its functionaries at the helm of the state. The "revisionist" view, incidentally also ascribed to Marx, was that if historical tendencies of capital were "socializing" it in terms of gigantic enterprises requiring accelerated numerical growth of the working class in proportion to all other classes, then, as long as polities were democratic, a working-class party would easily win at the ballot box and begin a peaceful, gradual transition from social democracy to socialism. Revolutions in what became the Soviet Union and China in the first half of the century seemed to settle the matter initially. But among major advanced capitalist economies, the advent, spread and staying power of the welfare state supported the perspective of a significant cross section of Left intelligentsia and their followers that Left political parties attaining state power would be able to strengthen social democracy in the direction of socialism. With the nearly

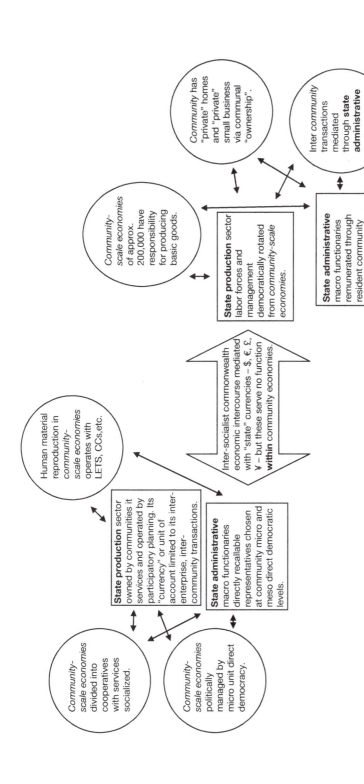

Figure 11.2 Flow of economic and political power

Community has "private" homes and "private" small business via communal "ownership".

Inter *community* transactions mediated through **state administrative** bodies.

Community-scale economies of approx. 200,000 have responsibility for producing basic goods.

State production sector labor forces and management democratically rotated from *community-scale economies*.

State administrative macro functionaries remunerated through resident community LETS and CCs according to democratic procedure.

Inter-socialist commonwealth economic intercourse mediated with "state" currencies – $, €, £, ¥ – but these serve no function **within** community economies.

Human material reproduction in *community-scale economies* operates with LETS, CCs, etc.

State production sector owned by communities it services and operated by participatory planning. Its "currency" or unit of account limited to its inter-enterprise, inter-community transactions.

State administrative macro functionaries directly recallable representatives chosen at community micro and meso direct democratic levels.

Community-scale economies divided into cooperatives with services socialized.

Community-scale economies politically managed by micro unit direct democracy.

simultaneous rise of neoliberalism and unceremonious collapse of the Soviet Union, claims on both sides were effectively mooted.

Following the attrition and eventual dismantling of the welfare state, along with undermining of much of the "foundational economy" of society by neoliberalism – and let us not forget the gathering clouds of climate-change Armageddon – a broad spectrum of Left constituencies for change took shape which posed two very different choices of roads to social transformation. The arguments face off as follows: On the one hand are those claiming the sheer planetary scale of problems is such that only a globally concerted movement toward change has any hope of salvaging humanity. On the other hand is the argument that, while the issue of planetary scale of challenges is real, change is more likely to be quickly realizable in more local and regional settings, and that these transformations will be catalysts for wider movements for change. It is further argued on the latter score that whatever the spark for change, environmental and climate change considerations will demand breaking down current geospatial scales of society.

Both sides marshal compelling arguments, and these cross-cut the various Left constituencies. Among environmentalists, for example, prominent Green Bill McKibben opines that "big is vulnerable. We are going to need to split up, at least a little, if we're going to avoid being subdued by the forces we've unleashed. Scale matters, and at the moment ours is out of whack with our needs" (McKibben 2011, 146–7). McKibben further places emphasis upon the fact that efficacious movements for change today eschew capital-*L* "Leaders" and centralization and instead tend to be amorphous in drawing together a multiplicity of organizations and small-*l* leaders in the necessary "all-encompassing fight over power, hunger, and the future of humanity on this planet" (McKibben 2013). Ecosocialists of various stripes similarly maintain that at all levels, including democratic deficits, patterns of inequality, the biospheric ravages of industrial petro-farming, worker alienation, planned obsolescence model of ever-expanding consumer mass consumption, and on and on, whether the social transformation unfolds under duress or through the popularity gains of Left ecosocialist political parties that accede to power through elections, breaking down current scales of economy and habitat along with generalizing agroecology for all basic food sustenance is an indispensable ingredient of a livable future (Baer 2016). However, even those supportive of the transformation of agriculture and society in ecosocialist directions warn against romanticizing "a particular form of peasant agriculture", as is plied today at the margins of the globalized economy under backbreaking conditions and without aid of either draft animals or basic mechanized appliances (Empson 2016).

All environmentalists, however, are not so sanguine over the prospect of "splitting things up". David Orr of Worldwatch, for example, suggests major reductions in scales of governance amount to "Thomas Hobbes's nightmare on steroids". Rather, he argues, "it will be necessary to enlarge governments both domestically and internationally to deal with the nastier aspects of the long [climate change] emergency" (Orr 2013, 287–8). The "enlargement" of government authority argument also lends itself to technocratic centralized strategies for combating climate change, such as those based upon geoengineering (Nicholson 2013). In an important sense, the global delay of climate-change action supports the foregoing as the de facto final solution. And, ever-ingenious, though potentially catastrophic, variants of geoengineering are increasingly attracting research funds and scientific interest (*Bloomberg* 2016).

Marxists, for their part, also challenge more "local" solutions to socialist change. Representative of this genre is work by William Robinson which points to world economic processes, euphemized as "globalization", leading to the emergence of a global or "transnational" capitalist class that today constitutes the organized force of capitalist rule (Robinson 2014). Hence, dismounting of this transnational capitalist class necessitates the forging of a global oppositional struggle for mass global revolution. Marxist doyen David Harvey similarly argues that "political unification of diverse struggles within the labour movement and ... dispossessed appears to be crucial for any movement to change the course of human history" (Harvey 2011, 247). Though Harvey holds fast to the position that seizing of state power in existing capitalist geospatial containers constitutes the minimal scale for embarking upon socialist change.

While the above vignettes hardly exhaust the new debate, what they do illustrate is that discussions of pathways to the future unfold at some distance from efforts at delineating the contours of the successor society with respect to how it will respond to the raft of dire ills humanity is saddled with and bring into being a world in line with the progressive, redistributive, eco-sensitive visions of the multiple constituencies calling for change. Indeed, if one hugely important insight into social change springs from the writings of Italian Marxist Antonio Gramsci, it is that revolutionary world views rise to hegemonic status not only through trenchant critique of the dominant order and the theoretical framing of a new progressive one, but also in social practices within a prerevolutionary society.

Current polities only reconfirm what has been well understood for some time: that under democratic electoral systems of the varying forms of representative democracy, the deck is stacked against any political party with a truly revolutionary program attaining power (Macpherson 2011). Nevertheless, as the phenomenon of Syriza in Greece illustrates, the possibility does exist when a cross section of social constituencies among a committed populace held hostage by brutal neoliberal austerity faces its demons head on. And, as suggested by Syriza member Costas Lapavitsas, if the ostensibly socialist party had a worked-out plan for organizing a new order rather than its "back-of-the-envelope" musings over "a parallel currency, or a parallel banking system", the outcome would have differed from the wretched capitulation of part of its elite leadership, giving immediate hope to other like parties (Lapavitsas 2016).

Noteworthy in the initially Greek-Syriza achievement of democratic consensus for an avowedly socialist party and referendum outcome of over

60 percent to say "no" to austerity and neoliberalism was its occurrence in a relatively small geospatial region with a population of around 10 million. But, what about the possibility of achieving such a consensus in a giant transcontinental society like the United States? Scholar and activist Gar Alperovitz reminds us that the early thinkers in the US democratic tradition had always expected democracy to thrive in more direct democratic settings and never would have imagined attempts to work it on such a scale as exists in the United States today without it gravitating toward centralized tyranny. Alperovitz further points out how, in more recent times of duress in the US economy, such as during the Great Depression of the 1930s, proposals emanated from both conservatives and liberals for breaking up the US economy and polity into more easily economically manageable and democratically governable regional units. In fact, President Roosevelt's Tennessee Valley Authority project and like plans for other regional authorities were the embodiment of an innovative, regional, publicly owned initiative reproducible today (Alperovitz 2011, 64–6).

Above, I made the argument that neoliberal-impelled abdication of responsibility by states for maintaining a "foundational economy" contributed, along with environmental concerns, to the new focus in transformatory thinking on matters of scale. However, the scorched earth of current trends euphemized as "globalization" has also given rise in the here and now to alternative economic forms, including LETS and CC communities as well as myriad cooperatives, which have picked up the slack in human material reproduction at more "local" and regional" scales. Within the European Union, in Spain particularly since the 2008 global meltdown, LETS and CCs have proliferated (Hughes 2015). Returning to the United States, besides LETS and CCs, estimates have it that over 140 million US inhabitants are members of cooperatives delivering services in everything from food to health care. Even 25 percent of energy in the United States is provided by locally owned public utilities and cooperatives, these also offering things like broadband service (Alperovitz 2013, 35, 58ff.).

To be sure, intense debate swirls around the question of whether cooperatives constitute beachheads to socialism or if their labor relations model those of future socialist societies (Marcuse 2015). The evidence points in two directions. On the one hand, cooperatives embody many of the ownership, individual empowerment and work patterns that socialist economies of the future will adopt. On the other hand, given the way many operate as cogs in global production systems, they also have a tendency to imbibe much of what is dysfunctional for humanity in these.

But even if it is agreed that LETS, CCs and cooperatives (of which the socialist village Marinelada in Andalusia, Spain, cited above, is representative) are the harbinger of economic modalities of the "foundational economy" which will form part of the tri-sector socialist design proposed here, we are still brought back to the question of how to get there. To answer this preliminarily, we must discount at the outset the simultaneous "global revolution" path. No galvanizing of global constituencies for change is on the horizon. Through the disintegration and disarticulation of global production, the commonality of interests that might have existed in an earlier period among working classes to foment such galvanizing has been exorcized. Electoral paths to socialism, particularly in large states like the United States, are also unlikely to be realized. What the Greek scenario does illustrate, to recapitulate, is that smaller states in both geospatial and population terms hold out potentialities, especially if supporting cultural and historical conditions exist, for the capture of the state by socialist parties. In Canada, to cite another partially supportive example, socialist parties have had success at provincial levels but not at the federal level.

Arguably, therefore, the optimal current pathway to the socialist future is for a combination of political and economic organizing which draws together existing LETS, CCs and cooperatives in given regions where these have spawned in greater numbers, indicating patterns of common economic need and potential for commonalities among social constituencies to be cultivated. Then the task for these communities of practice is to expand their scope through demonstration effects of the role they play in reproducing the material lives of the human beings in their communities and in the participatory, democratic ways of doing things they exhibit. Interconnections must also be facilitated among the foregoing forms and the many small businesses in communities such as restaurants, grocery stores, repair shops, bakeries, farmers, and so forth. I am in agreement with Richard Smith that continuance of activities of such small producers will be important for socialist transitions. The small-*m* markets within the ambit of *community-scale economies* discussed above that these businesses will become part of will not detrimentally affect them nor circumscribe the life chances of their owners and workers. Only large-scale property, that of major corporations in particular, will need to be nationalized or otherwise taken over by wider social communities during the process of social change (Smith 2016).

In itself, of course, the foregoing remains but a progressive island of economic intercourse in a hostile economic milieu that will seek to exploit it. However, the agenda of Left constituencies behind it must be to translate the economic demonstration effects into political capital to forge electoral constituencies in regions, provinces, or small states where victories can be won, use these victories to delink from globalization as it exists to the greatest extent possible, and then begin to put in place the kinds of modalities of economic and political organization advanced here. The earliest political struggles will likely involve provinces or regions attempting to politically disengage from unions in which theretofore they were ensconced. Though to the extent the successes of these breakaway regions are readily apparent in yielding a future increasingly stripped of current ills, populations in areas outside these regions will also be too divided to support wholesale suppression of such projects by their militaries.

Finally, autarchy is not the goal. It is simply a means of building the kinds of societies that will enter into different types of bonds from those now prevalent in the world of nation-states today. In the end, a global socialist commonwealth will need to be made to genuinely deal with the mounting global morass, economic and environmental, that now casts a dark shadow over the future of human life on the planet.

* This chapter received support of National Research Foundation (NRF) of South Korea grant: NRF-2013S1A5B8A01055117.

References

Albritton, R. (1999) *Dialectics and Deconstruction in Political Economy* (Basingstoke: Palgrave).

Alperovitz, G. (2011) *America beyond Capitalism: Reclaiming Our Wealth, Our Liberty, and Our Democracy* (Takoma Park, MD: Democracy Collaborative Press).

Alperovitz, G. (2013) *What Then Must We Do? Straight Talk about the Next American Revolution* (White River Junction, VT: Chelsea Green).

Baer, H. (2016) "Toward Democratic Eco-socialism as the Next World System", *The Next System Project*, http://thenextsystem.org/toward-democratic-eco-socialism-as-the-next-world-system/.

Bloomberg (2016) "Scientists Want to Give the Atmosphere an Antacid to Relieve Climate Change", https://www.bloomberg.com/news/articles/2016-12-12/scientists-want-to-give-the-atmosphere-an-antacid-to-relieve-climate-change.

Bookchin, M. (1990) *Remaking Society: Pathways to a Green Future* (Boston: South End Press).

Empson, M. (2016) "Food, agriculture and climate change", *International Socialism*, 152 (October) http://isj.org.uk/food-agriculture-and-climate-change/.

Engelen, E., Johal, S., Salento A. and Williams, K. (2014) "How to Build a Fairer City", *Guardian*, https://www.theguardian.com/cities/2014/sep/24/manifesto-fairer-grounded-city-sustainable-transport-broadband-housing.

Engels, F. (1954) *Anti-Dühring* (Moscow: Foreign Languages Publishing House).

Foster, J. B., B. Clark and R. York (2010) *The Ecological Rift: Capitalism's War on the Earth* (New York: Monthly Review Press).

Graeber, D. (2011) *Debt: The First 5,000 Years* (New York: Melville House).

Hancox, D. (2013) *The Village against the World* (London: Verso).

Harvey, D. (2011) *The Enigma of Capital: and the Crises of Capitalism* (Oxford: Oxford University Press).

Hobsbawm, E. (2011) *How to Change the World: Reflections on Marx and Marxism* (New Haven, CT: Yale University Press).

Hudis, P. (2013) *Marx's Concept of the Alternative to Capitalism* (Chicago: Haymarket).

Hughes, N. (2015) "The Community Currency Scene in Spain", *International Journal of Community Currency Research*, 19(A), 1–11.

Lapavitsas, C. (2016) "One Year On, Syriza Has Sold Its Soul for Power", *Guardian*, https://www.theguardian.com/commentisfree/2016/jan/25/one-year-on-syriza-radicalism-power-euro-alexis-tsipras.

Lenin, V. I. (1920 [2016]) "Our Foreign and Domestic Position and Party Tasks Speech Delivered to the Moscow Gubernia Conference of the R.C.P.(B.)", November 21, 1920, https://www.marxists.org/archive/lenin/works/1920/nov/21.htm.

Marcuse, P. (2015) "Cooperatives on the Path to Socialism?" *Monthly Review*, http://monthlyreview.org/2015/02/01/cooperatives-on-the-path-to-socialism/.

Marx, K. (1859 [2016]) *Preface*, https://www.marxists.org/archive/marx/works/1859/critique-pol-economy/preface-abs.htm.

Marx, K. (1867 [2016]) *Capital* Volume One, https://www.marxists.org/archive/marx/works/1867-c1/p1.htm.

Marx, K. (1875 [2016]) *Critique of the Gotha Programme*, https://www.marxists.org/archive/marx/works/1875/gotha/index.htm.

Macpherson, C. B. (2011) *The Life and Times of Liberal Democracy* (Oxford: Oxford University Press).

McKibben, B. (2011) *Eaarth: Making a Life on a Tough New Planet* (New York: St Martin's Griffin).

McKibben, B. (2013) "A Movement for a New Planet: Movements without Leaders", *Countercurrents*, http://www.countercurrents.org/mckibben200813.htm.

Mumford, L. (1961) *The City in History: Its Origins, Its Transformations, and Its Prospects* (London: Secker and Warburg).

Nicholson, S. (2013) "The Promises and Perils of Geoengineering" (Washington, DC: Worldwatch Institute).

Orr, D. W. (2013) "Governance and the Long Emergency" (Washington, DC: Worldwatch Institute).

Polanyi, K. (1971) *The Great Transformation: The Political and Economic Origins of Our Time* (Boston: Beacon Press).

Resnick, S. and Wolff, R. (1993) "State Capitalism in the USSR? A High-Stakes Debate", *Rethinking Marxism*, 6, 2, pp. 46–48.

Resnick, S. and Wolff, R. (1994) "Between State and Private Capitalism: What Was Soviet 'Socialism'?" *Rethinking Marxism*, 7, 1, pp. 9–30.

Robinson, W. I. (2014) *Global Capitalism and the Crisis of Humanity* (Cambridge: Cambridge University Press).

Sekine, T. (1990) "Socialism as a Living Idea". In Flakierski, H. and Sekine, T. (eds.) *Socialist Dilemmas, East and West* (New York: M.E. Sharpe).

Smith, R. (2016) "Degrowth, Green Capitalism and the Promise of Ecosocialism", *Links International Journal of Socialist Renewal*, http://links.org.au/degrowth-green-capitalism-ecosocialism-richard-smith.

Stiglitz, J. (1994) *Whither Socialism* (Cambridge, MA: MIT Press).

Westra, R. (2002) "Marxian Economic Theory and an Ontology of Socialism: A Japanese Intervention", *Capital & Class*, 78, pp. 61–85.

Westra, R. (2009) *Political Economy and Globalization* (London: Routledge).

Westra, R. (2014) *Exit from Globalization* (London: Routledge).

Westra, R. (2015) "In the Tracks of Imperialism", *Journal of Contemporary Asia*, 45, 4, pp. 677–692.

Williams, C. (2010) *Ecology and Socialism: Solutions to Capitalist Ecological Crisis* (Chicago: Haymarket).

12 Towards a posthumanist economics

The end of self-possession and the disappearance of *Homo oeconomicus*

Karin Schönpflug and Christine M. Klapeer

Introduction: bringing posthumanist thinking into economics

Michael Moffa in his 2016 *Posthuman Economies: New or No Economic Roles for Most Humans?* sees a posthuman era about to begin, where there will be a domination of

> "astoundingly and unimaginably sophisticated robots, A.I. systems, man-machine cyborgs, 'transhuman' and 'suprahuman' technologies, including GMO creatures and other surprises — all of them 'autoplasti-cally'-evolved or 'alloplastic' enhancements, competitors or replacements for 'traditional' humans." (Moffa 2016, n.p.)

But Micheal Moffa's posthumanism is what Cary Wolfe subsumes as a transhumanist rather than a posthumanist approach (Wolfe 2009, xi–xv). Wolfe is explaining how transhumanism is, in his opinion, the opposite of posthumanism, as transhumanism has its roots in the rational humanism of Renaissance and Enlightenment thinking, which then appropriates new findings of physics, mechanics, and genetics into altering human bodily existences. Transhuman approaches in that sense rely on human perfectibility, the belief that technology can transcend the limitations of the human body, brain, and agency aiming at transforming human bodies, a process Donna Haraway playfully and ironically describes in her Cyborg Manifesto (see Haraway 1991). Moreover, transhumanism as part of Enlightenment philosophy is based on the idea that the human condition can and must be improved through and by the domestication and/or manipulation of nature. In his famous utopia *Nova Atlantis* (1627), Francis Bacon, best known as the *father* of modern scientific methods, such as the experiment, imagined his ideal state as a community where modern science has succeeded over the wilderness of nature, describing the active improvement of animals, humans, and productivity through technical interventions (see also: Klapeer and Schönpflug 2016).

While transhumanism is perfectly compatible with modern economics, posthumanism, on the other hand, is where Michel Foucault insists that rather than "permanently creating ourselves in our autonomy", posthumanist thinking intends to change the nature of thought itself (Foucault 1984). According to Wolfe, posthumanism "oppose[s] the fantasies of disembodiment and autonomy" and wants to overcome the "humanity/animality dichotomy" where the human is "achieved by escaping or repressing not just its animal origins in nature, the biological and the evolutionary, but more generally by transcending the bonds of materiality and embodiment altogether" (Wolfe 2009, xv). Even more, not only should the split between humanity/ animality be overcome, but also the amputation and estrangement of humanity from all life, nature, the planet itself. Posthumanism as a critical theory and political, even ethical, project proposes alternative ways of thinking and living under, and as a critique of, the conditions of an advanced and global neoliberal capitalism, which is shaped by biopolitical, or, rather, necropolitical, patterns (Braidotti 2013).

As a critical approach, posthumanism has been prevalent in philosophy (see Braidotti 2013), science and technology studies (see Haraway 1997), physics (see Barad 2003), environmental sociology (see Hird 2010), ecofeminism (see Gaard 1997), and queer theory (see MacCormack 2009). However, a Google search on *posthumanist economics* yields no results (August 2016). Hence, this text aims to critically interlink posthumanist with economic thinking.

Beyond established dichotomies: overcoming the fiction of self-ownership

From a posthumanist perspective, the key to recreating another version of economics lies with a transgression of established dualistic thinking (such as mind/body, human/animal) and overcoming of those dichotomies which provide the basis (and legitimization) for modern capitalism, nation states, and many other unequal/exploitative relationships. What we consider as particularly important with regard to these dualistic categories is that they are intrinsically interlinked with modern conceptions of (holding) property (see also: Klapeer and Schönpflug 2015; Klapeer and Schönpflug 2016):

1 The rational mind holds property over the self and maintains self-control over his body and desires (self-ownership).
2 Rational (white) men acquire property over non-rational *others*, such as women, indigenous people, Blacks, and homosexuals.
3 Rational humans transform nature, land, animals, the planet into (private) property.

A posthumanist economics seeks to undo these hierarchical binaries in identity construction and the conception of private property (surpassing the Marxian definition of private property as capital (Marx 1844) by undoing the domination of (*free*) men over human *others* and all non-human beings and matter.

From a posthumanist point of critique, private property must surpass a capitalist's means of production (capital) and must philosophically start with the concept of self-ownership or property-in-self which originates with the works of John Locke. The great theorist of property-in-self, John Locke, employed the concept to designate the self-sovereignty of (free) men in their economic relations with other men. He conceived that "every Man has a Property in his own Person. This no Body has any Right to but himself" (Locke 1690, V-§§ 27). With property in his person, by fully owning himself, man can not only ward off the claims of others, but also, his "having property in his own person" is, according to Locke, a necessary requirement for the appropriation of all private property (of what in the natural state is firstly common property).

The significance which the concept of self-ownership holds for economic theory is revealed by a brief inquiry into the etymology of the word *property*. Kenneth Minogue highlights that the "etymological root of the term (proprius – one's own)", gives us the sense of the connection between a property and what possesses it, "that is, between the (self-)possessing subject and the objects or things possessed by that subject" (Minogue 1980, 11). Property thus becomes the condition for being *proper to* (or belonging to) a particular person. The properties of persons, the attributes they are possessing, therefore do not only make them distinctive but also mark the borders between the (self-)proprietor, all others, and the rest of the world.

In that sense *free* individuals have private property rights over themselves and their bodies and abilities in the same way as those persons can have private property rights over others who do not own their bodies, such as women (see Pateman 1988) or slaves (see Feiner 1988).

In this logic, the difference between self-proprietors and all others is necessarily based on a split between mind and body, a split which is essential to provide a basis for self-ownership, for the establishment of a free individual who is able to make contracts, to be a master and an owner. If separated enough, the mind/the ratio will govern the body/ the flesh/ the desires and therefore succeed as a true owner and, as the ideal political/economic subject (Klapeer 2014). If the split is not complete (as is the case with women and people of Color) or non-existent (as in the case of animals), the mind cannot own the body. Thus, women and people of Color have been perceived as *nature*, as non-rational beings being governed by their (sexual) desires and their bodies, unable to escape their embodied existence.

According to this logic, the body becomes the faulty party in a world view of "distrust of nature and materiality" (Barad 2003, 812), where the body is a symbol of the material, inconstant, disgraceful side of existence and regarded as a prison to the immortal soul. True wisdom and reality are thought to be on the other side, incorporeal and invisible (Praetorius 2015, 14).

If, then, a person or a being is coined unable to perform life as a separate self, with a mind split from the body, fewer or no personal rights (ownership, marriage, freedom of movement, education, health, voice, etc.) are therefore granted to this person. The work that may be performed by such individuals is seen as of lesser nature, and the value and remuneration of that work is considered insignificant and small. Finally, a whole set of values is derived from certain people's perceived "closeness to nature" and organized so that "value dualism are ways of conceptually organizing the world in binary, disjunctive terms" (Gaard 1997, 115). With humanist and Enlightenment thinking, "in the West, the human has been historically posed in a hierarchical scale to the non-human realm. Such a symbolic structure, based on a human exceptionalism well depicted in the Great Chain of Being, has not only sustained the primacy of humans over non-human animals, but it has also (in)formed the human realm itself, with sexist, racist, classist, homophobic, and ethnocentric presumptions" (Ferrando 2013, 28). In this way "the humanist image of thought also sets the frame for a self-congratulating relationship of Man to himself, which confirms the dominant subject as much in what he includes as his core characteristics as in what he excludes as 'other'" (Braidotti 2013, 67).

Tied to conceptions of self-ownership and a world view of binary hierarchies is the ownership over inanimate objects. John Locke explains how nature and the fruits of nature are transformed into private property when a *free* individual's labor is added to the natural abundance:

> God, who hath given the world to men in common, hath also given them reason to make use of it to the best advantage of life and convenience. [But …] there must of necessity be a means to appropriate them some way or other before they can be of any use, or at all beneficial, to any particular men. […] We see in commons[…] that it is the taking any part of what is common, and removing it out of the state that nature leaves it in, which begins the property; without which the common is of no use. And the taking of this or that part, does not depend on the express consent of all the commoners. Thus the grass my horse has bit; the turfs my servant has cut; and the ore I have digged in any place, where I have a right to them in common with others, become my property, without the assignation or consent of any body. The labour that was mine, removing them out of that common state they were in, hath fixed my property in them. (Locke 1690, 2/5, section 26 and 28, online)

Very important from a posthumanist point of view is that next to the doubtful non- consensual mechanism of appropriation that Locke describes as the root of creating property is to note that only the usage (such as harvest or mining), but not preserving or care of common goods, is the source for appropriation. At the marketplace consumption rights (rights for utilization) are traded, but the responsibilities tied to the use of a resource are not integrated into market processes or the establishment of property rights (Biesecker and Winterfeld 2011, 139ff.). Usage of property hence allows market production; the sale of produce yields monetary profits for the seller, and provides consumption and personal contentedness for the buyer. Economists term the pleasure yielded by consumption as *utility*; the satisfaction gained is measured in so-called *utils*.

This malevolent appropriation concept is responsible for income inequality and impoverishment of European common people in the process of industrialization, where commons were turned into pastures and small-scale herders and farmers were pushed from the countryside to the factories (Heilbroner 1999, 20). (Lower class) women were on the other side, being transformed into commons themselves, to common goods which can be consummed. Their work was being defined as non-labor, as natural resource (Federici 2012, 118).

Locke's logic also justified colonial appropriation in the "new world" and pushing indigenous nations (like Australia's first nations) permanently off the lands they had been preserving for thousands of years, as European settlers claimed that the "land was empty" (i.e., not utilized) (see also: McClintock 1995). A focus on usage rather than conservation finally sets a scene where environmental destruction and climate change are no-one's responsibility.

From a posthumanist perspective this whole aberrant of epistemes needs to be deconstructed and reframed:

1 The mind-body split of a privileged few *free* individuals that allows self-ownership, ownership over others and nature/the planet.
2 The creation of private property by those "free" individuals through usage rather than preservation of common goods;
3 The competitive creation of profit and/or utility by "free" individuals through the use of this private property.

Deconstructing the *Homo oeconomicus*: expanding feminist economics

Next to questions of androcentric conceptualizations of value and the gendered division of labor, feminist economics has for a long time been struggling with the ideas on the "free" individual. In mainstream economics the free individual constitutes itself in the concept of the *Homo oeconomicus*. That economic agent is seen as an autonomous identity, a separate self, "fully sprung from the earth" (Hobbes 1966 [1651]) and not dependent on the care of others, not even a mother to give himself birth. In the Hobbesian metaphor, economic agents are envisioned as mushrooms; more recently, the economic agent is seen as an independent adventurer, a Robinson Crusoe, shipwrecked on a lonely island (see Grapard 1995). In this metaphor the *Homo oeconomicus* is envisioned as a rational individual (whose mind rules over his body); he is utility-maximizing, and fully informed by the signals of the market.

Feminist economics is also deeply concerned with the consequences of establishing the "free" individual, the *Homo oeconomicus* as the economic subject, and with the placing the foremost value on the utilization of private property. Feminist economics clarifies that such a paradigm constitutes an economic system resting on invisibilized, un(der)valued, un(der)paid reproductive labor and the priceless exploitation of commons such as clean air and water. The dominant economic system "cannot respond to values it refuses to recognize. It is the cause of massive poverty, illness and the death of millions of women and children, and it is encouraging environmental disaster. This is an economic system that can eventually kill us all"[1].

Feminists, (proto-)feminist utopian thinkers, and feminist economists ranging from Christine de Pizan ([1405], 1999), Mary Wollstonecraft (1792), Charlotte Perkins Gilman ([1911], 1971), Marge Piercy 1997 [1976], Marilyn Waring (1988, 1995 and 1999), Marianne Ferber and Julie Nelson (1993) and Nancy Folbre (1991 and 1995) to countless others have for a long time criticized those core ideas of the current economics paradigm. Not only their manifestation in accounting practices, the distribution of labor, and incomes and wealth, but also the destruction of livelihoods, the environment and the planet as a habitat. They have called for a reconsideration of the current conceptions of value, care, and labor which are the foundations of androcentric and anthropocentric economics (see Schönpflug 2008).

Still, a shortcoming of feminist economics is that, while the dominant paradigms have been assessed and deconstructed at lengths, and while the category *woman* has been added to mainstream models and concepts such as GDP accounting and the evaluation of reproductive labor and welfare indexes have been expanded[2], truly alternative programs have – with some exceptions (see below) – largely been missing and/or have not been largely established (see Habermann 2010).

Feminist economists are aware of this shortcoming. Marilyn Waring, one of the second wave's more prominent feminist economists, originally argued for a (monetary) imputation of values generated by unpaid work or the environment. In her 1988 core book *If Women Counted. A New Feminist Economics,* she urged policy makers to bring to light "the invisibility of unpaid work and the ecosystem in the unidimensional growth paradigm" in national income accounting (Waring 1999, xx). Interestingly, in her book's second edition called *Counting for Nothing: What Men Value and What Women Are Worth*, Waring reconsiders her strategy of the first edition. She explains that because she was striving to save ecosystems and prevent environmental destruction, she was originally "prepared to use whatever tools could immediately empower my argument in the short term. Since economics was all powerful, the way in which I would empower our ecosystem was to give it a monetary value, to quantify it, to make of it a commodity. I desperately had to prove that the natural environment [...] had a value comparable with the alternative proposed exploitation. There was no time to battle the pathology of the economic mode" (Waring 1999, xx).

Therefore Waring's primary strategy was to align goods of a common nature or items of the nature-state (in the sense of Locke), which were not yet a private property, with commodities (e.g., objects exhibiting utility). But in 1999 Waring reflects on that strategy:

"My underlying agenda was to disable the system. I saw a mechanism for this in taking economics on at its own game. [...] I thought that the models would then be so overwhelmed, conceptually and statistically, that they would become inoperable, and even greater nonsense than they are. [...] I underestimated the willingness of the ideologues and practitioners to construct even more abstractions, regardless of the model's relationship to human experience. I underestimated their capacity for unreality" (Waring 1999, xxi).

Waring had in that sense originally planned to implode economic models by adding monetary value to non-commodities such as women's unpaid labor, environmental degradation and so forth, hoping the complexity would collapse the system. In this paper's final section, we are proposing this exercise again but in an even more systematic and explicitly posthumanist way.

Becoming other: transgressing anthropocentrism and human exceptionalism

The posthumanist critique of the mainstream economic paradigm strengthens the ecological concerns of feminist economics. Posthumanism even more explicitly pays attention to the divisive inferences between humans, non-human animals, the environment, and economics' focus on commodity consumption. Marilyn Waring refers to David Suzuki asking whether the "plethora of goods that our high production economy delivers so effectively provide the route to happiness and satisfaction or did the relationships between human and non-human beings still form the core of the important things in life" Waring 1999, xlviii). The link between feminist economic thinking and posthumanist critiques has so far not become dominant in the discourse. While feminist economics is to a large scale concerned with the androcentric divide in economic theory, ecofeminist and posthumanist thinkers are questioning the anthropocentric postulate in modern epistemes which position humans at the center of all scientific modelling, reasoning, and political organization. Furthermore, from their disciplinary standpoints they have been explaining the active connectedness of all life, e.g., humanity's symbiogenetic genealogy with microorganisms or the dependence of humans on an autopoietic system, which is a system capable of reproducing and maintaining itself.

Donna Haraway beautifully explains the symbiogenetic genealogy/ dependence in microscopic settings that may serve as a brilliant tool to dismantle the *Homo oeconomicus* concept as well as ideas of a free and autonomous individual:

> I love the fact that human genomes can be found in only about 10 percent of all the cells that occupy the mundane space I call my body; the other 90 percent of the cells are filled with the genomes of bacteria, fungi, protists, and such, some of which play in a symphony necessary to my being alive at all, and some of which are hitching a ride and doing the rest of me, of us, no harm. I am vastly outnumbered by my tiny companions; better put, I become an adult human being in company with these tiny messmates. To be one is always to become with many. (Haraway 2008, 3)

Such thoughts are therefore highly enriching for a mainstream economic thinking that postulates "free" men's autonomy and focuses on commodity usage, where a process of "thingification", of turning relations into "things" infects much of the way we understand the world (Barad 2003, 812). Adopting posthumanist thought in economic models would in that way completely change economic's understanding of growth, distribution, pollution, extraction of raw materials and exploitation of resources, people, and non-human entities.

The idea of humans as singular identities placed in an as environment of empty space is equivalent to the Democritean dream of atoms and the void (Barad 2003, 806). To unconsciously rely on bacteria, protists, and fungi is mimicked in the reliance on the invisiblized, un(der)paid work of "others" or the gratis exploitation and destruction of the commons and the environment. This blissful unconsciousness, omission, or even ungratefulness has been established as a (Western) societal norm with humanist and Enlightenment thinkers, but should be reconsidered with the realization of actual biological microscopic and macroscopic fact.

Myra Hird expands the microscopic view into something she terms *Gaia Theory*, an idea that explains our planet as an autopoietic system, where the multitude of organisms in the biosphere are working together like a superorganism that can regulate itself through positive and negative feedback. Pure consumers of matter, such as humans or animals, are not the central players in such a system; productive and symbiotic or symbiogenic organisms like bacteria, phototropes, chemotrops, or organotrops are. Organisms of such an autopoietic system have subordinated their functions to the goals of the system. An autopoietic planetary system where tiny organisms are the ones generating and determining life is a system where humans and their institutions are of no importance for the sustenance of that system. Humans "are not the central players in climate (or any other biospheric) regulation. Bacteria routinely cross species and geo-political boundaries, effectively trumping deep ecology arguments that environmental change respects no (human) national or political boundaries" (Hird, 2010, 9). Integrating that realization into economic theory should in that sense lead to a complete reconsideration of economic theories. Connecting again with the reflections on androcentrism and the mind/body split that were discussed above, Greta Gaard concludes from an ecofeminist point:

> [A]ll categories of the other share these qualities of being feminized, animalized, and naturalized, socialist ecofeminists have rejected any claims of primacy for one form of oppression or another, embracing instead the understanding that all forms of oppression are now so inextricably linked that liberation efforts must be aimed at dismantling the system itself. (Gaard 1997, 117)

Towards a posthumanist economics: the possibility of a practical utopia

Finally, with inspiration from feminist utopian thinkers such as Starhawk, who is building on the works of Marge Piercy ([1976], 1997), Shulamit Firestone (1970), Ursula Le Guin (1969), and Charlotte Perkins Gilman ([1915], 1997), this essay proposes first thoughts on a posthumanist economics as a practical utopia in an age of global crisis and austerity. This vision abolishes the idea of the individual/ the citizen/ the *Homo oeconomicus* populating (global) markets, nation states, and private households. Instead there is a focus on the connectedness of all life without insisting on the supremacy of humans, not even if they happen to be heterosexual, white, upper-class men.

In this section a key example of mainstream anthropocentric economic theory is exemplarily changed to fit a posthumanist frame of reference. We are choosing Gary Becker's model of the household, since it is a core building-block of microeconomic theory[3].

In his famous 1981 paper "Altruism in the Family and Selfishness in the Market Place", Becker models the gendered division of labor within a household, which is tantamount to a heteronormative family, where it is a rational decision for the wife to focus on housework and children and for the husband to specialize in paid work on the labor market. This gendered division of labor and working spheres is seen to be a successful strategy, since the husband is assumed to be driven by altruistic behavior and to share the monetary income (either like a benevolent dictator or due to rational cooperation between all household members) fairly amongst the members of the family. Becker states that "*a person (h)*", who is generally interpreted as the husband, "is given to be altruistic towards his spouse (w)", which means that *h*'s utility function depends positively also on the well-being of *w*. Becker formally states altruism in the family as such:

$$U_h = U\{Z_{1h},...,Z_{mh}, \Psi(U_w)\} \text{ and } \delta U_h / \delta U_w > 0 \text{ and } Z_h = I_h\text{-}y$$

U_h and U_w are the utilities of altruist and beneficiary, given by the consumption of a commodity Z; Ψ is a positive function of (U_w), which means that h's utility also increases if not only does he consume himself, but also he spends some (a fair share, as is later explained) of his income on w and on her consumption, which is visualized by the positive derivation of $\delta U_h / \delta U_w$. The husband's consumption is restricted by his income (I_h) and the amount spent on w.

In Becker's model, utility (U) of a commodity consumed (Z) is the center of the analysis. Based on the writings of Stanley Jevons, Leon Walras, and Alfred Marshal, standard microeconomic theory has, since the 19th century, worked with the utility concept, which suggests that when persons consume additional units of a commodity, their utility will increase by a certain amount of utils (e.g., if coffee is worth 100 utils and beefsteak 500 utils, depending on the person's preferences, the utility will increase by certain numbers of utils if more coffee and beefsteak are consumed). This cardinal view was in 1930 replaced by an ordinal construction of utility (using rankings rather than definite numbers, e.g., beef is preferred to coffee) by economic theorists such as John Hicks and R.J. Allen. Furthermore, it is essential to take into consideration that utility is considered to be diminishing, and there is a saturation if the amount of consumption of a certain good increases. This implies also that consumers will seek to harmonize consumption over all available commodities, given their money endowment. Individuals' welfare therefore increases with the consumption of well-balanced bundles of goods with a greater combined utility as compared to other bundles. Consumption depends firstly on prices and income, but also on preferences and taste (Tewari and Katar 1996, 14ff.). The micro-analysis of this behavior is then reflected in macroeconomic analysis, especially in the traditional GDP accounting which will focus only on market production and sales, i.e., the aggregate production and consumption of commodities within a nation.

This unidimensionality of measuring solely commodity consumption and monetary values in mainstream economics has not only been criticized by feminist economists such as the aforementioned Marilyn Waring, but also has been expanded with alternative approaches to welfare economics since the 1980s. Amartya Sen's capability approach added the importance of real freedoms, the ability to transform resources into valuable activities, the multivariate nature of activities giving rise to happiness, a balance of materialistic and nonmaterialistic factors in evaluating human welfare, and a concern for the distribution of opportunities within society to the agenda (Sen 2003) expanding utility accounting (desire-fulfillment, choice, and commodity consumption) with access to monetary (income, commodities, assets) and nonmonetary resources. Since 1990, capability-based indexes such as the Human Development Index (HDI), the Human Poverty Index (HPI), and the Gender Empowerment Measure (GEM) expand official GDP measurements by adding concern for health, education, distribution, or gender equality.

Still, for a posthumanist economics, those approaches of welfare economics need to be expanded to evenly include not only all genders, all races, and all classes, but also, at the same level of importance, all non-human entities and the environment.

At a first glance Martha Nussbaum's list on the Central Human Capabilities (Nussbaum 2003) is a good starting point, also from a posthumanist viewpoint, to expand those indexes. Nussbaum publishes a list of what she terms a "definite list of the most central capabilities". This list includes physical needs such as being capable of *"life"* (living without dying prematurely), "bodily health" (good health, food, shelter) and *"bodily integrity"* (including free movement without assaults, sexual freedom and reproductive choice). Items referring to emotional and cognitive needs on Nussbaum's list include "senses, imagination, and thought" (including freedom of religion, access to education, free expression in arts, etc.), *"emotions"* (in human association), *"practical reason"* (planning one's own life), and *"play"* (enjoyment of recreation).

The items "affiliation" ("being able to live with and towards others") and the institutional component "control over one's environment" (participation in political choices, holding of property, and working as a human being) relate to solidarity with fellow human beings, opportunity for political participation, and fair treatment concerning property and working rights. Finally the item *"other species"* ("being able to live with concern for and in relation to animals, plants, and the world of nature") surpasses the focus on humans (Nussbaum 2003, 41–42).

Still, when Nussbaum lists those most central capabilities, she anchors them in human action and humans' rights and human agency. Only one of those 10 items is concerned with non-human others, but those others (*"animals, plants, and the world of nature"*) are those that humans should *"be able to live with concern for and in relation to"*. Their rights become endorsed in the rights of humans as a passive right; therefore, this list of capabilities remains an anthropocentric guideline that is also primarily (in 9 out of those 10 list items) concerned with inter-human dealings. Nussbaum's concern with the *"truly human functioning"* in the sense of Karl Marx (Nussbaum 2004, 40) can in this way also be seen as a divisive marker.

"After all, 'truly human functioning' is only sensible when considering its contrast class, i.e. less than human functioning, or functioning that doesn't go beyond that of non-human animals" (Dorsey 2012, 24).

This may not only be a means of division but also a shortcoming, since Marx certainly focuses on human interaction, but he also foresees a bridging of the gap between humans and nature if capitalism and commodified desire-fulfillment are overcome. Marx considers to end man's alienation (*Entfremdung*) through the elimination of private property (capital) and commodity goods consumption so that

> *communism* as the *positive* transcendence of *private property* as *human self-estrangement*, and therefore as the real *appropriation* of the *human* essence by and for man; communism therefore as the complete return of man to himself as a *social* (i.e., human) being – a return accomplished consciously and embracing the entire wealth of previous development. This communism, as fully developed naturalism, equals humanism, and as fully developed humanism equals naturalism; it is the *genuine* resolution of the conflict between man and nature and between man and man – the true resolution of the strife between existence and essence, between objectification and self-confirmation, between freedom and necessity, between the individual and the species. Communism is the riddle of history solved, and it knows itself to be this solution. (Marx 1844, online)

In a posthumanist interpretation, it could be recounted that Marx sees people as separated from one another and nature through the organization of society in capitalist production – a split that he feels can be overcome by communism.

Engels also writes on the complicated interaction between man and nature; he describes a relationship where humans appear only as masters over nature but fail in the end when nature strikes back with disaster. The utilization of nature by man with all its limitations is still what distinguishes and privileges him from the non-human animal:

> In short, the animal merely uses external nature, and brings about changes in it simply by his presence; man by his changes makes it serve his ends, masters it. This is the final, essential distinction between man and other animals, and once again it is labour that brings about this distinction. Let us not, however, flatter ourselves overmuch on account of our human conquest over nature. For each such conquest takes its revenge on us. [...] Thus at every step we are reminded that we by no means rule over nature like a conqueror over a foreign people, like someone standing outside nature – but that we, with flesh, blood, and brain, belong to nature, and exist in its midst, and that all our mastery of it consists in the fact that we have the advantage over all other beings of being able to know and correctly apply its laws. (Engels 1883)

Engels incorporates the Lockean idea of labor transforming nature into private property, which also positions people over non-human animals, and which establishes civil contracts and separates man from non-human animals and nature. Engels also warns of the strike back of an ill-meaning monstrous nature that will punish men for its destruction.

Marx's view on the mastery of man over nature is less anthropocentric: Marx infers, "Man lives on nature – means that nature is his body, with which he must remain in continuous interchange if he is not to die. That man's physical and spiritual life is linked to nature means simply that nature is linked to itself, for man is a part of nature" (Marx 1844). Further on, he points to a utopian future of communism where "from the standpoint of a higher economic form of society, private ownership of the globe by single individuals will appear quite as absurd as private ownership of one man by another. Even a whole society, a nation, or even all simultaneously existing societies taken together, are not the owners of the globe. They are only its possessors, its usufructuaries, and, like *boni patres familias*, they must hand it down to succeeding generations in an improved condition" (Marx 1863–1883, online: 546).

Surpassing Sen's and Nussbaum's anthropocentric reading of Marx's "*truly human functioning*", a posthumanist economics must therefore put human and non-human needs on equal grounding. Another source to enrich mainstream economic theory is feminist utopian novels. Expanding the limited realm of economic theory is a scientific practice that actively overcomes the arrangement of isolation and autonomy which economics as a discipline often claims to inhibit. Utopian writing encompasses ideas from political science (e.g., concerning governance and political organizing), physics and mechanical engineering (e.g., about energy production and conservation) or gender and queer studies (e.g., on identity formation and personal relations), which are put together in a fictional model setting that may be of use to think outside the box. (To include such utopian thought into economic models will help prevent what Marilyn Waring warned about, namely, that mainstream economics will simply create more abstractions, add those new concepts and stir, rather than the system being completely rebooted).

One comprehensive example for posthumanist utopian thinking is Starhawk's utopian sequel *Maya Greenwood*. In Starhawk's utopian society, decision-making processes take place in a Great Council by actors of equal importance, where representatives of the four elements – air, water, fire, and earth – are speaking on behalf of non-human agencies (animals, plants, and nonliving matter) and are important parts in decision-making processes (Starhawk 1993, 45). In a 2002 handbook, Starhawk proposes a nine-point plan enriching Nussbaum's capabilities list with a posthumanist focus on economics. On top of her priorities (rather than at the bottom) is to "protect the viability of the life-sustaining systems of the planet" (Starhawk 2002, 237) where it is most important to "end pollution at its source, not just to mitigate or clean it up" (Starhawk 2002, 238). The protection of biodiversity, habitat, and the diversity of ecosystems is in this sense of the greatest importance. Secondly, she argues that there are things too precious to be commodified and which must be respected: those include places that have special meaning to indigenous cultures or local communities, and irreplaceable ecosystems such as old-growth forests or basic life resources such as water or air. Further points are communities' control over their own resources and destinies and responsibility and accountability of enterprises in local communities, and ends to discrimination and "opportunity and support for human beings to meet their needs and fulfill their dreams" (Starhawk 2002, 240). Those opportunities are connected to fair labor rights, common responsibility and increased democracy to ensure humans' basic means of life, growth, and development.

Starhawk integrates the economic visions of thinkers outside of the economic mainstream into her proposal. She mentions ideas of the "Mindful" *Market Economy*, plans of a *Restorative Economy* and the key concepts of *Participatory Economics* (equity, solidarity, diversity, and participatory self-management). The radical feminist concept of the *Gift Economy* is listed, and different models of state support, local sustainability, and networking are discussed. She summarizes those ideas concerning the role of the economy as such: "The job of the economy is to produce security and abundance for all, equably, efficiently, and sustainably, in a way that furthers human freedom and mutual solidarity, that strengthens our bond to place, and that protects the interests of future generations" (Starhawk 2002, 242).

By "security", she refers to standards of life that surpass survival; "equability" refers to feminist economics' demands for fair rewards of all kinds of market and non-market labor; "efficiency" is seen in the sense of Charlotte Perkins Gilman and refers to using as few nonrenewables as possible, enhancing sustainability (Perkins Gilman [1898], 1970; van Staveren 2003); and "solidarity" means mutual support in case of misfortunes. Finally, "abundance" replaces the key scare of scarcity of mainstream economics that was most firmly implanted by Malthus warning of a "population bomb" (Malthus 1798). Starhawk sees new inputs of energy, materials and labor, recycling, creativity, innovation, and sustainability-oriented efficiency as realistic sources to create abundance, i.e., pleasure and beauty on top of survival.

Inspired by these ideas, a posthumanist explanation of household behavior would finally change Becker's formal statement of household utility drastically:

Becker's equations:

$$U_h = U\{Z_{1h},...,Z_{mh},\Psi(U_w)\} \text{ and } \delta U_h/\delta U_w > 0$$

Posthumanist equations:

$$W_h = W\{P_h, E_h, \Psi[(W_{H-h}), (W_{1o},...,W_{mo})], \Phi(W_{planet})]\}$$

$$\text{and } \delta W_h/\delta[(W_{H-h}), (W_{1o},...,W_{mo})], \Phi(W_{planet})]$$

$$P_h, E_h = X_h\text{-}y$$

The idea of utility will in our posthumanist economic theory be replaced by the more encompassing welfare concept, referring to the fulfillment of Nussbaum's Central Human Capabilities; W_h therefore stands for the well-being of the human h. That well-being therefore depends on the described physical needs (life, bodily health, and integrity) $(P_{1h},...,P_{mh})$, the cognitive and emotional needs (senses, imagination, and thought; emotions; practical needs; practical reason; play) $(E_{1h},..., E_{mh})$. The Ψ is a positive function of affiliation with other humans (W_{H-h}) and concern for and relation with other species $(W_{1o},...,W_{mo})$, who are assumed to have similar needs P and E, and which makes the well-being of one human (h) positively dependent on the well-being of all other human beings (H-h) and the well-being of all other species (1o...mo). We are also adding the conservation and sustainability of all anorganic matter as a positive function $\Phi(W_{planet})$ to this equation. Where Nussbaum still gives value to the ability to hold property (land and moveable goods), which is expressed as commodity consumption $(Z_{1h},...,Z_{mh})$ in Becker's theory, a posthumanist economics will simply drop this factor as irrelevant. The positive derivation of $\delta W_h/\delta[(W_{H-h}), (W_{1o},...,W_{mo})], \Phi(W_{planet})]$ means that h's welfare also increases if he is not bettered himself, but spends some of his efforts on other peoples' and the planet's welfare. The human h's satisfaction of his physical and emotional needs is restricted by X, the organization of the society and the distribution of resources, and depends positively on h's efforts towards the well-being of all other humans and the planet. This factor X lastly implies that the binary and hierarchic organization of individuals in family households consisting of husband, wife, and children is an optional but not necessary or sufficient precondition to maximize the welfare of a greater community.

Conclusion

Key ideas of mainstream economics, starting with a privileged concept of self-ownership and property appropriation based on usage rather than preservation, need to swiftly be abandoned to make room for alternative economic systems oriented towards abundance, equably, efficiently, and sustainably, in an age of life-threatening global crises. A posthumanist economics therefore replaces the idea of the autonomous economic agent and his limited organization in nuclear families with an understanding of a human economics that is subordinate to a planetary autopoeitic system where humans depend on symbiosis with other species.

Notes

1 https://grunes.wordpress.com/2009/06/14/who%E2%80%99s-counting-marilyn-waring-on-sex-lies-and-global-economics-terre-nash-1995/
2 This led to whole branches of feminist and environmental economics working on making unpaid reproductive labor and environmental exploitation visible – for instance, in so-called satellite accounts.
3 Microeconomic theory aims at explaining what is happening within the smallest economic entities, such as individual households and firms. Mainstream economics explains household decision-making in a field called "New Home Economics", where decision-making processes within a household are a result of gendered comparative advantages.

References

Bacon, F. ([1608], 1834) "The Masculine Birth of Time or The Great Instauration of the Dominion of Man over the Universe". In: B. Montagu (ed.), *The Works of Francis Bacon* (London: William Pickerin: 223–224).
Bacon, F. (1627) *Nova Atlantis*. Online: http://www.fcsh.unl.pt/docentes/rmonteiro/pdf/The_New_Atlantis.pdf.
Barad, K. (2008) "*Post*humanist Performativity: Toward an Understanding of How Matter Comes to Matter". In: S. Alaimo and S. Hekman (eds.), *Material Feminism* (Bloomington: Indiana University Press: 120–154).
Becker, G. (1981) "Altruism in the family and selfishness in the market place", *Economica*, New Series, 48(189): 1–15.
Biesecker, A.; Winterfeld, U. (2011) "Nachhaltige feministische Einsprüche. Die Blockierung nachhaltiger Entwicklungen durch klassische Rationalitätsmuster", *Gender Heft* 2:S. 129–144.
Braidotti, R. (2013) *The Posthuman* (New York: Wiley).
Dorsey, D. (2012) *The Basic Minimum* (Cambridge: Cambridge University Press).
Engels, F. (1883) *The Dialectics of Nature*. Online: https://www.marxists.org/archive/marx/works/download/EngelsDialectics_of_Nature_part.pdf.
Federici, S. (2012) *Caliban und die Hexe. Frauen, der Körper und die ursprüngliche Akkumulation* (Vienna: Mandelbaum).

Feiner, S. (1988) "Slavery, Classes, and Accumulation in the Antebellum South", *Rethinking Marxism: A Journal of Economics, Culture & Society* 1(2): 116–141.

Ferber, M.; Nelson, J. (1993) *Beyond Economic Man: Feminist Theory and Economics* (Chicago: University of Chicago Press).

Ferrando, F. (2013) "Posthumanism, Transhumanism, Antihumanism, Metahumanism, and New Materialisms: Differences and Relations", *Existenz* 8(2): 26–32.

Firestone, S. (1970) *The Dialectic of Sex* (New York: William Morrow and Company).

Folbre, N. (1995) "'Holding Hands at Midnight': The Paradox of Caring Labor", *Feminist Economics* 1(1): 73–92.

Folbre, N. (1991) "The Unproductive Housewife: Her Evolution in Nineteenth-Century Economic Thought", *Signs* 16(3): 463–484.

Foucault, M. (1984) "What Is Enlightenment?" In: P. Rabinow (ed.), *The Foucault Reader*, (New York: Pantheon Books) Online: http://foucault.info/doc/documents/whatisenlightenment/foucault-whatisenlightenment-en-html.

Gaard, G. (1997) "Toward a Queer Ecofeminism", *Hypatia* 12(1): 114–137.

Grapard, U. (1995) "Robinson Crusoe: The Quintessential Economic Man?" *Feminist Economics*, 1(1): 33–52.

Habermann, F. (2010) "Hegemonie, Identität und der homo oeconomicus. Oder: Warum feministische Ökonomie nicht ausreicht". In: C. Bauhardt and G. Caglar (eds.), *Gender and Economics. Feministische Kritik der politischen Ökonomie* (Berlin: VS. Verlag).

Haraway, D. (1991) "A Cyborg Manifesto: Science, Technology, and Socialist-Feminism in the Late Twentieth Century". In: *Simians, Cyborgs, and Women: The Reinvention of Nature* (New York: Routledge: 149–181).

Haraway, D. (1997) *Modest_Witness@Second_Millennium.FemaleMan©Meets_OncoMouse™: Feminism and Technoscience*. (New York: Routledge).

Haraway, D. (2008) *When Species Meet* (Minneapolis: University of Minnesota Press).

Heilbroner, R. (1999) *The Worldly Philosophers* (New York: Touchstone Books).

Hird, M.J. (2010) "Indifferent Globality," *Theory, Culture and Society* 27(2–3): 54–72.

Hobbes, T. ([1651], 1966) *Leviathan, oder Stoff, Form und Gewalt eines bürgerlichen Staates* (Berlin: Suhrkamp).

Klapeer, C. (2014) *Perverse Bürgerinnen. Staatsbürgerschaft und lesbische Existenz* (Bielefeld: transcript Verlag).

Klapeer, C.; Schönpflug, K. (2016) "Die verborgenen Schätze müssen aus ihrem dunklen Schoß entrissen werden. Feministische und postkoloniale Reflexion zu gesellschaftlichen Natur- und Ressourcenkonzeptionen". In: K. Fischer, J. Jäger, and L. Schmidt (eds.), *Umkämpfte Rohstoffe. Aktuelle Entwicklungen im historischen Kontext* (Vienna: New Academic Press).

Klapeer, C.; Schönpflug, K. (2015) "Queer Needs Commons! Re_Visions to Challenge Capitalist (Self-) Ownership Logics and Macroeconomic Policies", In: N. Dhawan, A. Engel, C. Holzhey, and V. Woltersdorff (eds.), *Global Justice and Desire: Queering Economy* (London: Routledge).

Le Guin, U. (1969) *The Left Hand of Darkness* (New York: Ace Books).

Locke, J. (1690) *Second Treatise of Civil Government*. Online: https://www.marxists.org/reference/subject/politics/locke/ch05.htm.

MacCormack, P. (2009) "Queer Posthumanism. Cyborgs, Animals, Monsters, Perverts". In: N. Giffney and M. O'Rourke (eds.), *The Ashgate Research Companion to Queer Theory* (London: Routledge: 111–126).

Malthus, T. (1798) *An Essay on the Principle of Population*. Online: http://www.econlib.org/cgi-bin/printarticle.pl.

Marx, K. (1844) *Economic and Philosophic Manuscripts* of 1844. Online: https://www.marxists.org/archive/marx/works/1844/manuscripts/comm.htm.

Marx, K. (1863–1883) *Capital*. Online: https://www.marxists.org/archive/marx/works/download/pdf/Capital-Volume-III.pdf.

McClintock, A. (1995) *Imperial Leather: Race, Gender and Sexuality in the Colonial Contest* (New York/London: Routledge).

Minogue, K. (1980) *The Concept of Property and Its Contemporary Significance* (New York: New York University Press).

Moffa, M. (2016) *Posthuman Economics: New or No Economic Roles for Most Humans?* Online: https://www.recruiter.com/downloads/posthuman-economics-new-or-no-economic-roles-for-most-humans.

Nussbaum, M. (2003) "Capabilities as Fundamental Entitlements: Sen and Social Justice", *Feminist Economics* 9(2–3): 33–59.

Pateman, C. (1988) *The Sexual Contract* (Stanford: Stanford University Press).

Perkins Gilman, C. ([1911], 1971) *The Man-Made World or Our Androcentric Culture* (New York: Johnson Reprint Corp.).

Perkins Gilman, C. ([1898], 1970) *Women and Economics* (New York: Source Book Press).

Perkins Gilman, C. ([1915], 1997) *Herland* (New York: Pantheon Books).

Piercy, M. (1997, [1976]) *Woman on the Edge of Time* (New York: Ballantine Books).

Pizan, C. de ([1405], 1999) *The Book of the City of Ladies* (London: Penguin).

Praetorius, I. (2015) *The Care-Centered Economy: Rediscovering What Has Been Taken for Granted.* Heinrich Böll Foundation Publication Series Economy & Social Issues, Vol. 16.

Schönpflug, K. (2008) *Feminism, Economics, Utopia: Time Traveling through Paradigms* (London: Routledge).

Sen, A. (2003) "Development as Capability Expansion". In: S. Fukuda-Parr and A.K. Shiva Kumar (eds.), *Readings in Human Development* (New Delhi and New York: Oxford University Press).

Starhawk (1993) *The Fifth Sacred Thing* (New York: Bantam).

Starhawk (2002) *Webs of Power: Notes from the Global Uprising* (Gabriola Island, British Columbia: New Society Publishing).

Staveren, I. van (2003) "Feminist Fiction and Feminist Economics – Charlotte Perkins Gilman on Efficiency". In: D. Barker and E. Kuiper (eds.), *Toward a Feminist Philosophy of Economics* (London: Routledge).

Tewari, D.D.; Katar, S. (1996) *Principles of Microeconomics* (New Delhi: New Age International Limited Publishers).

Waring, M. (1988) *If Women Counted. A New Feminist Economics* (San Francisco: Harper & Row).

Waring, M. (1995) *Who Is Counting? Marilyn Waring on Sex, Lies and Global Economics.* Online: https://www.nfb.ca/film/whos_counting, 01.10.2015.

Waring, M. (1999) *Counting for Nothing: What Men Value and What Women Are Worth.* 2nd edition. (Toronto: University of Toronto Press).

Wolfe, C. (2009) *What Is Posthumanism?* (Minneapolis: University of Minnesota Press).

Wollstonecraft, M. (1792) *A Vindication of the Rights of Woman with Strictures on Moral and Political Subjects* (London: Joseph Johnson).

Index